CHOICES

**situations
to
stimulate
thought
and
expression**

THELMA ALTSHULER

Miami-Dade Junior College

Prentice-Hall, Inc.
Englewood Cliffs, N.J.

To Dick, David, and Julia

© 1970 by Prentice-Hall, Inc., Englewood Cliffs, New Jersey

13–133256–2

Library of Congress Catalog Card Number: 79–112913

Printed in the United States of America

Current Printing (last number):

10 9 8 7 6 5 4 3 2 1

PRENTICE-HALL INTERNATIONAL, INC., London
PRENTICE-HALL OF AUSTRALIA, PTY. LTD., Sydney
PRENTICE-HALL OF CANADA, LTD., Toronto
PRENTICE-HALL OF INDIA PRIVATE LTD., New Delhi
PRENTICE-HALL OF JAPAN, INC., Tokyo

CONTENTS

CHOICES situations to stimulate thought and expression

Drawing by Stevenson; © 1969 The New Yorker Magazine, Inc.

Drawing by Stan Hunt; © 1968 The New Yorker Magazine, Inc.

"I'll take one of each."

Life ought to be like

The first picture, because people should be free, as the signs invite them to be.

The second picture, because people need order, and directions prevent mis-understanding.

If you chose the first picture, answer these questions:

How would the city be changed if signs like these were really around?

How would a school be changed if it had signs like those in the picture?

What other signs, in the spirit of those in the first picture, could be added?

What signs could *not* be added to the picture without changing the **mood**?

Explain why you chose the first picture by adding to the reason given above.

What evidence is there in politics, songs, and news events that such signs represent the way people really feel these days?

If you chose the second picture, answer these questions:

How would neighborhoods be changed if there were more people like the customer in the cartoon?

In general, what would be the advantage of having more signs like those in the cartoon?

How is the reader expected to feel about this man? How do you know?

What effect would many of such signs have on human relations?

Tell why you prefer the idea of the second picture as an aid to society.

GENERAL CLASS DISCUSSION

What do the people who choose the first picture have in common with people who choose the second? (Or are they totally different?)

Once you have answered these questions, in speech or writing, you will have had a sample of how the exercises in this book move from a picture or an event to a theoretical discussion. A sample situation and choices will be found on page 2.

PREFACE

THE PROVOCATIVE

A double-parked automobile . . . a man who didn't show up for work . . .
a bookstore near a college . . . an expensive house in an all-white neighborhood . . . a poster showing a nude . . . a price tag on a package of
chopped beef . . . a crowded hallway . . . a park . . . a stop sign . . . a
flower . . . a baby crying . . .

The list above was made at random, with no intended connection among
the objects. Each is a familiar sight that arouses various free-association responses in people. For instance, the first, a double-parked automobile might
provoke these remarks:

"Some guys think they own the streets."

"Wish I had the nerve."

"I hope the driver gets caught."

"No wonder the traffic is unbearable."

"The police have a tough, thankless job trying to keep the streets clear."

"Somebody must have been paid off."

Behind each remark is a view of life, not necessarily consistent, but significant of belief if it recurs often enough.

Here are some familiar sounds that offer the same stimulus: "So I said
she should have known better . . ." "If he thinks he can get away with . . ."
"Why at your age, you should . . ." "I would have walked away . . ." "You
did the right thing." These are the sounds of values in action in ordinary
conversation which reveal underlying convictions about appropriate behavior. Such phrases are usually taken for granted to the extent that they
remain unquestioned. The person who is asked what he believes must pause
frequently to consider ideas which sound abstract or removed from his real

opinions and actions. But working from an object or a provocative anecdote (a "situation") one locates beliefs which have possibly not been recognized or articulated before.

For those who know how to look, everything has a meaning. People who are good at making observations, who move without apparent effort from the abstract to the concrete, are successful in composition classes. The most insignificant item assumes significance for them.

For those who don't know how to observe, nothing has quite enough "in it" to stimulate fluent expression. An honors class in English can spend an hour improvising an essay on a paper clip, a cat stuck in a tree, or the new music teacher who wears sandals. Other students have trouble composing as few as three pages on the history of mankind. The solution to this problem is to utilize personally held convictions. Just as a too lofty subject encourages empty words, so stopping with opinion is circular: "I believe this because everybody does who has any sense. . . ."

The examples in this book begin with opinion, the usually unexamined outburst of praise or complaint based on some concrete word, picture, or situation. Then they encourage the expression of a general statement to include the stimulus and others like it; an examination of the other opinions —or choices—not made; and a probing of personal experience and background to account for the choice made.

Out of such an approach to composition can come an improved ability to persuade and a greater knowledge of self. A bonus is the possibility that exchange of ideas through listening and sharing with others will bring about tolerance and understanding.

THE LOCATION OF VALUES

It may seem strange to begin with the familiar. Now that man has walked on the moon, his perspective, we are told, is interplanetary. Nevertheless, a major food company makes advertising claims that it fed the men on the moon; business remains somewhat as usual on the ground below. Despite the moon talk of the large abstractions—peace, progress, humanity, etc.— we still meet on the street, where people live; deal with each other; and make everyday decisions based on assumptions that are very earthbound indeed.

Never before have these assumptions been so important. It is no exaggeration to say that personal—and even national—survival may depend on the extent to which people accept or reject certain assumptions about race, economics, appropriate "roles," rights, freedom, and privilege. What do we accept? What must be changed? What is too trivial to be worth mentioning, or is locked in a custom not worth exploring? And what sights, sounds, and familiar events have a meaning based on the way people view progress and worth? What are the choices that matter?

The whole subject of values is often embarrassing. Most college students have memories of inspirational messages in high school assemblies or "the thought for the day" read out over the school public address system. Some have been exposed to sermons in church. All have heard the ideals stated or implied by a candidate seeking votes via television. Values have no place in many schools because they have too often been part of empty rhetoric or speech without participation by the audience. Nevertheless college catalogues claim to "improve awareness," "make life more meaningful," and "acquaint the student with the best that has been thought and said." Such statements are especially true of the claims made for courses in English and the humanities. So it is appropriate that a liberal education should be concerned with these matters. Indeed, there is good precedent for students to examine the nature of the good life, though Socrates is an outstanding example of the risks involved.

GOALS

Choices has been designed to enhance the following qualities in the students and teachers who use it:

1. To be intellectually curious and desire knowledge.
2. To be critical and question statements, facts, social norms, and their own behavior patterns.
3. To be able to think and work through problems independently.
4. To be able to see relationships for themselves—relationships between facts, concepts, images, and people; to be able to construct new relationships.
5. To be able to participate and question in any group of people.
6. To be open and receptive to criticism and ideas other than their own.
7. To express ideas with clarity and strength in speech and writing.

This book proposes to encourage participation and examination of belief by beginning with the familiar and to aid thoughtful expression by built-in choices of the sort a friend or tutor would ask in a dialogue. It begins with the object, the sound, the event.

Miami, Florida   THELMA ALTSHULER

ACKNOWLEDGMENTS

The customary acknowledgment of assistance includes thanks to those who helped in preparation of the manuscript. Such help usually consists in reading, criticizing, and finding errors or omissions. A textbook which does not convey information but rather encourages understanding of self in terms of response to provocative situations must have the assistance of innovative teachers, imaginative and sympathetic to their students' interests. It is to Editor Bill Oliver's credit that he recognized the special approach of this book and found the right kind of people to review it.

They are the following college professors: Helen B. Keller of Indian River Junior College, Lloyd A. Flanigan of St. Petersburg Junior College, Elisabeth McPherson of Forest Park Community College, Timothy G. Davies of Michigan State University, Karl K. Taylor of Illinois Central College, and Nancy S. Prichard of Shoreline Community College and the National Council of Teachers of English.

Valuable editorial assistance was provided by a young student, Kathleen M. Hassall, who reacted to existing situations and suggested others in keeping with the modern tempo. Special thanks to Martin J. Cohen for calling my attention to the goals formulated by students of Malcolm X College in a 1969 Summer Institute. Some of these goals are listed in the Introduction to the book. Appropriate quotations were suggested by Philip Rosenberg of the University of Connecticut and Carol Zion of Miami-Dade Junior College. And pulling it all together was Mirta Ortega, who did her usual fine job of typing and retyping.

HOW THIS BOOK WORKS

SAMPLE SITUATION

Carl E has just finished loading up his cart in the supermarket. He has beer, pretzels, some apples, a ham, spaghetti, tomato sauce, and potato sticks for a party at his place. As he looks over the groceries on the counter he realizes that one of the items is associated with a political project he had intended to support by boycott. It is three minutes till closing time, and the cashier is busily punching the cash register.

THE CHOICES

What should Carl do?

_____1. Lift out the taboo item and ask the cashier not to ring it up. Ask her to subtract the cost if she already has counted it. Give no reason. The boycott is really symbolic and private.

_____2. Turn it back as in choice 1, but tell the cashier why, in an effort to persuade her.

_____3. Let it go. One man's boycott doesn't count for much. He should find a more effective method of protesting.

_____4. Let it go, because of the convenience of having the food for the party.

The choices may represent nothing more than your mood of the moment. Nevertheless, the reasons behind each choice obviously mean more. They involve ideas about effective political action, embarrassment, self-deception, the private gesture, the importance of friends you'll be seeing in five minutes as opposed to a dream of progress you may never see fulfilled at all. It is important that the question here is not "What do you think about boycotts

2

as a means of supporting political policies?" Rather, it is "What should a person do who does want to support a certain policy and who . . .," a specific situation rather than a general survey.

Some people could begin developing a speech or composition from the choices alone. But added richness comes from factors such as age, geography, wealth, and other details. These other factors, found in the challenges, require more specific attention to the problem and help to clarify the views of the person who has made the choice.

THE CHALLENGES

Would you change your opinion if:

	Yes	No
The product originated in a Communist country?	____	____
The product was made or grown by a company that refused to bargain with a union?	____	____
The product was made by a manufacturer who publicized his political views on television?	____	____
The product was the main course Carl had been planning to serve his guests?	____	____
Carl lived in an area where few share his views?	____	____
Carl had already contributed money and passed leaflets for the cause?	____	____
Carl cared about the cashier's personal opinion of him?	____	____

Most considerations within the challenges will change with circumstances. While the choice is general, based on impulsive reactions, the challenge requires closer, more thoughtful scrutiny. The challenge asks:

Would you change your opinion if . . .

and allows room for a variety of possibilities including age, experience, and status of the person with a problem. For instance, most people say that they accept the general idea of honesty; but in actual practice, the return of money which does not belong to them depends on factors other than that belief. Many people will call a shopkeeper's attention to his having given change for a ten instead of a one-dollar bill, if he owns the store; but a similar mistake in a large chain store will seem like a bit of good fortune. There are also factors such as the relative wealth of a customer, chances of getting caught, and willingness to endure embarrassment.

3

Sometimes you will work alone. At other times you may defend your choices in a general class discussion, or in a group presentation with others who made the same choice. Together, you can prepare a more formal and varied defense than you might have been able to make on your own. At other times, groups who did *not* make the same choices may discuss their ideas.

It will soon be apparent, as you hear the opinions of others, that certain people tend to use the same kind of argument. One may insist on logic or statistical proofs; another person considers everything from the point of view of one special interest group, which makes him see everything in terms of race, sex, or occupation. Some are able to argue everything in terms of other situations ("I once knew a man who . . ."); others merely keep repeating the same idea but more loudly. There are also the *ad hominem* arguments familiar to anyone who has argued, from neighborhood bar to presidential campaigns ("With hair like *that,* how can his ideas be any good?"). Point out unfair approaches when you hear them.

The challenges may be included in the discussion. That is, someone may say, "I believe choice 2 would be all right if Carl lived in _____ (name of a local community with a particular voting pattern), but not otherwise. That's why I checked the 'yes' next to the challenge, 'Would you change your answer if Carl lived in an area where few share his views.' The person who cared that much about being in the minority might himself be challenged by someone asking what he is afraid of, why his own popularity is so important to him, and so on."

The situations may also be used as bases for writing. See the General Design for Writing below.

GENERAL DESIGN FOR WRITING

This plan is meant to suggest possible ideas and organization for composition. It is adaptable to many different lengths, according to the assignment. The writer should feel free to concentrate on any part which suits him and to omit instructions which do not.

Instructions for structuring themes are found in several assignments in each of the four chapters. At the beginning of each of the chapters are situations followed by questions which can be answered in such a way that a complete theme will result. Other assignments provide less help. But in every case, the General Design for Writing will provide added suggestions for those who have temporarily run out of something to say.

The General Design for Writing takes the same situation of Carl's choices through the various parts of a theme.

Beginning of Theme

Choose one of the sentences listed under Beginning of Theme. The sentence you choose will be general enough to cover the things you want to write about. General sentences deal with more than one person and more than one time. *Children, college students, usually,* and *never* are the kinds of words found in a general sentence. If they seem to apply to too many people, you have the chance to show why as you write your theme. If you don't like the choice of sentences at Beginning of Theme, write your own, or make changes in those you find in the book. A possible general sentence for the sample situation is

Hospitality for friends is more important than useless support of an ideal.

Body of Theme

RETELL THE SITUATION

When you retell the situation in the book, you may want to copy it just as it appears or shorten it. The purpose of retelling the situation is to begin with an example of an idea in action. The situation will be the only thing everyone will have in common. In class discussions or comparison of papers, it will be interesting to see how students who began in the same way then adapted the material to themselves.

TELL A SIMILAR SITUATION YOU HAVE
EXPERIENCED OR OBSERVED

Your own situation should belong to the general sentence and should be similar to the given situation. In the sample situation, the question concerns what a person should do about supporting his beliefs. It would be more convenient for Carl to purchase the item, but at the same time he would be going against a promise he had made to himself or an organization. A similar situation would have to deal with beliefs in conflict with comfort. A comment about grocery stores or high prices or politics or parties or cashiers would obviously be inappropriate. It would be taking a word out of context, missing the point, and misusing the situation as an excuse to talk about anything at all. Stay on the subject!

EXPLAIN YOUR CHOICE AND YOUR COMMENT

Examine your feelings about the right thing to do in the situation you have devised. Find whatever relationship there is between your choice for Carl and the choice in your own situation. You are not limited to the one situation, but can give several. Comment on the difference between one and the other. This is also the place to bring in any of your "Yes" answers to the challenges. Why would they have made a difference? Would different circumstances have changed your opinion about appropriate action in your own situation? Why? In what way?

EXAMINE YOUR OWN BACKGROUND

Try to determine what forces have influenced you to answer the choices and challenges as you did. In this example, what made friends or the feeding of them of such importance? Hospitality at home? A parent's refusal to allow friends to come in as often as you would like? Too much talk of news events? Some ill effects you have observed in the lives of politically active people?

This examination of personal background proves nothing which can be verified with statistics, but it should not be overlooked. It is a valid means of discovering the probable source of ideas many of us take for granted as being "natural" or based on "common sense," and therefore inevitably shared by any thinking person. At the same time, this probing leads to self-discovery; answering the following question may be just as interesting as discovering where you get your ideas: How did you get to be the way you are?

EXAMINE A PUBLIC APPLICATION OF YOUR CHOICE

What would happen if others behaved in the manner you are recommending? Would the world necessarily be better? What are the general advantages for people, not just for the one person in the Situation? Can you imagine everyone, or almost everyone boycotting the same product that Carl is concerned about? What would have to be done to persuade many people on a nationwide basis?

WHAT IS WRONG WITH THE CHOICES YOU REJECTED?
EXAMINE THE OPINIONS OF THOSE WHO DISAGREE
WITH YOUR CHOICE

Have the believers been taught falsely? Where do you think the "wrong" choices come from? What emotions are involved in the other choices? In Carl's situation, you might have thought that a wrong choice would have been to explain to the cashier why the product was being returned, that this would have been embarrassing for Carl the next time he went into the store, and that the store would be the wrong place to try political persuasion. People who checked that choice may, in your opinion, be apt to like argument and confrontation for their own sake without thinking about whether it does any good.

EXPLAIN THE POSSIBILITIES OF RECONCILIATION

How can people who believe as you do get together with people who don't? Emphasize what you have in common, what you can share, even if you cannot agree on all points.

Ending of Theme

The ending of the speech or theme should return to the main statement and restate it as persuasively as possible. It is not the place to introduce new arguments or examples, but it is the place to remind listeners or readers of the strongest points you have already made.

Consult this General Design for Writing whenever you find yourself with too little to say, or when you are repeating the points you have already made, or when you are straying too far from the main issues which began the situation.

BOTH SIDES

Before you begin to defend your own choices, consider the fair treatment given in the following selection to both rock musicians and the people who dislike them. This excerpt from a longer magazine article is a model for the presentation of two life styles in conflict. Sara Davidson does not claim that the wait-and-save people are better than the spend-it-now people. But she presents the impact of one group on the other with an understanding of each.

As you consider the choices you did not make, try to be as impartial as Sara Davidson in your presentation of the beliefs of others. It's better than sarcastic name-calling!

> Playing rock is a means of living out a definition of the good life that defies the American dream: never have a steady job, keep crazy hours, get stoned, play music, draw constant attention, and, if you do all these things well, make lots of money. The band members look at ads in the magazines—see the gray-haired couple in the rowboat, the happy wife is handing her happy husband a worm for his fishing rod. If you squirrel away now for the future you can retire at sixty and have a cottage on a lake. The reasoning behind this scene—years of working, saving, putting off, sacrificing—has no meaning to rock musicians and to an increasing number of young people who listen with puzzlement to job recruiters on the campus, talking of pensions and sick pay and medical benefits. They know people their own age who have bypassed the corporation jobs and are living at the rainbow's end of the work ethic—the mansion on Lake Mahopac. If young people can live in Big Sur, or Florida, or the Catskills, without saving for forty years at the Dime Savings Bank, what does this mean to people who have gone the other way, postponed their desires, worked at dehumanizing jobs? It means to some of them that maybe what they did was all unnecessary. Is it surprising that the man in

Boston is moved to rage when he sees John Finley with his long curls
and wallet full of money?

SARA DAVIDSON, from "Rock Style," Copyright © 1969
by Harper's Magazine, Inc. *Harper's* (July, 1969).

TIME AND SPACE

In using this book, all you need to find which choice you like is the quick
glance of impulse—and a pencil. The challenges take more time, but not
more space. A check in the *yes* or *no* column shows your answer. Then,
when you find a general statement that reflects your thoughts, claim it for
your own by marking it and using it.

When you begin to write, you'll have an idea, an opening line, a story to
show the idea in action, and some examples of important modifications.
After that, you're on your own if you want to be. If you can, develop your
ideas with reasons, other examples, a close look at your own experiences and
whatever else you find useful. Obviously, finding other things to say takes
more time than choosing ideas already there. And help is provided for this
body of the theme, if you need it. Look at the questions, and answer them
as completely as you can. At this point in your writing, a simple *yes* or *no*
will be less useful than *yes, if* . . . or *unless* . . . or *at times*. Slow up for
the questions. Speed is your enemy.

Because it was not possible to know how much space you would need
for your answers, only the questions were printed. But don't be fooled by
their appearance. They may be crowded together with no definite place to
write an answer, but at this point the answers must be thought out and
written in your composition. Say as much as you like, and when you have
nothing more for one question, go back for suggestions to stimulate more
writing.

In this way, you are on your own but you are not abandoned.

Your theme will include short answers and long ones, impulse and reflection.

CHAPTER I

What we think, or what we know,
or what we believe
is in the end of little consequence.
The only thing of consequence
is what we do.

JOHN RUSKIN

You have not converted a man because
you have silenced him.

VISCOUNT MORLEY

FREEDOM
AND
RESTRAINT

MINI-SITUATIONS

Hearing more than one "side" of a story is said to allow a fair person to judge what the truth is. On the other hand, it's hard to be fair when your sympathies leap to the defense of a member of a certain group—or when they automatically assume guilt. Everyone has automatic preferences and dislikes, based not on evidence but on identity. That's one reason it isn't easy to pick a jury.

In order for you to discover your own automatic sympathies, just imagine which party you would probably support—without knowing anything more. If you read these headlines in a newspaper, which party would you "like" before you knew more about what had happened?

My probable sympathies
would be with:

1. LANDLORD SUES TENANT
   FOR BACK RENT   _____

2. CAR-TRUCK COLLISION CAUSES
   EXTENSIVE DAMAGE   _____

3. MILLIONAIRE SUED BY
   INTERNAL REVENUE SERVICE
   FOR BACK TAXES   _____

4. SCHOOL BOARD WARNS
   STRIKING TEACHERS TO
   RETURN OR BE FIRED   _____

5. POLICEMAN ARRESTS TEENAGER
   ON CHARGES OF VAGRANCY   _____

6. PULITZER PRIZE-WINNING NOVELIST
   ARRESTED BY VICE SQUAD IN
   RAID ON "GAY" BAR   _____

7. IRATE CUSTOMER SLUGS BUTCHER   _____

8. WHITE "RADICAL" STUDENT
   TESTIFIES AT TRIAL:
   COP WAS RACIST   _____

9. NATURE LOVER TRIES TO HALT
   HOUSING PROJECT CONSTRUCTION
   IN WOODED AREA—REFUSES TO
   MOVE FOR BULLDOZERS   _____

10. UNION LEADER VOTED SALARY
    INCREASE—RANK AND FILE PROTEST   _____

11. LEGISLATURE SLASHES FUNDS
    FOR WELFARE MOTHERS   _____

12. IRISH ACTOR RETIRES TO NATIVE
    COUNTRY WITH FORTUNE
    MADE IN U.S.—AVOIDS INTERNAL
    REVENUE TAXES   _____

13. STUDENT CHARGES PLAGIARISM
    IN SUIT AGAINST SONGWRITER   _____

14. LOVELORN GIRL IN HUNGER STRIKE
    TO PROVE AFFECTION FOR ATHLETE
    WHO SPURNED HER   _____

15. Open Headline: _____

_____   _____

(You write one to try out on class.)

Now that you've marked your preferences, were you surprised by any of your answers? (Don't write your discovery. Just think it.)

Select five headlines which interest you and explain your preferences. Then try to figure out the circumstances which would make you change your probable sympathy to another person or institution in the headline.

The headline: _____

Why I chose as I did: _____

What would change my sympathy: _____

_____

(Do that five times. Try to be imaginative. That is, don't keep writing "If my man was guilty of using violence, I'd be for the other side." But if there is one action that you really dislike—enough to make any other facts unimportant—find out what it is. Do the same with economic, ethnic, or occupational identities.)

EXTRA:

What gets left out of headlines? What gets left out of trials? Imagine a situation (base it on a real one, if you like) in which you tell the events leading up to the confrontation, but the public hears only the explosion. Even though you may want your sympathies to show, describe the situation as fairly as you can, although you may not be able to refrain from expressing your feelings.

Explain: "I like what they stand for, but I don't like their methods. . . ."

Finally, complete a headline. You supply the ending which would make you unsympathetic to the person in the first part. Choose any two headlines, but have reasons ready for the two you didn't want to do!

1. HIGH SCHOOL STUDENT SUSPENDED FOR REFUSING TO (Play Dixie. Sing the National Anthem. Cut his hair. Pray. Turn in Student government association funds, etc.) _____

2. _____ REFUSED PERMISSION TO PARADE IN CITY (Is there any group you could put in here?)

3. MAN FOUND GUILTY, SENTENCED TO LIFE IN JAIL AT HARD LABOR FOR CRIME OF _____

4. ORGANIZATION REQUIRED TO PAY $100,000 FINE FOR CRIME OF _____

Explain your ending to each headline:

1. _____

2. _____

Explain why you chose not to do the two you omitted:

1. _____

2. _____

1

THE SITUATION

Charlie K is signing the loan papers for the purchase of a used car. He has hardly enough money for a down payment, and the monthly installments will take half his salary. As Charlie signs the conditional sales contract which sets forth the terms of payment, he doesn't notice the amount of actual interest nor the fact that if the car is repossessed he may still owe money which can be deducted from his wages. Besides, the car has been overpriced and will need expensive repairs.

Charlie's wife wishes he would spend his money on his home and children rather than on a car. The salesman is glad he is buying it.

THE CHOICES

Should there be laws to prevent Charlie from buying a car he can't afford?

_____1. Yes. There should be someone to help him get his money's worth, even if it means submitting details of the purchase to a special agency.

_____2. No. It's more important for him to have his freedom, even if it's freedom to make a mistake, than to have supervision of what he does.

_____3. No, but there ought to be restrictions on the sale and conditions of repayment of shoddy merchandise.

_____4. _____

(Your own statement of choice if you don't like any of those listed.)

THE CHALLENGES

Would your opinion change if:

	Yes	No
A consumer agency was run by local government?	___	___
The purchase of the car meant failure to pay the rent?	___	___
Restrictions on used-car agencies resulted in bankruptcy for some agents?	___	___
There were consumer-education courses available?	___	___
Driving the car will probably make Charlie feel more confident?	___	___
Charlie's wife told him not to buy the car?	___	___
Charlie was being protected from gambling, which he cannot afford?	___	___

Note: In each section, the first few theme assignments have the kind of help offered here. In others, there is less help, but the General Writing Design (pp. 4–7) is useful if you run out of ideas or lack a plan for organizing the material.

WRITING ASSIGNMENT

Beginning of Theme
(Choose one.)

People should have complete freedom, including the freedom to make a mistake.

Or

It is a mistake to pretend that misrepresentation and cheating are "freedom."

Or

_____

(Your own general statement if you don't choose either of the above.)

Body of Theme

Retell the situation, including your choice and answers to the challenges.

Continuation of Theme—Optional
(Select as many of the following as you need to develop a good theme on the wider implications of Charlie's situation.)

14

If some person or agency had the power to supervise a fair price for automobiles, what would make the plan work? What might go wrong? Should the federal government run such an agency? If not, what group might?

If Charlie buys a car with poor brakes and the car fails to stop at a crucial moment, is the car dealer partially responsible (morally, if not legally) for damages to life or property?

What responsibility do you think business has to protect the consumer? Does "protection" include prevention of a mistake?

Should there be rules for the purchase of automobiles as there are rules for the purchase of food, drugs, and cigarettes?

Should poor people be required to check with an authority before buying something expensive? Why or why not?

Should everyone study consumer education?

Should people have the freedom to drive an unsafe car?

Should poor people be allowed to gamble?

Should people be allowed to do anything considered dangerous or foolish or immoral if only the individual is involved? Comment on health habits, abortion, suicide, mercy killing, if you can relate those situations to Charlie's situation.

Ending of Theme

Restate your belief about purchasing rights and freedom.

2

THE SITUATION

Howard and Dolly have been invited to three different New Year's Eve parties. They plan to spend about an hour at each before drifting on to the next, and the last stop of all will be at a bar in their neighborhood, where they know a lot of the people and which usually has the liveliest crowd for the early morning hours.

One look at the first party convinces them that their plan will not work. Instead of a drop-in party which can be visited briefly and then left, this is obviously the kind of party at which they are expected to spend the entire evening. They can't get away without being noticed. Only two other couples have been invited, in addition to their hostess Grace and her boy friend. The dining room has been formally set for a midnight supper, and Grace, who has a reputation as a good cook, has apparently been preparing food for the past ten days. Howard and Dolly will have to hold up their part of the conversation, compliment Grace on each new goody she serves, and stay awake. They stare at each other.

THE CHOICES

What should they do about the evening?

_____1. Let it be ruined. Stay there and forget the other parties. There will be other New Year's Eves.

_____2. Proclaim sudden illness and beat a hasty retreat. There is a possibility the lie will be found out, but it's worth the chance for self-preservation.

_____3. Stay an hour, explain about the other parties, and abandon the other two couples to an even duller party than it would have been if Howard and Dolly had stayed.

THE CHALLENGES

Would your opinion change if:

	Yes	No
The other couples were unpleasant and boring?	_____	_____
Howard and Dolly had been fighting and they needed a lively evening to help get back together?	_____	_____
Grace had been giving Howard free tutoring lessons in math and was therefore entitled to a favor?	_____	_____
The invitation was made six weeks ahead of time?	_____	_____
Grace's boy friend had been accepting rides to and from school in Howard's car?	_____	_____
Dolly accepted the invitation and assured Howard they would not have to stay long because he had wanted to go somewhere else?	_____	_____

(Are your answers based on:

pleasure?
the strength or importance of the people?
obligation to a host?
The Golden Rule?)

Write a column describing the thoughts of Howard or Dolly as they walked into the room and heard there would be no other guests. Then write a column describing the thoughts of Grace and the kind of evening she hoped it would be. Make the couples any age you like.

Howard or Dolly	Grace

Howard or Dolly	Grace

GENERAL CLASS DISCUSSION

Who owes what to whom in this disastrous New Year's Eve? How do each of the choices really act as a disguise for the selfish motives people have on other occasions more important than parties—suffering, trying to cope tactfully, lying, telling the truth. Are Howard and Dolly likely to make the same choices for other difficulties? Do you?

3

THE SITUATION

Albert H is a high school senior in a class with more girls than boys. In his neighborhood the boys are less likely to finish school than the girls. Nevertheless, Albert has tried to be a "good student" with his eye on a better future. He delivers newspapers in the afternoon, sells tickets for school athletic events, and is working toward a college scholarship.

One day there is a school-wide strike against the food in the school cafeteria. The students spill out of the building and onto the school grounds. Bad lunches are only a part of their complaints. Albert is shouting slogans along with the rest of them and is caught up in a crowd in the front of the school. They ignore administration demands that they return to afternoon classes. Instead, three of the boys climb the flagpole and remove the flag. With help from police summoned to the school, the boys around the flagpole—including Albert—are disciplined by the school. They are suspended for the rest of the year. Albert's explanation that he had nothing to do with the flag incident is disregarded. He was in the area, and he got caught with the rest.

THE CHOICES

What are Albert's choices for the future?

_____1. Continue to fight for reinstatement to the school.

_____2. Go back to school in the following year, with the possibility that he will be able to clear his record and get a scholarship anyway.

_____3. Seek justice in the streets as a member of a militant group.

_____4. Decide to become a policeman, as a means of bringing more justice to the kind of incident he has just been part of.

_____5. _____

_____

_____

(Your own, different suggestion.)

THE CHALLENGES

Would your opinion change if:

	Yes	No
Albert really had taken down the flag?	____	____
Albert had been clubbed by police?	____	____
Albert's father was a policeman?	____	____
This story was about a black boy?	____	____
Albert was an indifferent rather than a good student?	____	____
The real culprit eluded police, and Albert knew who he was?	____	____

ACTION

If you selected choice 1, defend this idea: When you want something, you should go to a lot of trouble to fight for it, but within the legal system.

If you selected choice 2, defend this idea: The best way to handle a disappointment is slowly and steadily, without anger.

If you selected choice 3, defend this idea: Since there is little justice in the system, poor people need to make their own justice in their own way.

If you selected choice 4, defend this idea: Each man can make a better world by doing more than just getting by; individual idealism is needed.

If you selected choice 5—if you had a different reason for choosing one of the first four, write your own topic sentence here. Make sure it does not refer specifically to any person in the situation.

Follow the General Writing Design to complete the composition.

TIME OUT

a person whose position gives him the right to control, advise, or direct other people.

a definition of Authority

This priest has authority. He knows more about religious doctrine than his parishioners. He gives public sermons on morals and the good life. He answers private questions on personal decisions. His contribution to society (is, is not) worthwhile because

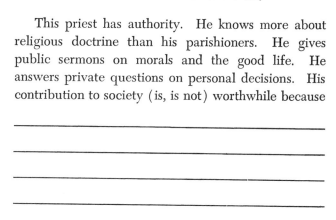

_____

_____

_____

_____

This policeman has authority. He keeps order, tries to prevent trouble before it happens, and places under arrest those whose violation of the law comes to his attention. His contribution to society (is, is not) worthwhile because

_____

_____

_____

_____

21

This dean . . . this parent . . . this employer . . . and so forth. Describe his duties, show him in action as he controls, advises, or directs someone else. Your situation should clearly show what you regard as the proper use of his authority.

Write the basic details of your situation here:

Try to understand your own attitude toward authority: Do you tend to accept without question? Resent in advance? What else?

Go beyond the situation you have just thought of, and write a theme defining authority—its rights, responsibilities, and abuses. When is it democratic? How does one qualify to use it? What is the best way to deal with it?

4

THE SITUATION

For the past several years, Dr. T has been the head of a volunteer organization. Now that he is retiring, he wants to thank the many people who have worked with him on various campaigns. In order to prevent the large, cold institutional quality of the gathering, Dr. T has decided to have four small informal parties at his home. In looking over the list, Dr. T notices a number of Jewish names and decides to invite all the Jewish people for one evening. He will figure out some other basis for grouping the others.

THE CHOICES

Is it a good idea to invite people of one religion to a party?

_____1. Yes, they'll feel more at home with their own kind.
_____2. No, they'll notice and feel discriminated against.

THE CHALLENGES

Would your answer change if:

	Yes	No
The grouping was according to general income level?	____	____
Age?	____	____
Neighborhood?	____	____
Profession?	____	____

Alphabetical order?

Length of time in the organization?

— —

— —

ACTION

If you selected choice 1, write a paper beginning something like this:

People tend to feel more at home with their own kind.

If you selected choice 2, write a paper beginning something like this:

Grouping people according to a label is insulting.

Follow the General Writing Design for additional suggestions.

GENERAL CLASS DISCUSSION

What is your opinion of grouping people according to designations as listed in the challenges? Are there voting blocs, special college courses, housing, etc., that are grouped according to these labels? Should there be? Be sure to make the distinction between what is and what ought to be.

OPTIONAL ASSIGNMENT

Write a personal essay comparing the behavior of people when they think they are "with their own kind" and when they think they are not. Include subjects discussed, language used, gestures, clothing, and so forth.

5

THE SITUATION

Professor Maxwell E is in charge of a crash literacy program, teaching reading to young men in their late teens and to older adults. He has found that students are not interested in most of the books with a limited vocabulary, but that they will read paperbacks about gang wars, prostitutes, and the wife-swapping clubs of the suburbs. Anything with action, either violent or sexy, seems to be popular. The professor believes that once the students start by reading anything at all, they will turn to other kinds of literature.

In ordering books for the coming year he will be using taxpayers' money to purchase books with titles like *Slum Sister, The Hooker's Revenge,* and *Torture Night in Cycle City.*

THE CHOICES

Should he order the books?

_____1. Yes. Anything the students read will develop the habit of reading.

_____2. No. They'd be better off not reading at all if that kind of book is all they'll touch.

_____3. No. The professor will probably get into trouble with a citizen's committee who are worried about the possible behavior of his students.

THE CHALLENGES

Would you change your opinion if:

	Yes	No
The books were antireligious?	____	____
The books used dashes instead of spelling out four-letter words?	____	____
The dropout rate has been high?	____	____
Some of the students have been in trouble with the law?	____	____
There were girls in the class?	____	____

Defend your beliefs about the professor's problem, or write an alternative suggestion for ways to encourage reading among his students.

6

THE SITUATION

At a night baseball game, the umpire was making calls which seemed outrageous to the manager of the home team. In addition to the standard "You're blind!" the manager yelled a great many unprintable accusations. After almost every decision, the manager was out on the field, waving his arms and letting the umpire know exactly what was wrong with his judgment, his looks, and his family background. The fans loved the argument. They were laughing at the manager's screams and threats, and soon they began to yell their own insults at the umpire. As far as the fans were concerned, the umpire couldn't do anything right. As the game continued, the home team suffered more and more, partly from their own blunders and partly as a result of some close calls against them. The game was crucial to the series, and the fans became increasingly serious in their anger against the umpire. Led by the manager, they called for his removal from the game, at the very least. The more ardent of them wanted the umpire to break his neck.

The home team lost. As the umpire tried to leave the field, several hundred fans headed toward him. The police were unable to protect him adequately, and a couple of big men picked up the umpire, shook him, and beat him up. He required a week of hospitalization for the lacerations he suffered.

The umpire brought suit against the team manager. He claimed damages on the grounds that it was the manager's insults which had instigated the anger of the fans and the riot which took place on the field.

THE CHOICES

If you were a member of a jury hearing the case, what do you think you would decide?

_____1. Award damages to the umpire from the manager, whose words had started the violence and who is therefore responsible for injuries.

_____2. Disallow damages, as the manager had not actually struck any blows.

THE CHALLENGES

Would you change your opinion if:

	Yes	No
The manager said "Hit him" to someone he knew, and that was the man who struck the umpire?	_____	_____
The attack took place without a crowd around?	_____	_____
The manager was not the only one yelling insults?	_____	_____

WRITING ASSIGNMENT

Beginning of Theme
(Choose one.)

The only person responsible for violence is the one who actually strikes a blow.

Or

The person responsible for violence is not only the one who strikes a blow but the one who stirred up the action in the first place.

See the General Writing Design for suggestions for further development of theme.

ACTION

This cartoon appeared in December, 1968. Allowing for the exaggeration of academic clothing for the man shining shoes, is the point still valid?

What answer do you think could be given by the man shining shoes?

Compose an answer that would be most persuasive for the customer.

Define Freedom or Restraint as it applies to this cartoon.

COCHRAN!

"Just what is it that you people want, anyway?"

7

THE SITUATION

Two young men live on the same block. One of the boys—Eddie—comes from a family that has strong, established rules and emphasizes order and obedience. Before a certain day when the summer season officially starts, they do not wear light clothes or go swimming, no matter how hot it is. No matter how late fall weather arrives, Labor Day is the time for taking out the dark clothing and ending summer activities. When Eddie is asked to write a composition in school, he looks up the things other people have said on the subject, using tried-and-true phrases. He does better-than-average work in school, and is always punctual and neat.

The other boy—Lionel—is almost the complete opposite of Eddie. When he wants to be, he is original, even eloquent. He refuses clichés, thinks for himself. He has won essay contests for his well thought out, creative ideas. He has failed science. While he understands the work, he often doesn't finish reports, because he is impatient with clerical details. When he is interested in a subject he can be at the head of the class; when he is not interested he zooms to the bottom.

THE CHOICES

If Eddie and Lionel had been students in your high school, which of the following would probably have happened?

_____1. Lionel would be in trouble with most of his teachers.

_____2. Lionel would be an honors student, in special classes.

_____3. Lionel would get help in organization from students like Eddie.

30

_____4. Eddie would have offers of jobs because his qualities are most in demand.

_____5. Eddie would represent the school at official functions.

_____6. _____

(Your own answer.)

THE CHALLENGES

Would your opinion change if:

The word *would* was changed to *should* in questions:	Yes	No
1.	___	___
2.	___	___
3.	___	___
4.	___	___
5.	___	___
6.	___	___

WRITING ASSIGNMENT

Beginning of Theme

Schools do not encourage independent thinking, and our contemporary society doesn't need it.

Or

Schools do not encourage independent thinking, and our contemporary society needs it badly.

Or

Schools do encourage independent thinking, but other qualities just as important must be encouraged, too.

Or

Schools allow independent thinking, but they don't encourage it from nonconforming students.

_____

(Your own statement, if you don't want to write about one of those listed.)

Body of Theme

Discuss any of the following as a means of developing your general statement.

Which of the boys do you think would be happier in schools as they now are? Explain any of your answers to the challenges.

Is it unfair for schools to develop originality when most students will have to take routine jobs when they leave school? In what ways is school a "preparation for life"?

What is the plight of the oddball or troublemaker in school? How can you tell when he is really creative rather than destructive? How much extra help, if any, should be available to him?

What is the plight of the C student? Is he generally overlooked as most attention is paid to the students on either end of the grading scale?

If you were running a school, what changes would you make to help all the Eddies and Lionels?

Follow the General Design for Writing for other suggestions.

Ending of Theme

End with some reference—serious or humorous—to the two boys whose situation began this examination of the real and the ideal in schools.

8

THE SITUATION

Jeff is an announcer at a local radio station. One of his jobs is the selection of which songs to play during the day. He must choose from many hundreds of records that come in. In recent months there have been complaints that some of the records are about subjects which teen-agers should not hear. The lyrics tell of narcotics and suicide and sex.

THE CHOICES

Do you think Jeff should allow such controversial songs to be played on the air?

_____1. Yes, because _____

_____

_____.

_____2. No, because _____

_____

_____.

_____3. In some cases, if _____

_____

_____.

THE CHALLENGES

If you selected choice 1 above, answer these questions:

Would you change your answer if it could be proved that listening to such records led to an increase in

> violence?
>
> drug addiction?
>
> promiscuous sex?

At what point does a total lack of censorship seem likely to bring about a backlash of strict control?

Bring in a current song sheet or records. Which of the songs do you think the censors might object to? Why? What is accomplished through the musical background, pauses, voice of singers?

Does your feeling about records include movies and books?

If you selected choice 2 above, answer these questions:

Have *you* ever changed your actions as the result of some songs you have heard? Do you know anyone who has been influenced? Tell how.

Would you change your answer if Jeff's competitors on the other radio stations were willing to play the songs he rejected?

If you selected choice 3, answer these questions:

On what basis can he decide? Give an example of something "too bad," or "really nasty." What about songs that sound harmless but have another meaning for those who know certain words? Can there be "a little bit of censorship," or does it get out of hand?

GENERAL CLASS DISCUSSION

If Jeff shows good judgment, what happens when he leaves the station? How can a code be formulated which would work for other announcers?

34

9

THE SITUATION

Tom W is a lawyer who has been asked to defend a young man charged with murder. The young man claims innocence and maintains that he never met the victim. Every time he tells the story, the facts seem to change. Tom is sure the man is lying, and thinks he's probably guilty of a particularly brutal slaying.

THE CHOICES

Should Tom defend the man?

_____1. Yes. Everyone is entitled to a fair trial, including the guilty.

_____2. No. Tom should not try to defend a man who can't even keep his story straight.

_____3. No. The man is probably guilty. Tom should not use the law to protect someone who has no respect for it.

THE CHALLENGES

Would your opinion change if:

	Yes	No
The man admitted to Tom that he was guilty, told him the whole story, and then asked for help?	_____	_____
The man was obviously lying, but it looked as though he hadn't committed the crime?	_____	_____

The man was accused of molesting children or murdering
seven different people?   ____ ____

GENERAL CLASS DISCUSSION

Is the reputation of some lawyers tied to the kind of clients they attract?
Give examples of outstanding (or notorious) trials in your own community.
Have any accused people had trouble getting a good defense?

10

THE SITUATION

Dan has been invited to a party by a boy he has met in class. When he arrives he recognizes several other people he has seen at school. He gets something to drink, and sits down to talk to a pretty girl. Some minutes later, he becomes aware that a number of the people on the other side of the room are smoking marijuana. He prefers not to, is enjoying his talk with the girl, but hates to risk arrest in a community where being near pot is as socially acceptable as manslaughter.

THE CHOICES

What should he do?

_____1. Leave right away and report what he has seen to the police. (It's his duty, both to the law, and to these people, who are doing themselves harm.)

_____2. Stay where he is and ignore them. (It's none of his business, and he's having a good time.)

_____3. Leave and forget about it. (After all, he was invited as a friend. Why should he be the informer or risk being implicated?)

_____4. Smoke along with the others. (The people in the room are his group. He should follow their code.)

_____5. _____

_____

(Other choice, if you prefer.)

THE CHALLENGES

Would your opinion change if:

	Yes	No
The girl Dan is talking to is the hostess?	___	___
The boy who invited Dan is a close friend?	___	___
Dan believes the laws prohibiting marijuana are unjust?	___	___
Dan has applied to law school, and getting busted will end his chances?	___	___

ACTION

Justify your answers to one of the choices and one of the challenges.

Further complications

Assume that the person who invited Dan to the party is the girl he is dating. Imagine the scene when Dan observes people smoking marijuana. If the fact that the girl herself was smoking is important or would change the things Dan says, add that information to the little "play" you make up.

Or

Suppose that the police arrive on the scene, arrest everyone there, and charge them all with possession of drugs. Describe a possible comment or explanation of three different people, chosen from among these:

Dan
The hostess
A policeman
Dan's father
A very drunk guest

TIME OUT

There is no one practice so fraught with danger as that which is called the Sunday evening out. Unless the girl is positively known to spend the time in the company of respectable friends, the privilege ought never to be granted. Make such arrangements as will allow her to go to Church in the morning or afternoon but not in the evening . . .

. . . Poverty and misery, be it remembered, are more generally the results of vice, laziness, and improvidence, than of misfortune.

These are quotations taken from a magazine printed in England during the 1860's. The advice to ladies about how much time off to give their maids is like the advice found on the women's pages of newspapers and magazines today.

The passage below contains some comments by a contemporary observer on what these quotes from one hundred years ago showed about the beliefs and attitudes of the time.

After you have read the quotes and the comments, you may be able to do the same thing—find a quote and comment on what it shows about the beliefs of the person making it.

The fact that some people were superior was an accepted and even a welcomed fact. God, if anyone, was to blame for any seeming injustice and a proper awareness of God's impeccable judgement did not admit of any criticism of the system He had ordained.

The poor were there to be alternately bullied and watched over. No sentimentality was lavished upon them, the attitude toward them being governed by a strict practicality. The working class as a whole were regarded with gentle disapproval, coloured by a suspicion that they were extravagant and drunken. The poor were viewed with active distaste except at Christmas time.

This comment and the quotation above were both taken from *The Queen,* a British magazine which began publication in 1861, as quoted in *The Frontiers of Privilege,* edited by Quentin Crewe.

ACTION

Add your own comments about what Victorian readers of this magazine apparently believed about themselves and the poor.

Can you find anything to justify any of their beliefs? Explain them with as much understanding as you can, even if you don't agree. Are there people today who would agree with all or part of these remarks? Explain.

What do *you* believe that the Victorians did not believe about servants, poor people, working people, or the middle class? What do you wish you could have told them? How are "poverty and misery" explained in your own group these days?

Imagine that you are an historian writing at some time in the future. How would you objectively explain some of our current beliefs?

11

THE SITUATION

Patrick F is against the welfare program. He believes that people who are too lazy to support themselves are enjoying paid vacations at the expense of the government, and that none of them will go back to work until the money stops coming in. He resents the fact that his taxes are being used, in part, to finance a program that he disapproves of.

Gene D is strongly opposed to the U.S. military policy of fighting in countries where he thinks "we don't belong." His eldest son will very soon be eligible for the draft. Meanwhile, the policies Gene hates are financed largely by American tax dollars. Gene hates the thought of paying for supplies, ammunition, and generals' salaries to prolong what he feels is militarism.

THE CHOICES

Without considering your own attitude toward their beliefs, do you think Patrick and Gene should refuse to file their tax returns?

_____1. No. The taxes apply to everyone. There are legal ways for change.

_____2. Yes. Patrick and Gene ought to do what they think is right. It's more important to be at peace with your own conscience than to obey blindly, and contribute to a situation you believe is wrong.

THE CHALLENGES

If you selected choice 1, explain how Patrick and Gene should go about changing the present situation. Don't be satisfied with easy answers:

If you selected choice 2, explain what would happen if everybody behaved according to individual beliefs in paying his taxes.

You may use the second sentence in each answer as the first sentence in your composition.

GENERAL CLASS DISCUSSION

Under what circumstances, if any, is disobedience to the law a valid position? Suppose that the law is made by an oppressor, an occupying army. If the *assumption* is made that a current law is immoral and that the public has neither the will nor the power to change it, what kinds of actions may follow? How could they be defended or attacked?

12

THE SITUATION

Wendy has gone downtown on a Saturday afternoon for a day of shopping . . . or shoplifting. She is about to step onto the sidewalk from the front doors of the department store when a store detective suggests that they go to the office for a little talk. A search reveals that Wendy is wearing a new bathing suit under her clothes. In her handbag are matching sun glasses. Both items are obviously from the store.

THE CHOICES

Some people who have been apprehended have used the following "explanations." Do any of them seem satisfactory to you? Which one?

_____1. "I was doing it as part of an initiation into a school sorority."

_____2. "I can't afford a new bathing suit. My family can barely get along with all of us working, and my mother's sick."

_____3. "Just tell me what the stuff costs. My father will send you a check— with a little extra for your trouble."

_____4. "You mean you're going to prosecute me? Why? I'll give you back the stuff. Isn't that enough?"

_____5. "I didn't take it from any person. This store has merchandise worth millions."

_____6. "I didn't do anything wrong. My only crime was getting caught."

THE CHALLENGES

Should the following people be subject to the same laws as ordinary criminals?

	Yes	No
Those who do something as a prank, or for friends.	⸺	⸺
Those who have always been poor.	⸺	⸺
Those who have always been rich.	⸺	⸺
Those who are willing to make restitution.	⸺	⸺
Those who take from the rich rather than the poor.	⸺	⸺
Those who don't recognize the difference between right and wrong.	⸺	⸺

ACTION

Did you check the choice 1 and challenge 1? Or number 2 for each? If your choice and challenge selections were the same, write a paper justifying the selections you made. How far are you willing to carry the excuses, though? What about crimes more serious than shoplifting?

Did you check choices and challenges whose numbers don't match? Explain why one kind of explanation seemed all right for the specific crime of shoplifting, yet you were unwilling to accept it as a general rule. (Are you often inconsistent? illogical?)

13

THE SITUATION

You are an adviser to a man with great power to reform. As Secretary of Health, Education, and Welfare, you turn your attention to the problems of sex and the family. There are unwanted children, children growing up in fatherless homes, frequent divorces, and widespread promiscuity. From your own knowledge of current problems, try to build a more perfect society in the future. Analyze the following possibilities for change. Next to each, write the main reason you chose it, or rejected it.

THE CHOICES

_____1. Legalized bigamy that allows more than one family to live together.

Reason for choice or rejection: _____

_____

_____2. Enforced separation of the sexes until some given age—18, 21, or 25.

Reason for choice or rejection: _____

_____

_____3. The abolition of marriage. Reason for choice or rejection: _____

_____

_____4. More difficult divorce laws. Reason for choice or rejection: _____

_____

_____

_____5. A limitation of the number of children in a family to a given number, with enforcement carried out by the state. Reason for choice or rejection: _____

_____

_____6. A curb on advertising that emphasizes the attraction of the opposite sex. Reason for choice or rejection: _____

_____

_____7. A license to breed, with permission denied to those with low intelligence or criminal records. Reason for choice or rejection: _____

_____

_____8. A continuation of most of our present rules for marriage and the family. Reason for choice or rejection: _____

_____

ACTION

Defend each choice. Include reasons why you think the idea is a good one.

Then, for each, make up a situation to show your idea in action. For example, imagine what families would be like if the father had more than one wife. What would mealtime be like? Which wife would supervise the children's homework? Would both wives stay home while Dad had a night out with the boys?

Or

Explain your rejections of the ideas you did not choose. Tell why they would not work, where the opposition would come from. Tell whether you believe "human nature" would prevent the idea from working or the church or people's ingrained habits, or some other influence you believe to be important.

Then, for two or three of your rejected ideas, make up a Situation illustrating why it would not work.

SURVEY

Which of the following kinds of movies, if any, do you consider dangerous?
A film showing:

_____ 1. A happy-ever-after ending for a bank robber, who keeps the money after outwitting police, and travels safely to a country without extradition laws.

_____ 2. A Cinderella story about a girl who sings about love and finds it.

_____ 3. A film about a girl who wanders from one lover to another, without caring for anyone; with close-ups of some of the lovemaking.

_____ 4. American pioneers portrayed as ignorant and greedy, intruding on the land of the Indians, who really had prior claim.

_____ 5. Sadistic torturers beating and burning their victims and obviously enjoying their work, their own lives ending violently on motorcycles in a gang war with a rival gang.

_____ 6. A film about a weak man who dreams of being rich and powerful, and has all his wishes come true through luck and accident—like happening to find a winning ticket on a race.

_____ 7. A film showing soldiers heroic, whose victory consists of "wiping out" the men on the opposing side.

_____ 8. A monster in a horror film about the destruction of the whole planet.

_____ 9. A film making fun of such authorities as school officials, police, the President.

_____10. (Your own example): _____

_____

_____

Do you go to see the films you consider dangerous for the general public?

Have you ever known anyone who keeps going to films he finds offensive? How do you explain his actions?

Does seeing a film make some people want to imitate the actions of people on the screen? If not actions, then attitudes?

What film censorship has there been in your community? What were the reasons for it?

Would you actually censor any of the above films if you had the chance? How? Would you restrict them for certain people? for instance:

children? _____

people with a history of previous mental disorder? _____

old people in a retirement home? _____

prisoners? _____

airline passengers? _____

high school assembly programs? _____

college film societies? _____

Name a movie you have seen which fits one of the descriptions in the list above.

What other factors have to be considered in addition to the basic story outline?

If you believe in some restrictions, do you believe the current ones are adequate?

Which censorship boards should there be:

federal government? _____

film industry owners? _____

religious organizations? _____

local citizens' groups? _____

your own committee? _____

If you believe in *no* restrictions, how would you answer arguments about the bad influence of movies on American life?

Would you use the same rules of judgment for what is shown on television as on movie screens? For books?

The reading selections on Freedom and Restraint are on pages 181–216.

TIME OUT

... much of the violence in the streets could be averted if more people of divergent views had a chance to air their views on television so that a nonviolent dialogue could be conducted.

In fact, this is where I see the crux of a potentially volatile situation within our present television system. Communication is man's basic social process. It is the process by which our societies are formed and by which they can as easily dissolve. It is a process so old and so instinctual to man that the slightest facial expression, gesture, or tone of voice carries meaning. The process of communication, like a great river, is continually shaping and changing our lives. Like a river, the process of communication can be dammed only momentarily. Television is the most powerful medium of mass communication man has ever toyed with. In its brief years, we have only begun to explore its vast social force. In denying people access to this medium, just as in damming a river, we have only placed a momentary check on the forces of change. And then, like that river, these forces can spill over and inundate a society. We see these forces today on our campuses, and we have seen them in our ghettoes.

The television industry freely uses artistic terms such as "taste" in their defense of censorship. They are not artists and have little cognizance of the semantic or philosophical blunder they are committing. What they are actually permitting or deleting in the name of art are human value systems. The values which they apply in their judgment of network television are clearly archaic. One CBS censor even let slip in a rare press interview: "Tom Smothers is right, you know, we're years behind the times."

TOM SMOTHERS, "Are the Brothers Being Smothered?"
The New York Times (June 29, 1969).

ACTION

To communicate is to inform. According to this article, what else can communication be?

Do you find that TV programs dealing with current problems leave you bored? Depressed? Enlightened? Or what?

Do you wish that they would tell and show more than they do?

What are the usual topics that TV comedians deal with these days?

Can you detect any political preferences in their jokes and skits?

State the case for those who oppose the views presented by Tom Smothers.

Have recent events made his ideas more or less valid? Explain.

CHAPTER II

Put your money
where your mouth is.
SOURCE UNKNOWN

The law
in its infinite majesty
forbids the rich as well as the poor
from sleeping
under bridges.
ANATOLE FRANCE

The satisfaction
that comes from purchases
lasts for three days.
ROBERT THEOBALD

MONEY

Getting it
Giving it
Keeping it
and
Using it

MINI-SITUATIONS

This is a jeweled pin. It is also:

1. expensive, but worthwhile for those who can afford it.
2. expensive, and a waste of money when you think of the important things that money could buy.
3. a token of affection from a man to a woman.
4. one of the beautiful objects that improve life.
5. the source of needless dissatisfaction to those who can't afford it.
6. a convenient way for thieves to take from the rich and give to the needy.
7. the only reason some women stay with a man.
8. an object of art.

Check as many of the above as happen to coincide with your views.

Now see what lies behind first impressions. Which of the statements above would probably reflect the "ideas" of:

A student radical? _____

An advertising manager for a magazine? _____

A young girl in love for the first time? _____

A cynical, much-married man with a mistress? _____

ACTION

Answer these questions as if you were one of the above "people." What do you believe about money, marriage, and "the good life" on the basis of that pin? Would you accept the idea that a free jeweled pin should be given to each bride? That the jewelers who make the pin should devote their time and energy to manufacturing more useful objects? That women should buy expensive jewelry for men? That advertising enriches our lives by encouraging purchases?

MISS PEACH

By Mell Lazarus

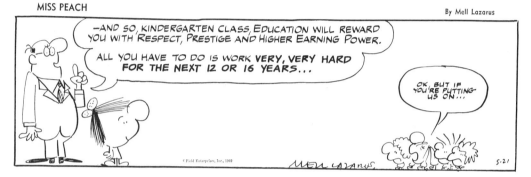

Miss Peach by Mell Lazarus.
Courtesy Publishers-Hall Syndicate.

ACTION

Name three famous people who probably agree with the older children.

Name three famous people who probably doubt, as the younger children do.

How would this comic strip "sound" as a serious statement? How would it be accepted by (1) the principal of your high school? (2) the first offenders in a home for juvenile delinquents? (3) you?

14

THE SITUATION

Mr. and Mrs. Allen have not seen their son-in-law's wealthy parents, the Baxters, since the wedding three years ago. Now they are in the city where the Baxters live, and all have gone out to dinner. When the check arrives, Mr. Baxter reaches for it. All conversation stops and he studies it. Finally he announces, "Let's see, that'll be twelve-fifty per couple, including tax and tip. He takes the money handed him by Mr. Allen and carefully counts out the exact change. Mr. Allen hands back fifty cents and says, "Here, this will take care of the parking fee." Mr. Baxter keeps it.

THE CHOICES

In your opinion, has Mr. Baxter been stingy?

_____1. No. He was accurate, honest, and fair. Unless there were definite arrangements that one or the other couple would pay for the whole dinner it was right to split the cost.

_____2. Yes. The restaurant was in the Baxters' home town. He should have insisted on paying for the whole dinner. His behavior was disgraceful.

_____3. _____

_____

_____

_____

(Another opinion.)

THE CHALLENGES

Would your answer change if:

	Yes	No
Mr. Baxter was much richer than Mr. Allen?	____	____
Mr. Allen was much richer than Mr. Baxter?	____	____
The price of the meal was much less?	____	____
Mr. and Mrs. Allen had been living as guests in the Baxter home for the past week?	____	____

WRITING ASSIGNMENT

Write a theme describing your own attitude toward who should pay for what when people eat out. Show what you think is stingy or generous and how you decided. Do the same rules apply to friends and family?

Beginning of Theme
(Choose one.)

The rules on how to treat others in money matters should come from etiquette books, because rules prevent confusion.

Or

Treating others should depend on the way people feel at the time the waiter brings the check.

Or

Hosts and guests should abide by the rules of common sense—if they can agree what those rules are.

Body of Theme

Choose one or more of the following, explain the exceptions, and answer the questions which interest you.

When the waiter brings the check, it is usually good practice for:

Each man to pay for his own. The waiter stands and waits while each counts his share. (When the waiter forgets to bring separate checks, are people annoyed by the amount of time it takes to figure each man's share?)

One man to handle the whole bill and for the others to settle up later. (Has anyone ever claimed the others owed him more than he actually paid?)

The bill to be paid by the one who can best afford it. Somehow it works out without anyone getting stuck with the bill too often. (Has anyone ever taken advantage of a steak dinner by "returning" it with hot dogs?)

The bill to be paid by one or two. (Do others get free entertainment more often than they deserve it?)

Some people not to have to repay with money because they are so much fun. (What would happen if people "paid" in personality instead of cash?)

What difference does it make if the entertaining takes place in someone's home instead of a restaurant? Suppose one person has a larger house or fewer people in the family or parents who allow more entertaining? What arrangements can friends make to enjoy his house for a party without taking advantage of him?

What are the disadvantages of too much watching out for stinginess, as when someone says "You paid last time. Now it's my turn."?

Have you noticed any change in the way people of an older generation and your own feel about money and hospitality?

Where did you get your ideas about who pays for entertaining? From newspaper advice columns? Etiquette books? Observation of others? Parental advice? Watching movies and television? Hearing the criticism of those who don't behave according to the code?

Ending of Theme

Write a statement or two explaining what seems a fair way for people to spend money for entertainment and hospitality. Include those with a lot of money and a little.

If you prefer not to write the theme suggested by the above questions, see below for an alternate suggestion.

Alternative Suggestion

Give an example of a situation showing the way a stingy person behaves. What does he do when it seems to be his turn to give a party or invite people out for a meal? What do his friends do about it? What would he say in defense of his habits about money? Call your account "Picture of a Stingy Man."

Now, on another page, describe someone who is more generous than the average. How does he entertain? How do his friends feel about his behavior? What would he say in defense of his habits about money? Call your account "Picture of a Generous Man."

15

THE SITUATION

A group of men who had been members of the same club for several years were in the habit of playing cards, betting high stakes on the outcome of each game. Two of the men—Arnold and Bill—were fairly consistent winners and used to tease the others, but it was all good-natured. The men were wealthy enough to afford their losses, and besides everyone used to win sometimes.

Then it was discovered by a private detective that Arnold and Bill had been consistently cheating, signaling confederates when to play or discard certain cards.

THE CHOICES

What should the victims do about the discovery? (Check as many of the following as seem appropriate to your own nature.)

_____ 1. Nothing.

_____ 2. Secretly take away club membership from Arnold and Bill.

_____ 3. Post news of the deception on club bulletin board, and spread the word in the neighborhood.

_____ 4. Bring a lawsuit for return of the money, if Arnold and Bill do not volunteer it.

_____ 5. Inflict damage—such as broken windows or fire—on their homes.

_____ 6. Bring criminal prosecution to put them in jail.

_____ 7. Get Arnold and Bill fired from their jobs.

_____ 8. Attempt to have their children boycotted socially.

_____ 9. Foreclose the mortgages on their houses and call in loans.

_____10. Beat them up, personally or with help.

ACTION

Do your choices have anything in common—like violence or money or hurt to the families of Arnold and Bill? Explain.

List the ten choices more or less in ascending order of punishment. Check with others to see if everyone agrees on the worst punishment, the next worst, and so on.

If you can think of evidence of what you actually did in a similar situation, tell what it was and how much your real behavior fitted your recommendation. If it was the same kind of action, try to make a general statement about yourself. If it was different, account for the inconsistency between what you did and what you have recommended in this case.

Or

Take any two choices which interest you and comment on what each shows about appropriate punishment. "Interest" may mean strong disapproval, of course; in that case tell why you believe the choice was unfair. How do you account for your rejection of one of the milder forms of punishment?

Or

Imagine a world in which one of the extreme choices listed here was selected more of the time. What changes might there be in our jails, churches, laws, etc.? For instance, if choice 1, doing "nothing" were always the reaction to offense, what might happen to people? to laws?

16

THE SITUATION

Karen R is working as a stock girl to earn enough money for the modeling lessons she takes every Saturday morning. The chances of her becoming a model do not seem very great because she is not pretty. Besides, there are many other places Karen's family could use the money.

For the price of a series of modeling lessons, her parents could reduce their debt to a loan company; or her sister, younger and prettier than Karen, could finish a course in nurse's training. The owner of the modeling agency tries to encourage all the girls to stay and says, "There is always a chance for everyone, even Karen." But then again, he benefits from the tuition money. As Karen works in the stock room, preparing price tags and climbing ladders to put away merchandise, she looks forward to the Saturday morning lesson.

THE CHOICES

Should Karen continue the modeling course when other members of her family need the money?

_____1. Yes. It's her money. She earns it. If she's foolish about spending it, that's her business.

_____2. No. The whole family is suffering because of Karen's impractical dreams. She owes something to them.

_____3. _____.

_____

_____

(Other choice, if you prefer.)

THE CHALLENGES

Would you change your opinion if:

	Yes	No
Karen's father was very sick?	——	——
Karen has spent money foolishly in the past?	——	——
Karen frequently feels inferior and shy with men?	——	——
The family may lose their home because of debts and back rent owed?	——	——
Karen has more practical skills she could be developing with the same money?	——	——

WRITING ASSIGNMENT

Beginning of Theme

Choose one of the following sentences (or one of your own) as the first part of your essay.

Nothing can cause as much trouble within a family as money.

Or

It's funny the way members of the same family can have different ideas about how to live.

Or

Every now and then, one "impossible dreamer" proves that dreams may come true.

Body of Theme

Retell the situation about Karen in your own words. Include your choice, the reasons you made that choice, and your answers to any of the challenges which interest you. Pay particular attention to your "yes" answers.

Or

Tell about another situation you know which fits the writing assignment you have selected. If your story has an end, tell what it is.

Tell of some famous person who has succeeded when no one thought he could. Does his success prove that others can do the same?

Tell what there is about your own background which may help to explain how you feel about this situation.

Ending of Theme

End it any way you want. If you have a good quotation, you may want to use it. Being funny may be appropriate. Perhaps you want a very short ending or none at all.

Alternative Suggestion

One of the ways of dealing with Karen's situation is to ignore the choices and concentrate on the people. Describe the way Karen's action appears to her—the way she sees herself, what she dreams about, how her friends appear to her, and what she probably thinks about as she attends to her duties on the job. You may not want to describe her outward appearance at all, but rather concentrate on what she thinks about when she is alone and with other people. You may want to furnish her with a boy friend, or you may want to show an encounter between Karen and an employer or another member of the family—but don't try to do them all. That would make a full-length novel. Call the paper something like:

Karen—Inside and Out

or

Karen—Dream and Reality

If you decide to concentrate on her thoughts, try to make them sound natural. That would mean allowing her mind to jump from one subject to another at times, rather than putting all similar thoughts into one paragraph.

TIME OUT

There's no real social value in sports. It's all part of the Protestant ethic, all shot through with capitalistic values. The funny thing is, I'm a prisoner of the ethic myself. I have to win.

JAMES SIMON KUNEN—SDS member;
ex-star athlete (lacrosse, football,
softball, lightweight crew team at
Columbia) as quoted in "Letter from
the Publisher," *Sports Illustrated*
(June 16, 1969), p. 6.

_____1. I agree. Schools spend money on spectator sports which could be spent on helping the poor.

_____2. He's right. But the Protestant Ethic has done a lot of good in our country.

_____3. I disagree. By his own admission he likes winning as much as anyone.

_____4. Athletes should play ball and not talk politics.

_____5. _____.

_____

(Some other comment.)

ACTION

Compare Kunen's statement with:
(a) the views expressed toward sports in your campus newspaper.
(b) your own views toward the value or uselessness of sports.

OPTIONAL

Explain how someone can be "a prisoner" of values he does not accept, just as Kunen thinks he has to win when he doesn't believe in winning. Tell of a situation (real or imagined) in which someone else finds himself acting according to principles he thought he had abandoned.

In a recent speech, a retired football coach had these things to say about the lack of "fair play" in American society:

> People on the street should show the same sportsmanship and interest as players on the field. Too many people spend their lives warming the bench.
> In all my coaching days, I have never been associated with beatniks. And it was not beatniks who went to the moon and back. It was the type of Americans who have the same spirit you see on the college football fields—the real American spirit.

ACTION

Write another statement you think the football coach would probably make:

_____

_____.

Define "American spirit" or "beatnik" as you think the coach would define it: _____

_____.

If you have a different definition, tell what it is: _____

_____.

What is "warming the bench"?

What is "playing the game"?

Imagine the coach discussing his beliefs with another person. What would he say?

63

17

THE SITUATION

For the past three years, Clyde has been attending a special workshop designed to prepare men for the next step up the executive ladder within the organization for which he works. He has attended the classes, taken the tests, and been overlooked each time there was a vacancy in a higher job. This year, once again, the course is announced on the office bulletin board. If he takes the course he will once again be eligible for promotion, but he will also be giving up his vacation time with no guarantee that the promotion will come through. If he does not take the course, his name will not be considered for promotion.

THE CHOICES

Which would be your recommendation for Clyde?

_____1. He should take the course. It's worthwhile to give up a vacation in hopes of more money and a better position.

_____2. He should take his vacation and forget the promotion within that company. His pride should prevent his looking so eager for a better job. If they don't recognize his abilities, that's the company's loss.

_____3. He should try to find out what is wrong with himself. The company management must know what they are doing if they have overlooked his promotion in the past.

_____4. _____

_____.

(Your own recommendation.)

THE CHALLENGES

Would your answer change if:

	Yes	No
Clyde was single?	___	___
Clyde was married to an ambitious woman?	___	___
There seemed to be a lot of favoritism in the company promotions?	___	___
In the previous years there were outstanding men who have since been promoted or left the company?	___	___
Clyde was happy in his present job, though it pays less money than the one for which the course is designed?	___	___

GENERAL CLASS DISCUSSION

How much immediate pleasure is worth giving up in hopes of something better? Have the special classes, school admissions, scholarships, job offers, wage increases, or other opportunities in your experience been as represented? better? worth waiting for? or disappointing? How can these standard methods of improvement be made more attractive to more people? *Should* they be?

WRITING ASSIGNMENT

Beginning of Theme
(Choose one.)

Most decisions in life work out better without consideration of pride or enjoyment; it is best to keep trying if the goal is worthwhile.

Or

Most decisions in life work out better if the choice is based on what makes you feel good at the time. Too much time and effort are wasted in dreams which may or may not come true.

Body of Theme

Retell the situation involving Clyde. You may add details of your own, such as the name of the company, nature of the job, and other people in the office. Be sure to explain your choice and answers to the challenges. For example, "Clyde would be better off staying in a job which made him happy unless his wife happened to be very ambitious for him."

65

Continuation of Theme

Choose those which interest you.

Tell a personal situation you once experienced or observed which required someone to make a choice between his immediate personal comfort and long-range plans requiring sacrifice. If he waited, what did he gain—graduation, a girl, a job, a trip? What did it "cost" to wait—evenings out, friendship, clothes, etc.? If he did not wait, what did he gain or lose?

If you have ever read a story dealing with a similar situation, tell about it. Was it a story with a definite moral? What do you think really would have happened, which didn't happen in the story?

Why didn't you check one of the other choices? What was wrong with it?

What changes would there be if most people were unwilling to look to the future? For instance, if nobody was willing to give up a vacation for a training course, would there still be good workers around?

You've probably heard about the grasshopper who regretted wasting his time while the ants stored up food for the winter. Make up a similar story that proves either the advantage of trying hard or of living from day to day.

Ending of Theme

Write a concluding statement which incorporates the beginning position and any changes.

18

THE SITUATION

Once upon a time there was a land in which the Gleefs held control. All important posts were held by Gleefs. Schools were run by and for the Gleefs. Money, the chance to travel, the best foods, the most interesting uses of leisure time—all were reserved in large quantities for Gleefs. Being a Gleef was hereditary. It was impossible to *become* one.

The non-Gleefs, needless to say, lived totally different lives. They were called Yooms, and they did the jobs rejected by the Gleefs. The ones who didn't work at all were put in jail or allowed to starve.

A change in government took the power from the Gleefs. The new governors found that the clerical jobs were still done most efficiently by the Gleefs. Captain Klojj is now hiring a staff for his office. Even though he has been told to make every effort to hire Yooms, as repayment for their previous years of suffering, he is tempted to hire Gleefs. They spell better, are more punctual, and more accustomed to working. The captain knows that his own promotion depends in part on his skill as a manager.

THE CHOICES

Do you think that Captain Klojj should hire Gleefs to do the work in his office?

_____1. Yes, the important thing is getting the job done. No matter why a person is better suited, the job is more important than the person who does it.

_____2. No. The Captain should hire the more deserving Yooms and give them a chance. People are more important than efficiency.

_____3. No. The Gleefs must be punished for their years of oppression. They should not be given jobs or privileges until the score is evened out—next generation maybe.

_____4. Yes and No. A temporary use of Gleefs, with a massive training program for Yooms.

THE CHALLENGES

Would you change your opinion if:

	Yes	No
This story took place in Ireland?	_____	_____
The "Yooms" were really blacks in American ghettos?	_____	_____
The "Yooms" were physically handicapped?	_____	_____
The "Gleefs" were really a group of people with power, of which you are a member?	_____	_____
The "Yooms" were war veterans?	_____	_____
The "Yooms" were unprepared students?	_____	_____
The "Yooms" were members of a despised caste in India?	_____	_____

GENERAL CLASS DISCUSSION

Compare your answers to the choices and challenges. Note different ideas on what *oppression* is and who have been the various victims. Make parallels with recent news events where it is appropriate.

WRITING ASSIGNMENT

Beginning of Theme
(Choose one.)

People should be hired on the basis of their ability to do the job.
Or
People should consider a man's past and his potential as well as the cheapest way to do the job.

Body of Theme
(Divide into sections A, B, and C.)

Retell the situation at the beginning of this exercise, using the nonsense words "Gleefs" and "Yooms." (Section A)

Tell which answer you selected as being the right attitude to take toward Captain Klojj's choice. (Section B)

In Section C explain each "Yes" you checked. Explain any of the "No" answers which interest you.

Answer and comment on whichever questions interest you from the following. Remember to change paragraphs each time you move to another topic.

Write an example of your own which deals with the same general subject of offering jobs on an equal basis or keeping back jobs from one group in order to give special help to another group. This might include a story about what happened to you or a friend when you applied for a job and why you think you (or the friend) did or did not receive it.

Tell what there is about your own background which may help to explain why you feel as you do. Include whatever stories you have heard from your parents or through outside reading.

Tell what is wrong with one of the answers you did *not* choose.

Ending of Theme

Make a general statement in which you are careful not to tell who the Gleefs and Yooms are.

ACTION

The Volkswagen advertisements have excited admiration for their direct-ness, cleverness, and refusal to make the ordinary appeals. This one has deliberately been reduced to a picture and a headline, in order for you to write your own. Add whatever text you think would be appropriate. The choices you make about what to emphasize will also reveal something about your own interests and values.

VOLKSWAGEN OF AMERICA, INC.

Live below your means.

19

THE SITUATION

Jackson and Babs have been sharing an apartment. The lease is in Jackson's name, but Babs pays one-third of the rent. Lately they have not been getting along. One night Babs goes out alone, and Jackson falls asleep before she gets home. He wakes up the next morning to discover two people in Babs' bed instead of one. She has brought home a male friend. Babs maintains that she pays for one-third of the apartment and she can do anything she wants in her third. Jackson, furious, says that he paid for the bed and he wants both of them out. He tells Babs to start packing.

THE CHOICES

Who is right?

_____1. Jackson is right. It's his apartment, and he's being made a fool of.

_____2. Babs is right. Jackson doesn't own her. They aren't married, so she has the right to do as she pleases.

_____3. Neither. Both are wrong, because _____

_____.

THE CHALLENGES

Would your answer change if:

	Yes	No
Babs was not contributing to the rent?	_____	_____

71

Jackson had been the one to bring home a friend? _____ _____

The major argument between Babs and Jackson had been
over his refusal to marry her? _____ _____

They shared the rent equally? _____ _____

Babs was paying two-thirds? _____ _____

Babs and the new friend had made love at his place rather
than coming back to the apartment she shares with Jackson? _____ _____

If you selected choice 1, make the speech that Jackson might make
to Babs when he found her with the other man. What does Jackson apparently assume about women, money, and people's obligations to each other?

If you selected choice 2, make the speech that Babs might make to
defend herself. What does Babs apparently believe about men, money,
and people's obligations to each other?

If you selected choice 3, tell how the whole confrontation could have
been avoided if both Babs and Jackson had acted differently at an earlier
time. What assumptions are *you* making?

WRITING ASSIGNMENT

Explain *all* your answers, and write an essay on the general subject of
Unmarried Couples. (Narrow your topic to manageable size.)

TIME OUT

In an interview, a young industrialist was quoted as saying the following:

My wife and I, we're decent people. We like tennis, art, music. We have three children. We're not really bad at all.

It took me three months to make my first big business deal, and I had to come back from my honeymoon to sign it.

My father was unusual in that he was always satisfied with what he had and he never wanted more.

On the basis of the three quotes above, do the following:

Write another quote that you think the young industrialist might make.

Define "decent people" according to the person making the above statements.

Define "unusual" according to the person making the above statements. Tell in what ways you agree with or disagree with this person as to the nature of the good life and goals.

OPTIONAL

Write the dialogue or act in a little play that shows a person with these beliefs in discussion with another person. Some suggestions for the other person:

His father

The girl he didn't marry

Another industrialist on the commuter train

His physician

A social worker

You as an interviewer who could ask him any questions that would reveal more about his beliefs and their implications for others.

20

By this time, perhaps there have been enough situations for you to be able to make your own, see several sides of an issue, choose one, and see larger implications, if any. This is not a situation, but rather the raw materials for one if you use them properly.

Add together as many of these as you need to make a situation:

A small country town; people who have lived there most of their lives

An eight-year-old boy named Stanley

His sister Theresa, age eleven

A mother who wears revealing clothes, cooks indifferent meals, and leaves the house unswept, sometimes for days

Hillbilly accents and bad grammar

Some incidents of theft of toys and broken play equipment

Neighbors

A school

An automobile

THE SITUATION

THE CHOICES
(Include a sentence that gives a reason for each.)

____1. _____

_____

____2. _____

_____

____3. _____

_____

THE CHALLENGES
(Include your "yes" and "no" answers.)

Would you change your opinion if:

                                                        Yes   *No*

_____   ____   ____

_____   ____   ____

_____   ____   ____

_____   ____   ____

_____   ____   ____

_____   ____   ____

76

WRITING ASSIGNMENT

Beginning of Theme

Write at least two possible beginning sentences to go with the material you have created so far.

Now choose one of the general statements, and complete the theme.

21

THE SITUATION

Gordon is offered a job he really wants, in a field that has always fascinated him. There is a chance for advancement, and he likes the people he would be working with, but the salary is very small. It is not likely to increase for some time. On the other hand, he can work for his brother-in-law, who has offered him a fairly important, though boring, job at a high salary. He is not particularly fond of his brother-in-law. Gordon has a wife and a young son. If he takes the first job, there will be enough money for essentials, but not for any luxuries for awhile. The second job would support them all handsomely.

THE CHOICES

Which job should Gordon take?

_____1. The one he likes.
_____2. The one that pays better.

THE CHALLENGES

Would your opinion change if:

	Yes	No
Gordon's wife had come from a well-to-do family, and expected a fairly high standard of living?	_____	_____
Gordon was single, or childless?	_____	_____

The second job was offered by someone other than his
brother-in-law?

_____   _____

_____   _____

(Write your own challenge and answer it.)

GENERAL CLASS DISCUSSION

Discuss the kinds of satisfaction provided by jobs in this country.   Include
the implications of the answers to the above questions.
   How can these be important?

> Size of company
> Attitude of worker
> Status of occupation
> Scarcity of employment
> Usefulness of the work
> Attitude of management

WRITING ASSIGNMENT

Beginning of Theme

> Job satisfaction is less important than responsibility to family.
> Or
> Responsibility to family is less important than satisfaction with a job.
> Or
> Neither job satisfaction nor responsibility to family is important.

"I'm rich, yes, but not rich beyond my wildest dreams."

Drawing by Whitney Darrow, Jr.; ©
1969 The New Yorker Magazine, Inc.

22

THE SITUATION

Mr. R is an old man with two grown children, a son and a daughter. The son has grown wealthy while working in his father's business. He accepts his father's instructions about where to live and how to spend money. His wife (whom his parents helped him to select) also consults her in-laws before making an important decision. Privately, the son and his wife tell their friends that they don't like following orders. They want to move away, go into some new business, but the old man has threatened to disinherit them if they move. They live under his supervision and wait for him to die.

Mr. R's daughter has just enough money to get along. She accepts money from her father sometimes, but she follows no orders. Several times she has lost large sums because she would not take advice, and she has seen her brother get much more. Her house is much smaller than her brother's house, and her children will need scholarships to continue their education. Sometimes she is resentful of her own comparative poverty, but most of the time she forgets that she is the daughter of a rich man who will not give her money.

THE CHOICES

Which of Mr. R's children has chosen the better way to live?

_____1. The son. He has the money. Refusing to obey his father would be an expensive way to get independence.

_____2. The daughter. She lacks the money, but she has her freedom.

_____3. It's too hard to tell. It depends on how long the rich old man continues to live!

THE CHALLENGES

Make up your own. Then answer the questions you made up. Would you change your opinion if:

	Yes	No
_____	____	____
_____	____	____
_____	____	____

ACTION

Imagine:

Mr. R discussing his son and daughter with Mrs. R.

The daughter in a moment when she is wondering if she should change her attitude toward her father's money.

The son in a moment when he is wondering if he should change his attitude toward his father's money.

Now make a tape or a live speech which will let an audience hear the thoughts.

Imagine that you have been given an unlimited budget to change this story into an outline of a story for television. What would happen

in a show designed to be shown around Christmas?

in a show designed for one of the late-night mystery thrillers?

in a show designed for the ladies' afternoon crowd?

SURVEY

Situation

14 Allens, Baxters

15 Arnold, Arnold's friends

16 Karen, Karen's family, owner of modeling school

17 Clyde, Clyde's employer

18 Captain Klojj, Yooms, Gleefs

19 Jackson, Babs, Babs' friends

20 Stanley, Theresa, the mother

21 Gordon, Gordon's brother-in-law, the wife, society

22 Mr. R, his son, his daughter

Which person in each situation did you find least likable? Put a circle around his name in the list above.

Which person in each situation did you find most likable? Put an X over his name in the list above.

Explain one of your circled names and one of your X'd names in a way that goes beyond the situation to show a general belief about human actions.

Now look at the choices you almost made. Try to see what they reveal about you.

This is a choice I almost made in this section: _____.

I almost chose it because _____

_____.

I decided against it because _____

_____.

What would you do with an extra thousand dollars? _____

_____.

Did your plans include investment? If so, what kind? Would you spend it immediately? If so, how long would the money last?

Do you agree with the people who say that the new generation is unwilling to work as hard or as long as the older generation did?

_____1. No, I don't agree. (If you checked this choice, how do you account for the widespread belief that young people today are less interested in work than young people once were?)

_____2. Yes, I agree. (If you checked this choice, how do you explain current lack of interest in hard work or jobs?)

If you had to describe your beliefs about money in one word, which of the following would you choose:

CAREFUL   GENEROUS   EXTRAVAGANT

STINGY   RESENTFUL   UNINTERESTED   _____?

Explain what you meant by each word you chose.

Find a choice you made after reading one of the situations in this section which showed your word in action.

Which of your choices made after reading a Situation probably did *not* fit the word you selected to describe your belief? How do you account for this difference?

Comment on any class discussions in which ideas different from your own were revealed. Did you want to learn from those people, or stay away from them? Or something else?

Describe your own views on spending. Select situations which show you in action—for instance, buying clothes, sharing expenses on a double date, borrowing or lending money, gambling. If you are sometimes "stingy" and sometimes not, try to explain why you feel as you do.

Have you ever known anyone who decided to retire, at a relatively young age, with a fixed income? Does he like his life? Can you imagine your own early retirement? How much do the opinions of others influence your desire to work, or be productive?

Are people who choose not to work generally disapproved of by your friends? By other people?

Is work always a necessary part of life? Without work, how might people spend their time?

Give an example of someone who works for something other than money. How do you know he does? Would you?

The reading selections on Money are on pages 217–241.

CHAPTER III

All you need is love.

LENNON AND McCARTNEY

Love is like the meazles; we kant have it
bad but onst, and the later in life we have
it the tuffer it goes with us.

JOSH BILLINGS

LOVE-HATE
AND
OTHER
STRONG
FEELINGS

MINI-SITUATIONS

If you can, answer each of the following with a simple yes or no. If you think, "It depends on other circumstances," tell what they are.

	Yes	No

A man with a wife and two children goes to several business conferences each year. Because he handles contracts for large purchases of supplies, he is offered the best food, entertainment, and women—either as decorative companions at dinner or anything else. Does "anything else" include a harmless way to spend the night, with no effect on the man's marriage?

It depends: _____

Many years ago in a change of will a sick father made on his death bed, most of a sizable inheritance was left to the son who was living with the father at the time. The daughter, who received very little money, suspects but is unable to prove that her brother exerted undue influence on the father who did not realize what he was signing. Should her resentment continue to keep her apart from her brother?

It depends: _____

A roommate leaves his clothes, papers, and food lying all over the place. Should his neater roommate, whose warnings have been ignored, take drastic action—like burning the stuff?

It depends: _____

A man knows that one of his coworkers has been taking the afternoon off for a golf game from time to time, instead of being out of the office on the official appointment he has announced. If the coworker is likely to get a promotion soon, should the rival find a way to call the attention of his superiors to the goofing off? ____ ____

It depends: _____

The invitations to a big party were made two weeks in advance. One girl, usually a member of the crowd, was not invited until the day before the party. Should she pretend to have something else to do, even though she wants to go? ____ ____

It depends: _____

A woman has married for the second time, and her new husband does not get along with the six-year-old son of her first marriage. If she returns him to his father, she will have to renounce all claim on him. Should she give up the son or the husband? ____ ____

It depends: _____

A patriotic organization offers free turkey dinners to families on welfare every Christmas. All are invited to walk in the Memorial Day parade to the cemetery. One of the families receiving a free turkey does not want to march. Should they? ____ ____

It depends: _____

ACTION

Choose three of the mini-situations and explain your answer. Include statements which would apply to other cases as well.

THE SITUATION

Glenn and Peter have been friends since childhood. They have liked the same things, had the same ideals, and fought for the same causes. A recent change in their government has made those causes illegal. The penalty for continuing to meet, petition, and argue the need for change is a long prison sentence. Those who help the revolutionaries are regarded as equally guilty. Glenn has accepted the new law, and the severe penalties have caused him to stop working in politics. He finds the new regime oppressive, but feels powerless. He has tried without success to make Peter stop, too. Glenn's argument is that the state is strong, the chance for arrest and conviction too great. Peter rejects the argument, saying that the beliefs they both share are worth the risk of fighting against an unjust, repressive government.

Now, Peter is considered a wanted criminal. There is an order for his arrest. He phones Glenn, doesn't identify himself, and asks for help. If he is caught the entire resistance organization is in danger, and it will be a long time before the movement can be rebuilt.

THE CHOICES

How should Glenn answer his friend's appeal for help?

_____1. Refuse to help. It is the job of every citizen to obey the law.

_____2. Give all help possible, even at personal risk to himself. His memory of the cause and the bonds of friendship are stronger than fear of the state.

_____3. Try to help in some safe way, such as sending a letter to a General

Delivery box or sending money through a friend unaware of the contents of the envelope. A man's first obligation is to save his own skin. Help without peril is all right.

THE CHALLENGES

Would your answer change if:

	Yes	No
The penalty for aiding Glenn was death?	___	___
The penalty for aiding Glenn was a fine?	___	___
Those in power were freedom-loving democrats while Glenn belonged to a group believing in totalitarianism?	___	___
Those in power were dictators while Glenn belonged to a freedom-loving group?	___	___
This took place a generation ago or longer?	___	___
This took place in the United States?	___	___
This took place outside the United States?	___	___
The crime was *personal* rather than political? (e.g., Glenn had lost his temper, committed murder, and was seeking help to escape.)	___	___

GENERAL CLASS DISCUSSION

How important to your own immediate circle is loyalty to a friend? How do you know? Does it include the replacement of something lost? Sharing? Helping with an assignment, repairing something owned by the other person, lending money? Risking personal loss? Risking punishment?

What loyalties, if any, are considered more important than loyalty to a friend? What physical evidence is there that there are other loyalties? Remember, you are describing a group belief as well as your own.

WRITING ASSIGNMENT

Beginning of Theme
(Choose one.)

The claims of friendship are stronger than the claims of government.

Or

The claims of the government are stronger than the claims of friendship.

89

Body of Theme

Retell the situation involving Glenn and Peter. Tell what you think each man should do.

Note your answers to the challenges and explain. For example, "If this story took place a generation ago or longer, my answer would still be the same. The rules of courage and friendship do not depend on time or place."

Tell a personal situation *you* once experienced which called on you to make an important choice between a friend and the law. Which did you choose? How do you explain what you did? Do you regret your actions, or would you now behave the same today if you had another chance?

Make the Glenn-Peter story longer. Turn it into a more detailed story of your own by placing it in a particular city or country, with names for the authorities and the rebel group.

What story have you ever read that deals with a similar situation? How did it end—in glorious death for the person who stuck to his principles of friendship? If so, did the sacrifice seem worthwhile to you? to the dead man's friends?

What is wrong with the choices you did not select? If everyone behaved in the way you recommend, what changes would there be in society? (Imagine, for instance, a nation based on loyalty to friends rather than the law, or a society in which the state was so important that friendship did not count at all.)

Ending of Theme

Describe your views on friendship and obedience to the law in as general a way as you can.

THE SITUATION

Norah has an unusual job and an unusual marriage. She is a veterinarian with a good income—quite a bit better than her husband's. For the past few years, Frank's business—a store that sells novelties and party favors—has been earning hardly enough to meet expenses. Now the landlord has raised the rent, and Frank is thinking of selling his merchandise through the mail. That way he will be able to work at home. The mail-order business will take only a few hours a day, and the rest of the time he can work in the garden, clean house, and have a good meal ready for Norah when she comes home.

THE CHOICES

Should Frank stay home while his wife earns most of the money?

_____1. Yes. Why not? The important thing is to enjoy your work, no matter where it is. Old-fashioned distinctions between men and women are not suited to the modern world.

_____2. No. The marriage probably won't survive that kind of arrangement. It's bad enough that his wife makes more money than he does. If he starts to keep house he might as well call her the head of the house.

THE CHALLENGES

Would your opinion change if:

	Yes	No
There were children in the family?	____	____

Frank made as much money as his wife?   _____ _____

This couple lived in a very small town?   _____ _____

The wife's profession was more traditionally feminine—
dressmaker or beautician?   _____ _____

The situation remained the same, except that Norah did the
cooking?   _____ _____

Frank was very dependent on his mother?   _____ _____

WRITING ASSIGNMENT

Beginning of Theme
(Choose one.)

Sharp distinctions between the work of men and women will soon no longer be valid for the modern world.

Or

One of the last things to change should be the traditional roles of men and women.

Body of Theme

Retell the situation at the beginning of this exercise, and show which choice you believe to be appropriate. Note any changes in your attitude according to the *yes* answers under challenges.

What is another situation that involves an unusual job for a man or a woman? What effect has that job had on the marriage? What do their friends think? Their in-laws? Their children?

How might a teen-age son of Frank and Norah feel? Imagine the conversations he would have with friends in school. Describe a scene showing their son as a very conventional boy embarrassed by his parents. Then imagine a son just as unconventional as his parents—including his clothes and hair. What difference might there be in the acceptability of the parents to the boy?

What if Frank didn't try to work at all but simply lived on what his wife earned? If she was happy with him, would their living arrangements still be of interest to others? Describe the possible effect on most of their neighbors. What would be an ideal neighborhood in your city for this arrangement?

How much do money and pride seem to be related? Think of at least three short examples to explain your answer.

Ending of Theme

If you can, be humorous. If not, restate the general principle stated in the beginning.

25

THE SITUATION

In recent years, computers have changed jobs, helped get men into space, and brought couples together. Suppose that colleges were equipped with match-making computers which brought together the right student with the right professor. If the student had a tendency to hand in assignments at the last minute, he would get a professor who admired that trait—or who would know how to be gentle about correcting it.

THE CHOICES

Put a check next to the traits you think should be punched out for the professor who would help you to be the most effective student. Put an X next to the one who sounds as if he would be the least effective for you.

_____ 1. Lectures most of the time, rarely asks for discussion, but has lectures packed with interesting information.

_____ 2. Sometimes plays "games," like pretending to believe something in order to challenge class.

_____ 3. Follows the syllabus or textbook page for page, with little deviation or change of pace. Dependable. Gives excellent preparation for objective and departmental tests.

_____ 4. Gives essay tests that allow much freedom to create and bring in information the student regards as most important.

_____ 5. Allows extra-credit reports in class or research outside.

_____ 6. Gives unexpected "pop" quizzes which reward those who keep up with the work and trap those who put off the reading.

_____ 7. An entertaining speaker, with many comments about current happenings and personalities in class.

_____ 8. Grades on the "curve," so that some percentage must always get A's or F's, no matter how good or bad a particular class may be.

_____ 9. Insists on punctuality from students and himself.

_____10. Is a very strict monitor who allows no cheating when tests are being taken.

_____11. Has "group" work in which a panel presents material and all share the grade.

_____12. Can be persuaded to postpone an announced test if enough students request extra time.

ACTION

Explain why you made three or four of the choices you did. Include whatever good or bad personal experiences you may have had to show why the computer would be "wise" to match you with the traits you checked.

Or

Describe three of the professors suggested above as each might describe himself to one of his colleagues. Make him defend his way of doing things by telling what is wrong with other teachers' methods.

TIME OUT

Miss Carol Remington-Worthing, daughter of the late Philip Charles Remington-Worthing, Special Envoy to Iran from 1947 to 1958, and the late Mrs. J. Edward Arthur, was married here yesterday to Robert M. Fuller, son of Mr. and Mrs. Fuller of Palm Beach, Nob Hill, and Dallas.

Over three hundred guests attended the ceremony at Grace Episcopal Church and the reception at the Colony Club, among them many well-known personalities.

The gifts included a diamond-encrusted silver peacock, the gift of the Shah of Iran, the bride's godfather.

After a wedding trip around the world, the couple will make their home in Paris, where Mr. Fuller is European District Manager for Ardrex Electronics.

Do the bride and groom sound attractive? Why or why not? Do you envy, admire, or resent them? (The news story on this wedding appeared, complete with pictures, on the society page of a very large metropolitan newspaper. The names of people and places have been changed in the above shortened account.)

This story covered four columns. Do you think that was too much space for its importance? If so, do you think the emphasis on the event is due to public interest in the wedding? the prominence of the bride? the prominence of the guests? the interest of rich people in reading the story? the interest of the general public in reading the story?

What do you think each of the following would notice most about this article:

A switchboard operator engaged to an Army corporal.

A labor leader who helped organize a union twenty-five years ago.

96

A student of economics in graduate school at Harvard.

A mother with three marriageable daughters.

What assumptions are made by the story, in your opinion, about the American attitude toward rich people, their looks, possessions, brains, sports, and importance as a model for the rest of us? Are they really our royalty?

THE SITUATION

Sam J has answered an advertisement in the Help Wanted column and has been told to report for an interview at a certain time. He misses the bus which would have dropped him off at the office building a little ahead of time. Now, late for the appointment, he has trouble finding the address and the office number. Someone in the lobby told him to take an elevator which didn't stop at the floor where the company was located. When he arrives at the company, he finds a roomful of applicants. He gives his name to the personnel assistant and is told, "You're late."

THE CHOICES

If you were Sam, what would you probably do?

_____1. Angrily explain that I would have been there on time if I had been given accurate instructions about the location of the offices.

_____2. Apologize and say that I am ordinarily punctual but I had bad luck to miss the bus.

_____3. Look the man in the eye and lie: The bus I took was scheduled to arrive ahead of time, but it broke down.

_____4. Tell the man to forget the job, then walk out. With a bad beginning like this, I probably would not get it anyway.

_____5. Nod and say nothing.

_____6. _____

_____

(Your own choice.)

THE CHALLENGES

Would your opinion change if:

	Yes	No
The personnel assistant was smiling?	____	____
Sam had been out of work for two months or more?	____	____
He was just applying for the job in order to satisfy his family's demands?	____	____
He is used to getting what he wants by crying and apologizing?	____	____
He has a lot of confidence in himself?	____	____

GENERAL CLASS DISCUSSION

The choices have been in answer to the question "What would you probably do?" But in general, what strategy would probably work best regardless of your own first impulses?

WRITING ASSIGNMENT

Beginning of Theme

There is a right and a wrong way to apply for a job.

Or

No job is worth the humiliation some personnel people make the applicant go through.

Or

When you want something, you have to change your approach to suit the situation.

Body of Theme

Retell the situation involving Sam, and explain which choice you made. Give your reason for the choice. Explain your "yes" answers to the challenges.

Optional
(Select as many of the following as you need
to develop your ideas.)

Tell about another situation related to this one. Show how the behavior of that person was like the choice you checked in this situation, and what the result was for him.

What is there about your own experience or background that you think had an effect on the choice you made?

Tell about your own observations of your feelings about being places on time or not. Would you rather arrive fifteen minutes ahead of time or five minutes late? Which places? Under what circumstances would it make any difference to you? Do you feel uncomfortable when you break your usual pattern?

Look at one of the choices you did not make, and tell what you think was wrong with it.

Look at one of the choices you almost made, and tell why you were attracted to it.

Discuss the whole atmosphere of applying for a job and whether the interview has much to do with the kind of work people do later.

THE SITUATION

Edward and Mike have been friends for a number of years. They are neighbors, and Mike's wife often cooks dinner for Ed, a bachelor. Now Mike has been asked to join a local men's club. He likes a few of the members, and belonging to the club would help him both professionally and socially. The club's membership board has made it clear that they want no part of Edward. Also, belonging to the club will probably occupy a lot of Mike's time.

THE CHOICES

Should Mike join the club that won't accept Edward?

_____1. Yes.
_____2. No.

THE CHALLENGES

Would your opinion change if:

	Yes	No
This took place in a small town?	____	____
Edward is being excluded for reasons of race or religion?	____	____
Edward is being excluded because the club members simply do not like him? (Mike's other friends, too, have remarked that Edward has a tendency to be loud, and tells bad jokes.)	____	____

Edward says he doesn't care about clubs? ____ ____

Edward has been trying to join the club for two years? ____ ____

Mike will probably be too busy to keep up with his old friends? ____ ____

Edward once lent money to Mike and saved his business during a crisis in Mike's life? ____ ____

WRITING ASSIGNMENT

Beginning of Theme

When a man gets the opportunity to improve himself, he should leave the past behind.

Or

There can't be a reason good enough to abandon an old friend.

Or

Exclusive clubs are forces for both good and evil.

Body of Theme

Retell the situation about Edward and Mike.

Explain the answers you gave to the choices and challenges.

Tell of a situation you experienced or heard about which is similar to this one, perhaps involving a fraternity and two friends.

Optional

In your opinion, is the interest in social organizations generally worthwhile?

What seems to be the appeal of special clubs with restricted memberships?

How would the two men sound if they happened to meet six months after Mike had joined the club which excluded Ed?

Have you been able to form any judgments on the differences between joiners and nonjoiners? If so, what are they?

Is friendship between men generally understood these days in America without insinuations of homosexuality?

Ending of Theme

Sum it up.

28

THE SITUATION

Phoebe and Toba went to the same high school, but their social lives were totally different. While Phoebe was active in scholarly and religious activities and didn't have a date the whole time she was in school, Toba didn't miss a party or a dance. She had begun going out with boys when she was eleven, had her first child when she was sixteen, and her first husband at seventeen.

After graduation, Phoebe had a series of dull, quiet jobs. She traveled for self-improvement to shrines of culture, took care of her aged parents, and put her extra money in the savings bank. She considered most men crude, rough, and forward.

Toba received her diploma in the mail. She had to stay home with the baby and couldn't attend the graduation exercises. She had a series of husbands and lovers, lots of excitement and romance and an equal amount of tearful accusations and abuse.

THE CHOICES

How do you believe this "story" would end? Choose one ending for each girl.

_____1. Phoebe met a fine man, a dentist with three grown children, and lived a happy, respectable, comfortable life.

_____2. Phoebe met a fine man, a dentist with three grown children, but he turned out to be a difficult, demanding tyrant and was too tired to give her much love and affection.

_____3. Toba lost her looks before she was thirty-five. As a result of too much drinking and debauchery she has a number of ailments, and is currently a lonely, discarded woman trying to make a living for her many children.

_____4. Toba eventually met a man who admired her gaiety and spirit. Better looking than ever, she now presides over a large house, has a loving husband, devoted children, and a respected place in the community.

The challenges are omitted in this exercise, because there are already so many different ways of telling the story.

WRITING ASSIGNMENT

Beginning of Theme

Instead of writing an opening general statement, this time begin with the situation. If you make the story more detailed, it may become the body of the theme as well as the beginning. Make the story detailed in *one* of the following ways:

Imagine that each girl, after twenty years of one kind of life, tried to change drastically. Show the difficulties each would encounter in unfamiliar surroundings. You may want the scene to be a high school reunion party. Add friends, husband, whatever characters you need.

Or

Imagine that a reporter for the local newspaper is interviewing the only surviving members of that graduating class, Phoebe and Toba. How will each woman describe herself for the benefit of the public? What will the reporter observe that he will not write? Show the interview and the final story as it appeared in the paper.

Or

Imagine a weekend which Toba and Phoebe spent as roommates at a resort hotel. There has been a mixup about reservations and they are forced to share a room. Describe whatever phone calls, visitors, arguments, and chats you need to show the contrast between these girls. (Assume that neither is married at the time of their meeting.)

Or

Criticize the whole situation of Phoebe and Toba as being contrived, extreme, unreal—whatever you believe about it. Give an example of a more "real" situation you either know about through experience or make up.

Ending of Theme

Write a brief comment describing current beliefs about "good" girls, "bad" girls, and the kind in between.

ACTION

Write about this advertisement.

Would you enjoy a Swingles Week?

Would you go if you won a free trip? What if you had to save up for it?

What part of this advertisement appeals most to you? Least?

In what way is this related to love?

Courtesy Hilton International

THE SITUATION

When Mrs. McW got a divorce from her husband, the settlement agreement included a certain amount to be paid to her for each of the three children. Mr. McW has sent a check on the first of each month, and has seen his children on weekends.

Now Mrs. McW has taken the children and run off with a man she met. They may or may not get married, but they have left the state. Mr. McW no longer sends in his child-support payments.

THE CHOICES

What decision would you like to have the judge make about the child support?

_____1. Order Mr. McW to continue to make support payments for his children. A father must support his children, no matter where they live or how their mother behaves.

_____2. Order that the children be turned over to their father. Any mother who runs off with another man has demonstrated that she is unfit to bring them up properly.

_____3. Allow the children to stay with Mrs. McW and her lover, but without the father's support. A man should not be required to support children he can no longer enjoy.

_____4. _____

_____

(Your own choice.)

THE CHALLENGES

Would your opinion change if:

	Yes	No
Mrs. McW was an alcoholic?	___	___
Mr. McW was struggling to make a living and Mrs. McW's lover earned a lot?	___	___
Mr. McW has been unfaithful too?	___	___
The children were very young?	___	___
The children were old enough to prefer one parent over the other?	___	___
The children like Mrs. McW's lover?	___	___

WRITING ASSIGNMENT

Beginning of Theme

Use the general statement included in the choice you made.

Body of Theme

Retell in your own words the situation about Mr. McW and his wife. As you retell the story, you may add details of other people, places, amounts of money, and occupations, if you like. Be sure to include the answers you have already checked under the choices and challenges. Explain all answers that you think are important.

Continuation of Theme

Select one or more of the following suggestions for developing your ideas:

Write another example about child support or a father's responsibility for his children. Use either a real or fictional case.

Or

Who do you think should make decisions about child support—social workers? judges? the people who live next door? the grandparents of the child? the child himself? What would be the advantages and disadvantages of three of these possibilities?

Or

Is the child usually better off with his mother? Why? When might he be better off with neither party? with a poor parent?

Ending of Theme

Restate your general belief about parents and the support of their children. Include whatever exceptions you have thought of during the writing of the body of the theme.

For instance:

"I believe that children should stay with the parent who is best for them —and that would usually not be a woman who had run away with a lover."

Or

"I believe that the welfare of the child is most important. Money should not interfere at all."

Or

_____

_____

_____

30

THE SITUATION

Curtis H, a community leader, wants to see Justin Wise elected mayor. He has decided that no other candidate is really qualified for the job. Justin Wise believes in the causes Curtis H supports. The preelection polls have predicted a very close race.

Although Curtis wants to help Wise get elected, he really can't stand the campaign manager. The manager is bad-mannered, conceited, and extravagant. Curtis disapproves of the way he's running the campaign. Some of his friends, who feel the same way, are unwilling to work with such a man.

THE CHOICES

Should Curtis work with the campaign manager?

_____1. Yes. Work to get Wise elected, even though it means working under the direct supervision of the man he dislikes.

_____2. No. Donate money to the campaign fund but stay home. One man more or less won't make much difference.

_____3. Yes. Try to take control away from the current campaign manager.

_____4. No. Reconsider his support for a candidate with the poor judgment to choose such an unpleasant manager.

_____5. _____

_____

_____

(Your own choice.)

THE CHALLENGES

Would your opinion change if:

	Yes	No
Rather than trying to get a particular man elected, Curtis was concerned about air or water pollution, and it was the head of the Conservation League that he disliked? (In other words, what if a permanent rather than a temporary campaign were involved?)	____	____
The current campaign manager was using illegally obtained campaign funds?	____	____
The current manager, despite his personality, seemed to be very effective at gaining new votes?	____	____
Curtis was a fairly lazy man?	____	____
Curtis has been overly sensitive in the past?	____	____

GENERAL CLASS DISCUSSION

What excuses do people make when they don't want to be bothered with a cause?

How do leaders lose the allegiance of possible helpers by the way they conduct meetings or assign tasks?

How can people learn to keep their eyes on what is more important than differences in human personalities?

Tell about your own recent experience with causes and the personalities of the other workers.

WRITING ASSIGNMENT

Beginning of Theme

In a worthwhile cause, personal feelings count less than winning.

Or

Personal feelings are more important than issues or candidates.

Or

There is often a practical solution to conflicts within a volunteer cause.

31

THE SITUATION

Rudy K married Lily before he went into the service. He was sent overseas after basic training with only a brief leave home. In actual time spent together, you could say their married life has been short. But Rudy feels married, and has been having his allotment checks sent to Lily.

Now Rudy has his discharge from the Army. Within a week of his return he can tell that something is wrong. The friends he knew in high school seem glad to see him, but they don't talk to him the way they once did. There are special looks when Lily's name is mentioned, and it doesn't take him long to realize that his wife has been unfaithful and with more than one man.

His suspicions are confirmed when his sister assures him that Lily ran around a lot. She even supplies names and other details until Rudy tells her he doesn't want to hear any more.

THE CHOICES

How would you like this story to end?

_____1. Rudy should forget about what Lily did while he was away. Even though she was wrong, they can work things out. The marriage vows should not be lightly set aside.

_____2. Rudy should confront Lily with his suspicions. Give her a chance to defend herself, even though there is a good chance she will lie.

_____3. Rudy should get a divorce. What Lily did proves she was not serious about Rudy. A man's pride does not allow him to stay with a woman who has made a fool of him.

THE CHALLENGES

Would your opinion change if:

	Yes	No
Lily was the most beautiful girl Rudy has ever known?	___	___
Rudy has a chance for an out-of-town job?	___	___
There is a child?	___	___
Rudy is a gambler and a spendthrift, and Lily helps him save?	___	___
Rudy was unfaithful while he was in the service?	___	___
This story took place one hundred years ago?	___	___

Write a one-page essay explaining your choice and your answers to each of the challenges.

Or

Write a longer essay that explains your choice, your answers to each of the challenges, and other questions in the general writing design. Try to separate your own personal beliefs from the values of your society. That is, if you personally believe one way and you think most people would not agree with you, mention the reason.

ACTION

Tell about the feelings involved. Make a little story using as many of the challenges as you need. Begin this way:

When Rudy heard that his wife had been running around with other men while he was in the service, he decided to _____

_____

_____

(You take it from here.)

Or

Tell about Rudy and Lily as if you were a social worker who is describing the effect on society of many marriage break-ups, and who desires change. Recommend whatever you think would help. Use the form of a newspaper interview. Begin this way:

When _____, the well known social worker, was interviewed at
      (your name)
a luncheon recently, the expert was asked about causes of marriage break-

down in this country. _____ said that _____
                                (your name)

_____

_____

(You take it from here.)

TIME OUT

A man, engaged to a girl who is away at college, goes into a "singles" bar where he meets another girl. They are attracted to each other.

A happy ending for this little tale would be:

_____1. The man talks to the girl in the bar, but decides not to follow it up with any activity which might lead to his forgetting his fiancée.

_____2. The man invites the girl to dinner and attempts to make love to her, under the belief that the way he feels about this girl has nothing to do with his marriage plans.

_____3. The man pursues this girl as much as possible, including lovemaking and plans to see her in the future. If the attraction is strong enough, maybe he's engaged to the wrong girl.

Explain the answer you have chosen. Was your answer based on impulse, live-for-tonight-and-forget-tomorrow? Did you weigh the consequences of your recommendation thoughtfully and reasonably?

My views have been distilled not only from my private life and my training as a minister but also from my first-hand observations of young people. In their intimate relationships, for example, I frequently have seen a tender trust and depth of commitment that in my judgment is a tribute to humanity. This is not true for all of them, of course; some are still exploiting each other, as the two sexes have been doing for centuries. But the unconventional behavior of many young men and women today is an expression of their search for genuine moral values. In effect they are saying to their parents: "I'm not intentionally trying to hurt you, but I must risk it while trying to find my own way in a society that constantly preaches love but does not exemplify it."

RONALD M. MAZUR,
Protestant Chaplain
State College at Salem, Mass.,
from *Commonsense Sex*, Beacon Press.
Reprinted by permission.

ACTION

Choose one of the following statements and explain what you think the author means. Make up a situation you think appropriate. Indicate your own approval or disapproval of the ideas expressed here only after you have first explained and have then shown them in action through the situation you describe.

_____1. ". . . the unconventional behavior of young men and women today is an expression of their search for genuine moral values. . . ."

_____2. ". . . some are still exploiting each other, as the two sexes have been doing for centuries."

Young people often ask of sex more than it can possibly give. Rejecting society's values and traditional ways of looking at things, which, they say, have gotten the world into the mess it's in, they turn to sex as a magic key to understanding themselves and others, to investing even casual relationships with meaning. But sex alone cannot bear so heavy a burden, and when this becomes apparent, the resulting disillusionment can shadow a future marital relationship.

DR. JOYCE BROTHERS, psychologist,
from *Good Housekeeping* (June, 1969).
Reprinted by permission.

_____1. I tend to agree. Dr. Brothers is warning people not to expect sex and love to be the same. The warning is needed by a lot of people.

I particularly like the following quote: _____

_____2. I tend to disagree. Young people look at sex so differently these days that people of an older generation usually don't make sense when they write about it. I particularly disagree with her statement

that _____

_____3. I agree with most of what Dr. Brothers says, but I prefer that love be written about in a different way. I find that the following parts of this excerpt have the wrong tone: _____

_____

This code as it currently concerned young people might have been roughly summarized as follows: Women were the guardians of morality; they were made of finer stuff than men and were expected to act accordingly. Young girls must look forward in innocence (tempered perhaps with a modicum of physiological instruction) to a romantic love-match which would lead them to the altar and to living-happily-ever-after; and until the "right man" came along they must allow no man to kiss them. It was expected that some men would succumb to the temptations of sex, but only with a special class of outlawed women; girls of respectable families were supposed to have no such temptations.

FREDERICK LEWIS ALLEN,
from *Only Yesterday* (1931). Reprinted
by permission of Harper & Row,
Publishers, Inc.

ACTION

The above was written by a social historian describing attitudes in the 1920's.

Describe current attitudes toward sex as if you were a social historian two hundred years in the future, trying to describe the way people thought and behaved during your own era, the third quarter of the twentieth century.

Write a little story, complete with dialogue, showing some imaginary characters putting into action the code described above.

Write a theme in which you make clear your own beliefs about the advantages and disadvantages of the code described above. If you like, comment on the way the author did or did not manage to keep his own feelings out of his writing.

32

This is another make-your-own situation. Use as many of the following characters as you would find useful. Be sure to allow for a point in your story when different choices will reveal a different belief about the way people should act.

Phyllis, a waitress on the night shift

Chester, a new policeman in the precinct

Leo, the ex-husband of Phyllis

Leon, a salesman for a drug company

Catherine, a drug addict

Make your own setting and action. Try to create a situation that would allow others to think of similar situations making the same point.

THE SITUATION

THE CHOICES

_____1. _____

_____

_____2. _____

_____

_____3. _____

_____

THE CHALLENGES

Would you change your opinion if:

	Yes	No
_____	____	____
_____	____	____
_____	____	____

WRITING ASSIGNMENT

General sentences for Beginning of Theme:

_____

_____

_____

Or

Beginning with Ideas

Choose one of the following propositions and defend it in any way you choose. Be sure to include at least two situations which illustrate what you mean?

1. Love is not the answer to big problems.
2. There should be education in controlling emotions.
3. An important gift in dealing with people is the ability to save pride.

Organize your theme by beginning with one of the above statements and then including an example of what you mean by telling a situation which fits the statement.

Or

Organize your theme by beginning with a situation which fits the statement you have chosen but have not mentioned to your readers yet. Then tell how you interpret the situation to fit the statement.

With either method of organization, include some of the suggestions of the General Writing Design to develop your theme.

33

THE SITUATION

One day when Sid T wanted to go to the racetrack but didn't have the time, he asked his friend Dennis to place a bet for him in the third race. If the horse won, Dennis was to bet the money on a horse running in the fifth race.

Dennis did as he was told, placing the money on the horse in the third race. The payoff was fifty dollars. He looked at the tip sheets and decided against placing the money on the other horse. It seemed too risky, and he was sure Sid would rather have the fifty dollars.

When he got home he had the unpleasant task of telling Sid that he had failed to carry out his instructions and that the horse he didn't bet on had won $425.00.

THE CHOICES

What action should Sid take?

_____1. Require Dennis to pay the money for a winning ticket.
_____2. Let it go.

THE CHALLENGES

Would your opinion change if:

	Yes	No
The money loss was less?	____	____
The money loss was greater?	____	____

Dennis was Sid's employee?   ____ ____

Sid is a man with a low income?   ____ ____

The two men have known each other for a short time?   ____ ____

Sid has heart trouble?   ____ ____

_____   ____ ____

(Your own challenge.)

ACTION

Retell the situation, emphasizing Dennis' point of view at the track, on the way home, and in conference with Sid.

Or

Discuss the limits of friendship. Have you ever been the victim of a friend's carelessness, stupidity, or bad judgment? How much did you lose? How did you react—resentment, numbness, delayed anger—and what effect did the incident have on your friendship?

GENERAL CLASS DISCUSSION

Is this story primarily psychological or economic? To what extent do you think the actions and feelings of people are controlled by their income or prospects for the future? Think of examples of people doing a noble deed because they could "afford" it.

34

THE SITUATION

When Oscar and his friends go to the beach, they try to meet girls. One day they were lucky enough to sit near some pretty girls who seemed friendly (they pushed their blankets closer) and available (they allowed Oscar to buy them hot dogs and soft drinks). One of the girls—Lottie—seemed like a distinct possibility for a date later that night. She sat close to Oscar, and they listened to the transistor radio together.

The dream-buster who came along was a tall, handsome fellow with a big, colorful, inflated beach ball to sit on and bounce all over the beach. Soon he was lifting the girls on top of the beach ball and showing them how it worked. They squealed and fell off, but they loved it—Lottie most of all. At this point, Lottie has had two rides, is first in line for the next, and the stranger's arm is around her shoulders.

THE CHOICES

What should Oscar do?

_____1. Go home. When you're beaten, you can save time, money, and grief by admitting it.

_____2. Complain loudly to Lottie—even if it embarrasses her. A man should never let a girl make a fool of him.

_____3. Find a knife or a nail and deflate the ball. Where there's a will there's a way.

_____4. Quietly talk to Lottie. Carefully selected words and a soft tone can be very persuasive.

122

_____5. Ask his friends what went wrong. Some men seem to be born losers when it comes to women.

_____6. _____

     (Your own choice and reason if different from the above.)

    Each of the choices has two sentences in it. The first sentence (go home, complain loudly, find a knife) suggest the kind of action some people might take.

    The second sentence (when you're beaten, a man should . . .) offers an explanation for the action.

    Look at the second sentence of the choice you checked.

    Do you really believe that sentence?

    If you answered *no,* write a better explanation to tell why you chose the action you did.

    Was your recommendation for this situation emotionally like the one you chose for Sid in the previous situation? Explain why or why not.

35

THE SITUATION

The year of Donna's seventeenth birthday, she had her first love affair—a summer romance with a camp counselor. It lasted through the Christmas vacation. But distance and other people at school were as responsible as anything else for ending it. Only one other man beside the camp counselor was important to her before she and Phil got engaged. Both her affairs ended amiably. She doesn't feel "used" or exploited, but she has reason to believe that it is important to Phil that he marry a virgin.

This question gets asked at least once every season in the newspaper advice columns. It is being asked again here.

THE CHOICES

If Phil asks about men she has known in the past, should Donna tell him the truth? (Remember, you are not being asked whether or not you approve of Donna's actions. The question has to do with what is *told*, not what was *done*.)

_____1. Yes. The marriage should begin honestly.

_____2. No. It would be kinder and more practical to pretend inexperience.

_____3. Neither. She should not marry Phil because _____.

ACTION

Which of the following were important in helping you to make your choice?

_____ Common sense

124

_____ Listening to gossip

_____ The code of your own group

_____ The advice of women's magazines

_____ The advice of men's magazines

_____ The temperament of the man

_____ The temperament of the woman

If you selected choice 1, explain your reasons. Be as general as you can. That is, if possible, form a "rule" which would apply to other situations. In your rule, you may include exceptions.

Be sure to consider these matters:

Should a person look forward to a lifetime of doubt and suspicion for the sake of getting something off his (her) conscience?

Or

How important is honesty when weighed against the benefits of a happy marriage?

If you selected choice 2, explain your reasons. Be as general as you can. That is, try to form a "rule" which will apply to other situations.

How good is a marriage that begins with deception? What about the risk that someone who knows—or the lover himself—may appear at some time in the future?

If you selected choice 3, explain your reasons. Be as critical of yourself as possible. Think of a Phil with the qualities the world may consider ideal for a husband. Think of the effect of your reasons on teen-age girls. Try to formulate a general rule to support your choice.

36

THE SITUATION

Ellen, a widow in her forties, has worked actively for her church for many years. She has taught a Bible class, sold tickets for church suppers, and helped to fry the chicken and bake the pies that are served and sold at the fund-raising affairs. Although she has never held an office in the church organizational groups, she does expect some recognition for her work. Recently she was very hurt to learn that the minister of her church held a large party in his home. Present were all the inner circle—the deacons, committee chairmen, and the rich members of the congregation. However Ellen was not invited, and neither were her two closest friends who are hard-working but poor like herself. They have never been invited to a purely social affair given by the minister.

At the time to plan the Spring carnival, the minister tells Ellen that he expects her to contribute her wonderful cooking again, and he knows she'll be able to help out as usual—at one of the booths during the daytime and in the kitchen at night.

Ellen looked at the minister but did not answer. That night, though, she began to wonder if she should continue to work for the church that had meant so much to her all her life.

THE CHOICES

Should she take on this new volunteer job?

_____1. Yes. Her work for the church is more important than the minister's failure to give her recognition.

_____2. No. She has done enough. Let him get work from one of his social friends.

_____3. Yes, but she should tell him how sad and hurt she has been.

THE CHALLENGES

Would your opinion change if:

	Yes	No
The minister's wife selected the guests for the party at his home?	____	____
The church was very poor and had only a small congregation?	____	____
Ellen didn't get invited to other parties either—perhaps because of her looks and behavior?	____	____

ACTION

Write the note that you think Ellen should write to the minister. Be as shy, angry, or self-righteous as you like.

Or

Describe the lack of appreciation and the hurt feelings in a similar situation that happened to you or someone you know.

Or

Tell the advantages of doing good works without caring about any reward.

SURVEY

Look at the choices you have made for some of the situations in this unit (only some are included). Was your choice based on impulsive action or restrained consideration? Check the appropriate column.

My answer was:

Situation	Impulsive (based on immediate feeling and unconsidered reaction).	Restrained (based on a care for the future, anxiety, a sensitivity to others, the appearance of respectability).
27 Should Mike join the club that won't take his friend?	_____	_____
31 How should Rudy react to his wife's unfaithfulness?	_____	_____
30 Should Curtis work with the campaign manager?	_____	_____
26 How should Sam react to the accusation of tardiness?	_____	_____
34 How should Oscar react to Lottie's desertion?	_____	_____
23 How should Glenn answer his friend's appeal for help?	_____	_____
24 Should Frank work at home?	_____	_____

On the basis of your answers to the above questions, would you call yourself generally impulsive or restrained? Give an example of your behavior in a situation out of your own life that shows either your impulsiveness or your restraint. Was there any advantage to acting as you did? Any ill effects? Did you form any resolutions for the future? Write a theme on what you learned about yourself.

Or

Write a theme recommending a general kind of behavior. Refer to at least two of the situations in this section.

The reading selections on Love and Hate are on pages 242–269.

CHAPTER IV

We don't want you to tell lies.
We think there are two truths—
a positive truth
and a negative truth. We want you
to be positive, to say it was a good play
rather than bad.

TELEVISION OFFICIAL TO
SPORTS ANNOUNCER

MINI-SITUATIONS

Many situations offer the opportunity to lie—from the little tactful evasions of friendship to the large-scale lies of life and death. The following situations suggest some of those common opportunities, large and small. Select the answer you consider to be right for each of them. Indicate when you think the truth should be told and when it should not be. For borderline cases, explain

Tell the truth   Tell a lie (or evade)

_____1. A mother-in-law gives an ill-fitting hand-knitted sweater to a bride. She asks the girl, "How do you like it?" What should the girl say?   _____

_____2. A co-worker has the unpleasant habit of snapping chewing gum. His desk is next to yours. He asks if you mind the noise, which was mentioned by someone else. Do you tell him the truth about his gum?   _____

_____3. A teacher asks for a frank evaluation of a course he has taught for the first time. The person he asks has an average of *B*, on the borderline of being an *A*. Does the student mention what is wrong with the course content or the method of presentation?   _____

_____4. A girl it too incompetent to get a job on her own, but an employer will give her the chance to get some work experience as a secretary if her parents secretly provide the money. He will then put it into a pay envelope and pretend that it is her salary. Should the parents tell the girl the truth about who is really paying her salary?   _____

_____5. A teen-age boy will probably never realize his dream of

132

becoming an engineer. He lacks the money and the mathematical ability. He has come to a school counselor for guidance on his next year's schedule of courses. Should the counselor attempt to persuade him to study an easier course that is more in keeping with his abilities? ____

____6. A man gets a well-paying job with an insect-spray company, though he knows the spray can be harmful to the people who eat the fruit. He tells himself that if he doesn't do the job, someone else will. Is he telling the truth? ____

Which of the following affected your choice:

The insignificance of the situation?

The consequences of the lie?

The desire to prevent someone from being hurt?

The age of the person?

The difficulty of facing the truth?

If not these reasons, then what others?

If you can, write the main reason for your choice in each of the mini-situations.

What might have made you check a different column? Write an example of a circumstance which would have made the mini-situation sufficiently different for you to have changed your answer:

Situation: _____

The Change: _____

Why? _____

Optional

Get together with some classmates and do a skit that shows someone facing the choice between telling the truth and lying. Use any of the situations in this book, or make up one of your own.

Give the characters names, and make up a specific place (dime store, apartment, bar) for the setting.

Just before the ending, in which the choice is made clear, stop the skit and have the announcer ask the class to write down an ending they would like to see. Then finish the play with the ending you have decided on. Be prepared to defend your way of ending the play against the arguments from the people in class.

37

THE SITUATION

Mike, a top salesman for a construction company, has been claiming too much money for hotels, restaurants, and transportation on his expense accounts. The newly hired efficiency-expert Lester has vowed to cut waste, and Mike is clearly wasting the company money. All the salesmen are likely to "remember" expenses that they really didn't have and they pocket the extra money. Lester has been firm with them—the practice must stop. If he insists for them, he won't be able to make an exception for Mike. If he presses Mike too hard, Mike may take an offer from another firm. The padding runs into hundreds of dollars a year, but Mike brings in business in the thousands.

THE CHOICES

Should Lester insist that Mike's padded account come closer to the truth?

_____1. Yes. All the people on expense accounts should be honest, for the sake of company morale. There can be no exceptions to a strict accounting. Besides, the money adds up and can result in loss.

_____2. No. A star salesman like Mike is irreplaceable. The efficiency-expert would best serve the company by looking the other way when he suspects that the expense account is more fiction than fact.

_____3. Not really. Lester should let Mike think he is getting away with fraud, because Mike apparently likes to live that way; but the employers should allow the extra expense-account money to substitute for the raise or the bonus they would give him for his outstanding service.

134

THE CHALLENGES

Would your opinion change if:

	Yes	No
The amounts claimed were much larger?	____	____
The amounts claimed were much smaller?	____	____
Lester, the efficiency-expert, is married to the boss' daughter?	____	____
Mike runs up big gambling debts?	____	____
Mike doesn't get along with the other salesmen?	____	____

GENERAL CLASS DISCUSSION

What are the human, as well as the material, values involved in this situation?

Beginning of Theme

Choose one of the following statements and include it (restating it in your own words) in the first paragraph.

Rules of honesty should be the same for all.

Or

Rules of honesty should not be the same for all.

Body of Theme

An example to illustrate your views can be found in the situation about the extravagant claims on the expense account. Take whatever parts you need and tell whether you think the salesman should be allowed to continue his practice.

Continuation of Theme
(Choose those which interest you.)

Put another example—or several—of related items of business honesty and dishonesty in the next paragraph.

Tell what would happen if everyone behaved in the way you are recommending.

Are employees entitled to take what they can in retaliation for the way the company takes either from them or from the public?

Explain how there may be personality clashes between Mike and Lester because of different life styles for a salesman and an efficiency-expert. What would tend to separate them in other decisions, besides expense accounts?

Tell some abuses of expense accounts that you have heard about or personally experienced. Beginning with office paper clips and stamps for personal use, note other forms of employee dishonesty.

In what ways can the stubborn insistence on a rule result in financial loss? Should the rule be followed anyway? What happens if there is no rule except the individual good judgment of the workers?

Ending of Theme

Restate the idea you have been defending.

38

THE SITUATION

Once upon a time there was a country which required each person, at the age of eighteen, to stand in a line that would determine the kind of knowledge he would have for the rest of his life. Those standing in one line would receive Truth, no matter how painful. In all the affairs of their life, they would be able to see clearly. They would know when people were lying to them, would know the extent of the affection their families had for them, and would clearly recognize their own mistakes. Those who stood in the first line would often be good scientists who could work toward new discoveries. While they could laugh at many things, they would not be easily amused by empty entertainment. Their special gift of clarity would prevent ordinary avenues of escape.

Those standing in the other line would receive a special, painless application of an electrode which would keep them perpetually ignorant and happy. The electrode would be like a permanent tranquilizer.

THE CHOICES

Which line do you think would have more people in it?

_____1. The first line. People want to know the truth, even at the expense of happiness. The insistence on knowing the truth is one quality which has made men proud of being human ever since they began to think.

_____2. The second line. Very few people care about truth, very few are curious, very few have inquiring minds or want them. Pleasure would impress most—and if someone who started to go in the first line saw the larger number of people in the second, he'd probably move over.

THE CHALLENGES

Would your answer change if:

	Yes	No
People in the Truth line were stronger or more beautiful than the others?	___	___
The choice was temporary, and at the age of twenty-five a person could change?	___	___
The people who insisted on truth were in the majority?	___	___
The people who insisted on truth regarded themselves as an elite group?	___	___
The country went to war?	___	___
The choice was made at age thirty-five, rather than eighteen?	___	___

WRITING ASSIGNMENT

Beginning of Theme

It is expensive and painful to know the truth—but it is worthwhile.

Or

It is expensive and painful to know the truth—and in most cases it isn't even worthwhile.

Or

The lines of truth and falsehood are hard to define.

Body of Theme

Retell the situation, including your choice.

From the following ways of developing this essay, select one that interests you.

Discuss some reading you have done which dealt with a great man's search for truth. Did the author favor truth? Did he seem to think most people do? What was the result of lying—war, flattery, happiness?

Examine closely one of the challenges. How would it change the situation? Think of another challenge—or circumstance—which would affect the number of people in one line or another.

What happens to the truth during a national crisis? If the public had known the facts, would they have been able to change what happened?

If you have ever been on the scene of a big news event or on the inside of a campaign, tell the difference between what you know or saw and the way it was reported. *Why?*

Describe the newspapers, magazines, and/or movies available in a land in which more people chose pleasant lies than painful truth. Include examples of "escape" entertainment you know about.

Describe a scene between two lovers who had both elected to stand in the first line. (If both saw clearly, would they still be lovers?)

Ending of Theme

If it seems appropriate, write a summary statement of your beliefs about truth and the public.

If not, let the body of the theme speak for itself.

39

THE SITUATION

Anthony B, a student, hails a cab, and then notices that the driver doesn't seem to be very alert. The cabbie runs a red light, and almost turns the wrong way onto a one-way street. The student asks the driver if he's all right, and the driver replies that he's just gotten out of the hospital. He explains that two black men had gotten into the cab and forced him at gunpoint to drive to a deserted section of town. They told him to pull over to the side of the road, and get out of the cab. They beat him up and took his wallet as well as his cab. He got the cab back eventually, but it was badly damaged. He spent three weeks in the hospital. The police have failed to find the two men. He tells the story angrily, referring to the two men who beat him up in racist language that angers the student.

THE CHOICES

How should Anthony react to the racist remarks?

_____1. Tell the cabdriver to stop the cab immediately. Notify the driver that he intends to report him for racist remarks. Note his i.d. number, and write a letter to the cab commission.

_____2. Continue to ride in the cab but point out the foolishness of judging an entire race by one incident. (Optional: If he thinks he has persuaded the driver, shake hands and leave a generous tip.)

_____3. Say nothing and leave no tip.

_____4. Express sympathy and seem to agree with the victim's grievances.

THE CHALLENGES

Would your opinion change if:

	Yes	No
The drive took place at night in a deserted section of town?	____	____
The student was a girl?	____	____
The student was black?	____	____
The cabdriver was an old man?	____	____
The student was studying to be a clergyman?	____	____

GENERAL CLASS DISCUSSION

Is the inclusion of a situation involving black criminals a display of racism on the part of the author of this book? Can racist remarks such as the cabdriver's be understood? forgiven? changed?

WRITING ASSIGNMENT

Beginning of Theme

Bigotry must be fought wherever it appears.
Or
You have not changed a man's mind just because you have silenced him.
Or
There is more than one way to express disapproval.

40

THE SITUATION

Nicholas R is a film critic for a metropolitan newspaper. The film he is currently reviewing cost over six million dollars to make. It had two different directors, was made on three different continents, and has been four years in the making. There has been a lot of advance publicity and the producer and stars are making cross-country tours for interviews in all the media.

As Nicholas watches the picture, he takes note of the stars, the expensive background, and some implausible events and acting.

THE CHOICES

What should be Nicholas' guide when he writes the film review?

_____1. To let his readers know whether they would probably enjoy it or not. He should also include warnings of scenes they would consider offensive.

_____2. To make every effort to praise such an expensive picture. It will probably be considered "important" during the Academy Award nominations.

_____3. To judge the film according to its own aims—that is, if it sets out to be nothing more than a silly, senseless comedy, praise it for being an excellent example of its type.

_____4. To judge it against a model of perfection—what it might have been as well as what it is.

_____5. To go by his own personal mood at the time. People don't really expect serious film criticism anyway.

THE CHALLENGES

Should his opinion change if:

	Yes	No
Nicholas works for a conservative paper?	____	____
Nicholas was once a drama major in college?	____	____
Nicholas writes for a small-town paper?	____	____
The star is a favorite of his?	____	____

ACTION

Describe your own basis for choosing a movie and judging it. Are you ever influenced by critics? publicity? the opinions of friends? Explain.

41

THE SITUATION

Jack W is a man who has had the usual share of disappointments. He has learned that the beautiful girl you marry grows less beautiful as the years go by, and often reminds you of your faults; friends would rather see you in good times than bad; and business deals lack the kind of courtesy and fair play Jack had been led to expect when he was a child. Jack blames his parents for giving him the idea that life would be like a happy-ever-after story.

Now that his younger brother is in his teens, Jack would like to prepare him for what to expect in life. They often play games and sports together, and Jack is reminded that competition in games is a lot like the competition he has found in the outside world.

THE CHOICES

How should Jack play the game to prepare his brother for "real life"?

_____1. He should try as hard as he can to beat his brother, even before the boy develops skill. In that way, the boy will learn not to expect advantages from other opponents.

_____2. He should take every advantage of his brother's carelessness including a look at his brother's cards or a deceptive play.

_____3. When they are playing a game, Jack should be gentle with his brother and deliberately allow him to win sometimes. In this way, he will encourage the boy to have confidence in himself, and with that confidence he will be able to face disappointments when he grows up.

144

THE CHALLENGES

Would you change your opinion if:

	Yes	No
Jack's mother disapproved?	____	____
The boy were much younger?	____	____
Jack's family had an income considerably higher than average?	____	____
Jack's family had a very low income?	____	____
The boy seemed to be a crybaby who was teased by other children?	____	____
The boy had refused to play any more games with his brother?	____	____

WRITING ASSIGNMENTS

Imagine the way Jack looks at his brother during one of the games they play. What is Jack thinking about? What does he want for his brother? Now imagine that his brother knows what Jack is doing and why. Explain what the boy thinks as he watches Jack play a game—cards, handball, Monopoly, or any other competitive game. Write one page for Jack's thoughts and one page for the boy's.

Or

EXPOSITION OF EACH. Explain the advantage of each choice and what is wrong with it as preparation for "life." Include examples of adults or children you have observed. Make your own preference known after you have examined all three.

Or

COMPARISON OF LIFE AND BUSINESS. Explain the importance of playing games as a means of understanding life. In what ways is business "played" according to rules found in games? Are there penalties for cheating? What skills are rewarded? Which game is most like life: poker, baseball, or tennis doubles? How do the games differ for different temperaments or social levels?

Or

CONTRAST OF LIFE AND BUSINESS. Explain why games and business have too little in common for there to be any relation between the way Jack teaches games to his brother and the skills needed for success in the world. Who keeps "score"? What are the rules? How do you learn them? What is a "foul"? What is winning? Who is on the bench?

Begin like this: "It is tempting to say that life is 'a game,' but there are important differences."

TIME OUT

Mrs W is a hypocrite. She claims to be charitable, but donates to the poor only to get personal recognition. She attends charitable functions to show off her expensive clothes, but when asked for an anonymous donation says, "My husband gave at the office." She is an active supporter of fair employment and equal opportunity but pays her maid barely a living wage.

Mr E is a hypocrite. He claims to be a pillar of the community, and is on the "save-our-town" committee. He is active in church groups and organizes youth clubs. But his wife never knows when he'll be home for dinner and his own children never see him.

Mr A is a hypocrite. He claims to love animals, but keeps his expensive Irish setters in undersized cement-and-wire pens and at times forgets to feed them.

Professor S, Miss L, Congressman R, Doctor J are all hypocrites. It's easy to find examples of hypocrites; they're all around. Write about them. Show any one of them in action by giving a situation that illustrates why your person is a hypocrite.

Optional

Act out your portrayal of a hypocrite either alone or with a friend, or in front of the class.

Bring in a record, poem, or other art work which shows a hypocrite in action. A few seasons ago, Jeannie C. Riley had a hit record called the "Harper Valley P.T.A." that told of a mother who refused to be reprimanded for her morals by people whose behavior was no better than hers. And a number of years ago, Robert Browning wrote a poem, "Soliloquy in a Spanish Cloister," about a monk who claimed to be religious but was actually very irreligious in his hatred for a fellow monk.

42

THE SITUATION

Gloria has been bored by (you name a course) class since she enrolled. There is nothing about the subject or its presentation that she finds at all appealing, and it's hard for her to understand why the professor seems to think his course is important. One day, near the end of the semester, the teacher looks around the class and asks if there are any questions. Gloria has a strong impulse to say, "This course has nothing to do with my life. I'll never need to know any of this, and it doesn't do me any good. My question is, what am I doing here?"

THE CHOICES

Should Gloria ask the question?

_____1. Yes, she should ask the question. She genuinely wants to know.

_____2. No, she should not. The professor will be insulted, and it may hurt her grade.

_____3. Maybe. It would depend on what course it was.

THE CHALLENGES

Would your opinion change if:

	Yes	No
Gloria had asked the question in different, more tactful words?	_____	_____

Gloria was the class troublemaker?   ____   ____

Gloria had previously not had much to say?   ____   ____

Gloria had selected a different time and place?   ____   ____

The professor seemed to be the kind of man whose feelings
are easily hurt?   ____   ____

If you answered "yes" to challenge 1, tell what words Gloria should use to make her question acceptable.

If you answered "yes" to challenge 2, or to challenge 3, explain what difference it makes who asks the question and what tone of voice is used.

If you answered "yes" to challenge 4, explain how you think Gloria should have handled the situation. Change the scene, and tell who would be there, as well as what would probably be said. Explain whether it would be wise to ask the question close to the end of the semester.

If you answered "yes" to challenge 5, tell how a student can judge the mood of a professor, or guess how much his feelings might be hurt. Include what you think might be the reactions of other students.

If you answered "no" to all the challenges, explain your original choice. Tell why you think the answer you chose is the best one for Gloria.

43

THE SITUATION

Leon R has had to stop working because his doctor has told him he has emphysema. The disease will become progressively worse until he dies, and Leon will have to stay home where he can be close to a mechanical device to aid his breathing.

Added to Leon's problems is his wife, Clara. That is, Leon isn't sure if she is a problem or not, but finding out will be expensive. Having been married twice before, Leon knows how it feels to have a marriage break up. Now that he is no longer able to make a living, he fears that Clara will leave him and he will be left to the care of strangers.

Leon's only income is his small monthly social security check for total disability. His wife earns some money as the manager of a small dress shop. If she stays with him and adds her income to his, they can get along and can afford doctors' bills and the special equipment Leon needs to stay alive. Without her, Leon will probably live with much less comfort and for a shorter length of time.

THE CHOICES

What can Leon do to assure his wife's staying with him?

_____1. Rely on her love for him. Tell her the truth—that he has no resources.

_____2. Pretend to have an insurance policy for $10,000 with Clara as beneficiary.

ACTION

If you selected choice 1, explain why you think Leon should tell the truth about his finances to his wife. Show what would happen if Clara abandoned him and what his thoughts would be. Show what their life would probably be like if his wife continued to stay with him despite his lack of money. Give a general principle showing what you believe about honesty in marriage. If you know of a related situation, tell it. Tell what is wrong with choice 2.

If you selected choice 2, tell why you think Leon should hold out the promise of insurance money in order to encourage his wife to stay with him. Show Leon's thinking which led him to the decision that you believe to be right, and try to imagine Clara's thoughts when she discovers there has never been an insurance policy! Will the knowledge that he is deceiving his wife affect the way Leon gets along with her? Give a general principle showing why you believe survival is more important than anything else. If you know of a related situation, tell it. Tell what is wrong with choice 1.

44

THE SITUATION

Larry has a new job as a clerk at a large business firm. He is in charge of ordering business supplies. The man in charge of Larry's department has been with the firm for a long time. He hints that Larry should order extra supplies. The department head has been using these extra supplies for his son and his son's classmates. Larry knows that if the boss finds out, he will probably lose his job.

THE CHOICES

What should Larry do?

_____1. Refuse to order the extra supplies. It is better to get yelled at by the department head than to risk losing his job.

_____2. Do as the department head says. It's his job to obey his superiors and the supplies are only worth a few dollars.

_____3. Pretend that he has sent out the extra order and claim that the supplies never arrived.

_____4. Go to the head of the firm, and tell him the whole story.

_____5. _____

_____

_____

(Write your own suggestion.)

THE CHALLENGES

Would your opinion change if:

	Yes	No
The amount of money for the supplies was larger?	____	____
The department head was also a new employee?	____	____
Petty theft seemed to be common in that office?	____	____
The department head was a severe disciplinarian?	____	____

WRITING ASSIGNMENT

Beginning of Theme
(Select one.)

In general, it is a good idea to obey orders from a superior.

Or

In general, it is a good idea to obey only those orders which suit your own conscience and well being.

Or

Special privileges make special problems.

Body of Theme

Retell the situation about Larry and the department head. Explain your choice and your answer to the challenges.

ALTERNATE BODY OF THEME

You may prefer to think of an entirely different situation, in another kind of job, in which someone has to make a choice *like Larry's*. Make it a situation with advantages and penalties to either choice. The choice should be serious and the power being obeyed or rejected should be strong.

Here are some suggested characters if you decide not to retell the situation about Larry and the department head:

A maid and her employer

A man of draft age and his draft board

A king and his subject

An actual historical character, such as Joan of Arc

An entertainer and his producer

A student and teacher

A sergeant and a major

Include the place and the time it happened.

Ending of Theme

Tell in some detail what your views are on obedience, privilege, and possible penalties.

The next few situations have something in common—men, women, and the chance to face the consequences of truth. If you vary your own stance as you move from one to the next, try to understand why it is necessary.

45

THE SITUATION

A nineteen-year-old girl named Sara W has left the small town where she grew up in order to work in a large city in the same state. She is able to support herself, and pays the rent for her own apartment without help from her parents. Recently she has become serious about Steve, a young man she has been dating steadily. Though uncertain about their future plans, neither dates anyone else. They usually end an evening by sleeping together. One night, Sara invites friends and co-workers to a party, which goes on for hours. Steve is there to greet guests, pour drinks, and perform the other duties of a host. When the guests begin to leave it is very late and Steve is still there. If he remains after the last guest has left, it will be obvious to everyone that he plans to spend the night.

THE CHOICES

How should Steve handle the situation?

_____1. He should be careful to leave with the last of the guests; otherwise he endangers Sara's reputation.

_____2. He should say goodbye to the other guests with Sara and stay. Make no explanations.

_____3. He should announce that he is going to stick around and help clean up.

_____4. _____

_____

(Your own choice, if different from those above.)

THE CHALLENGES

Would your answer change if:

	Yes	No
Sara and Steve were over twenty-five?	____	____
Sara had been drinking heavily at the party?	____	____
Sara and Steve had announced their engagement?	____	____
Rather than a large party, it had been a small gathering of close friends?	____	____
Sara's guests were all quite casual in their own affairs?	____	____
Sara's older relatives were among the guests?	____	____
Her employer was among the guests?	____	____

GENERAL CLASS DISCUSSION

The discreet action for Steve to take, according to one expert on behavior, would be to leave before the other guests or with the last guests, even if he and Sara both knew he would be back. Does this seem like discretion, hypocrisy, or protection against public opinion? Does the recommendation that he appear to leave have its counterpart in any other similar action you have heard of?

ACTION

Write a paper on "Honesty" in the sense of being true to yourself, without regard for the opinions of others.

Or

Discuss the effect of television dramas and commercials on what young men and women now believe to be right. Include etiquette books and the advice of newspaper columnists.

46

THE SITUATION

Geraldine and Lennie are college students who have been living together in an apartment near the campus. Lennie's allowance buys the food and they are sharing the rent. Geraldine has told her parents she is rooming with another girl. Now, Geraldine's parents are coming to visit their daughter. They have never seen her apartment. Geraldine has asked Lennie to move out for the time that her parents are in town.

THE CHOICES

Should he?

_____1. Yes. His moving out will save a lot of trouble with her parents.

_____2. Yes. His moving out will save the girl's reputation.

_____3. No. It would be hypocritical for them to pretend.

THE CHALLENGES

Would your opinion change if:	Yes	No
The parents planned frequent visits?	___	___
Geraldine was under the legal age of consent?	___	___
Geraldine's allowance was supporting them both?	___	___
Geraldine and Lennie were both over twenty-one?	___	___
Geraldine's father had a history of heart attacks?	___	___
Both Lennie and Geraldine have been avoiding facing up to reality all their lives?	___	___

47

THE SITUATION

Janice is spending the summer at an exclusive ski resort with her parents. She is thirty-five and has never been married, although her parents have introduced her to countless eligible young men. She has a good deal of money and stands to inherit even more. Now she meets the man who manages the pharmacy at the resort. He seems to be a kind man, a little older than she is.

THE CHOICES

Which of the following endings do you think is most likely?

_____1. Janice and the pharmacist fall in love. He doesn't know she is rich when he proposes, and he refuses to spend her money.

_____2. Janice and the pharmacist fall in love. He doesn't know she is rich, but is pleasantly surprised and delighted that she can set him up in the business he has always wanted.

_____3. Janice is ready to leave without a proposal from the pharmacist. When she lets him know that she has money, he agrees to marry her.

_____4. Janice's father tries to arrange for the pharmacist to marry his daughter. Janice gets angry, leaves her family, and decides to get along without their meddling.

Explain your choice. Then look back at the other choices and comment on each. Which is least true-to-life? Why? In which choice does the pharmacist appear least attractive? Why? What do these choices and your answers reveal about the American attitude toward romantic love?

Optional

Retell this story with the following changes (use as many as you like, or add others of your own):

The girl is younger than thirty-five.

The man is a ski instructor instead of a pharmacist.

The heiress had been married once.

_____

(Your own changes.)

GENERAL CLASS DISCUSSION

It has been said that college students want to read about "people like themselves." Does this mean literally wanting to read only about other college students?

Do you have difficulty imagining or understanding the situation of a thirty-five-year-old unmarried woman? Does it seem to be only humorous?

TIME OUT

"*I've rarely seen a candidate concede less gracefully.*"

In the cartoon above, a defeated candidate seems to be doing what comes naturally to him. He's telling his own truth. If this public display of honest feeling were usual, or accepted, this situation would not have been made into a cartoon.

ACTION

For at least five of the following, think of the possible kinds of emotional display and the acceptability of each to the general public and to you.

A husband and wife arguing on a bus. (How loud can they get before they attract attention? Is the attention generally amused or disapproving?)

A man in a crowded garage, complaining about what he thinks is too high a bill for automobile repairs. (Would anger help get the bill reduced? Can the loud complainer go back to the garage and do normal business? Is he likely to be overcharged in the future?)

The mayor of a town, greeting men back from overseas at a public reception. (What kind of public display of emotion would be acceptable? What would be unacceptable? When are a man's tears considered a sign of weakness?)

An actress being interviewed on the same television program with a younger woman now married to the actress' ex-husband. (Would most people admire the actress for maintaining her composure? Would it help her popularity if she publicly slugged the other woman?)

A young couple in love, at a church service. (Hand-holding? . . . What else? What limits are there on behavior in other public places?)

For the following, indicate the extent of honest emotion that might be displayed as opposed to the decorum demanded by our society. Give a real-life example where possible.

A candidate for public office being asked in a television interview how he feels about his son's recent arrest for possession of illegal drugs.

A soldier facing court martial for being AWOL.

A man whose doctor has just told him that the x-rays reveal he will not need a dreaded operation.

A girl on a date with a boy who seems to be crazy about some very loud popular music that does nothing at all for her.

A man and his wife's mother discussing the new baby.

162

48

THE SITUATION

The wife of a national leader said in an interview that her husband used to beat her in the early days of their marriage and that he often went with other women. Now that they are older and the husband is politically very powerful, he comes home more often but does not talk to her. He plays cards a lot and tries to tell his fortune with them. The wife does not look forward to the retirement years. "He is not an interesting person," she told the press. "Living alone with him won't be fun."

THE CHOICES

In your opinion, should the wife have spoken this way to the press?

_____1. Yes. It is refreshing to hear such honesty from the wife of a public figure. The public has a right to know the truth.

_____2. No. The wife's remarks would damage public confidence in the husband. He has a right to expect his wife to hide such ugly facts from the newspapers. He should be presented to the public in a dignified way.

THE CHALLENGES

Would your opinion change if:

	Yes	No
Her husband were running for reelection?	____	____
She accused her husband of extravagance?	____	____

She has reason to believe his leadership would be dangerous
for the country?   ____ ____

Her husband's opponent was also spoken about frankly by
his wife?   ____ ____

Her husband is unopposed and liable to be reelected for an
indefinite period?   ____ ____

ACTION

Imagine an interview with the wife of some national figure you know about.
For some reason (advice from a friend, drinking truth serum, or blackmail)
she has to tell the truth about her marriage. Up to this point she has the
reputation of being the sort of perfect wife of the candidate who only nods
to crowds and smiles and tells how much she enjoys cooking for her husband
and family. Tell about the things she might say in a truthful interview.
If you like, add enough details about the public reaction to make a brief
story of the situation.

Or

Find examples from interviews with the wife of some successful man to
show how most comments actually sound. Almost any newspaper—particularly on Sunday—has this kind of interview. So do the women's magazines.
How does she want to make herself appear to be? How does she spend her
spare time? Does she sound real? Like anyone you know? Is her behavior
admirable or just dull?

Or

Tell why you made the choice you did. What are the advantages of the
public attitude you selected? What are the disadvantages of the other
choice?

Note: The official's wife mentioned in this situation was actually Mrs.
Eisaku Sato, wife of the Premier of Japan. She was quoted in a United Press
International article. According to the article, the Japanese people enjoyed
hearing her comments, and did not think less of her husband. Can any
American understand that? Can you?

49

THE SITUATION

A film made by a European director has been proclaimed by critics as "sensitive," "provocative," and "a most honest depiction of real human emotions." It deals with a fascinating woman, loved by two men who have remained friends through the years. The woman is restless and has several affairs, including one with the friend of her husband. Nowhere in the movie is the lovemaking shown explicitly, though it is clearly happening. The film is concerned more with the moods and the feelings of the people than in making a moral statement.

THE CHOICES

Which of the following statements about the film is closest to your own belief?

_____1. An honest film about real life is beneficial to people of all ages who see it.

_____2. The woman in the film is so unusual that the film would appeal only to certain people.

_____3. The film deals with adultery and therefore condones it. It should not be shown widely.

Now (and this is harder) explain why you think a person might have picked an answer other than the one you did.

Name three recent controversial movies, and explain your beliefs about one of them.

GENERAL CLASS DISCUSSION

A student once wrote the following about the film in this situation: ". . . I'm not exactly priesthood material myself, but I still have some grain of moral value in me. . . . I am not denying that this type of thing goes on in the world today, if not much worse. . . . I feel that a person should be taught in a more subtle way."

What do you think he meant by

"priesthood material"?

"if not much worse"?

"a person should be taught"?

What does he assume a film should do? Does he include himself among those who can be corrupted? Do you share his objections? If you do, strengthen his argument. If you don't, tell what is wrong with his position.

If you could interview him for further information, what questions would you like to ask him (for example, whether he thinks movies should ever end with the unfaithful wife being shown happy)? What answers would you expect him to give for each question? (For example, in answer to the question above he would probably say, "No, because others would be encouraged to imitate her actions.")

ACTION

Rewrite the situation in a way that is obviously sympathetic to (a) the film, or (b) to the censors.

50

THE SITUATION

When Andy P applied for a job with a large corporation, he was asked a question he found hard to answer. He had already passed the physical and mental tests, the aptitude tests, and the personal interview. The job was one he wanted very much, and he was sure he would be hired. The personnel director was explaining salary, hours, and fringe benefits when the manager of the company walked in and asked Andy this question:

"Suppose you are in a telephone booth. You have just hung up the receiver when ten dollars' worth of coins spill out of the slot. What would you do with the money?"

THE CHOICES

What answer do you think Andy should give the boss?

_____1. He should say that he would dial Operator and find out how to return the coins, even if he knows that he would probably keep them.

_____2. He should tell the boss the truth on the grounds that the answer is a test of his honesty—not just the honesty with coins but with answering questions.

_____3. He should tell the boss, "I would keep the coins and walk away without telling anyone." Any other answer would make him sound too naive to be trusted on the job.

_____4. He should refuse to answer the question because it is an invasion of privacy and has nothing to do with how well he would perform his duties.

THE CHALLENGES

Would your answer change if:

	Yes	No
Andy really thought he should return the money?	____	____
Andy really thought he should keep the money?	____	____
The job itself was with the telephone company?	____	____
The person interviewing Andy was manager of a wholesale liquor company?	____	____
The interview took place in a small town?	____	____
The interview took place in a large city?	____	____
A lie detector was used on all applicants?	____	____
Andy is tired of being considered unsophisticated by his wife and friends?	____	____

ACTION

Explain your answers to the choices and challenges in a paper on one of the following.

What Honesty Means These Days

Honesty Equals Innocence (or Strength, Wisdom)

Changing with the Situation

Out-thinking a Job Interviewer (coach, scholarship committee)

Honesty in School

(For the daring: Comment on the validity of the problem set up in this situation. How honest have *you* been in answering, how aware of the way your answers would sound to others in the class?)

168

51

THE SITUATION

Four-year-old Brian is eating breakfast alone in the kitchen when he re-members a television cartoon show and takes his bowl of cereal into the living room. No eating in the living room is a firm rule for the whole family. When he hears his mother approaching he pushes the bowl in back of him in an effort to conceal it. The milk and cereal that splash out are clearly visible to his mother.

THE CHOICES

What should she do?

_____1. Ask Brian if he has been eating in the living room, with a lighter punishment if he tells the truth.

_____2. Tell Brian to clean up the mess.

_____3. Angrily dismiss Brian while she goes for the sponge and paper towels.

_____4. Hit Brian hard enough to make him remember.

_____5. Tell Brian how hard she works to keep the house clean, in order to make him sorry he had done wrong.

THE CHALLENGES

Would your answer change if:

	Yes	No
Brian was between five and ten years old.	_____	_____

Brian was between two and four years old. ⎯⎯ ⎯⎯

Brian spilled ink rather than milk. ⎯⎯ ⎯⎯

This was the third time this week he took food into the
living room. ⎯⎯ ⎯⎯

Brian used a forbidden word rather than spill milk. ⎯⎯ ⎯⎯

The parents often ate in the living room. ⎯⎯ ⎯⎯

ACTION

Describe your views on the disciplining of children. Choose one of the
following words as being the most applicable to you and show it in action
through at least two other examples in addition to Brian.

Strict   Firm   Consistent   Flexible   Patient

52

THE SITUATION

Young Harold C has his first teaching job at Laurel Mountain Township, a small town with a beautiful school and students who generally do well. The salary is good.

Harold has already been in trouble with the principal because Harold assigned his class to read a book that dealt with problems in the slums. The principal pointed out that there was no point in bringing such unpleasantness into the lives of the children of Laurel Mountain, and besides some of the language was quite indecent. Harold agreed to withdraw the assignment.

Now he is in trouble again. His trouble stems from one of the following assignments. (Since this is a semi-do-it-yourself Situation, choose Harold's troublesome assignment.)

_____1. A comparison between capitalism and communism.

_____2. A comparison of the effects of marijuana and alcohol.

_____3. An invitation to a controversial speaker to address the class.

_____4. A field trip to an unsavory part of town.

_____5. An exposé of early Laurel Mountain Township history.

_____6. An unpopular attitude toward American foreign policy.

_____7. _____

_____

_____

(Write your own suggestion about something which Harold assigned. Make it an idea, rather than improper social behavior on the part of the teacher.)

THE CHOICES

Assume that Harold got into trouble by saying or doing something regarded as outrageous by the parents of Laurel Mountain Township, in connection with one of the troublesome assignments above. What should he do about it?

_____1. Quit his job and look for one that gives him greater freedom of expression. Leave, even it it means loss of money.

_____2. Stop talking about unpleasant subjects. Schoolteachers should concentrate on neutral skills and leave controversy to the outside world.

_____3. Stay on the job until he has to leave. He should risk the displeasure of the principal and fellow teachers as well as the parents. If he is fired, perhaps he can claim money damages for breach of contract.

Justify your choices.

53

A MAKE-YOUR-OWN SITUATION

Given the following hints, fill in the needed information in any way you like. Then write a situation leading toward a point having to do in some way with Truth and Lies.

A new product or invention: (You name it.) _____

Its function. (Tell what it does.) _____

The opposition to it. (Why.) _____
Characters:

    An inventor

    A manufacturer

    A committee

    Others: _____

THE SITUATION

(Take a main "character" from one of the above.)

THE CHOICES

(Try to give some merit to each, and be prepared to offer a fair argument for each choice.)

_____1. _____

_____2. _____

_____3. _____

WRITING ASSIGNMENT

(Give your own opinion as you justify your personal choice.)

SURVEY

How are the following objects and events connected to ideas about honesty?
Write some comment after each. Then select any five for an essay about
the general attitude toward honesty in America. Include those instances
in which Americans generally expect to act honestly and to be treated
honestly.

Amateur tennis _____

Department store clothing sale _____

Traffic court _____

Popular movies _____

Insurance claims _____

A drugstore cash register _____

Nightclub whiskey _____

College board exams _____

Prize fights _____

A garden club flower show _____

Packaged meat in a supermarket _____

College professors _____

In several of the situations you have just read, there have been opportunities to do the genuinely honest thing as opposed to the honest-ap-
pearing action. In which of them did you recommend the genuinely
honest action? That is, one for which there was least chance of getting

credit—honesty almost entirely for its own sake. In your answers, include honest emotions as well as respect for private ownership.

In which were you mainly interested in appearances?

Were there any in which your choice was based on something other than honesty?

Several of the situations dealt with honest revelations involving the relationship between a man and a woman. Were you consistent in your recommendations? In which cases did you consider appearances important?

Is there one law for everyone? Should there be the same punishments for poor as well as rich people who steal?

Write your own situation involving a choice between something people called honest and dishonest.

Choose any ten situations in this book. In which of the choices have you recommended:

Devious methods _____

Open confrontations with an opponent _____

Doing nothing _____

Retreating from what was wanted _____

Talking one's way out of a difficulty _____

Here are some of the general ideas included in this book. Which of them have been important to you? Put numbers indicating the one you think are most important.

Making a good impression _____

Being willing to take a chance _____

Choosing an orderly life _____

Choosing an unstructured life _____

Coming to terms with authority _____

Planning for the future _____

Outmaneuvering a threat _____

Bringing about change _____

Which of the above has seemed least important? Put an X next to it.

Write a theme on what you know about your own values as a result of your answers.

The reading selections on Truth and Lies are on pages 268–304.

David Evins

"I don't care what happened yesterday. Neither does The News."

Mr. David Evins, with a face that looks like Fernandel, sat on the couch of his office, surrounded by a jumble of brilliantly colored fall leathers and held up the shoe he had designed for next winter. "The toe will be slightly rounded," he said. "And the heel a little higher.

"The News has pulse. It has tempo. It's alert. I like that. Since I'm in the fashion business," said Mr. Evins. And he stretched. Elegantly. Mr. Evins' elegant shoes go up to $185.

"I read The News at breakfast." Breakfast is served in a 9-room duplex on Park Avenue. "As soon as I can get it away from my wife and son. I refuse to buy more than one copy.

"I read it from front to back page. From the news reports to the baseball scores to the financial page. I don't have to delve through 1800 stocks to find what I'm looking for."

With that Mr. Evins turned to his new thigh-high stretch boots to be sold soon at I. Miller for about $125.

Over 1,140,000 News readers are in families with incomes of $12,000 to $25,000. If you have something *these uppers* want to buy, give them the message in The News.

The News is what's happening.

N.Y. people like the N.Y. News.

Courtesy *New York News.*

TIME OUT

What Makes a Happy Life

What makes a happy life, dear friend,
If thou wouldst briefly learn, attend—
An income left, not earned by toil;
Some acres of a kindly soil;
The pot unfailing on the fire;
No lawsuits, seldom town attire;
Health, strength with grace; a peaceful mind;
Shrewdness with honesty combined;
Plain living; equal friends and free;
Evenings of temperate gayiety;
A wife discreet yet blithe and bright;
Sound slumber that lends wings to night.
With all thy heart embrace thy lot,
Wish not for death, and fear it not.

MARTIAL

Write a theme comparing the beliefs expressed in this poem and those expressed in the advertisement on page 177.

INTRODUCTION TO
READINGS

In the complete stories and essays that follow, basic situations and choices are concealed by the writer's art, but are nevertheless present. The characters act according to their beliefs in a moment of decision which determines consequences large and small. Sometimes nothing more is at stake than a temporary job, a date for the weekend, or a way to spend free time. At other times the decision affects acceptance at a prestige college, the continuation of a marriage, or the beginning of a riot.

In each case, it is possible for the reader to see how the person making the choice might have behaved differently. The stories provide the easiest examples of "choices," because at some point in each story the character can continue as before or take the action described. What he does is determined by who he is, and the good author makes the action seem inevitable by the way he presents his people. In this sense the "situation" determines the choice, because the characters are no longer shadowy people identified only by names. They exist in a time and place, and the reader can see why they did what they did. What the *reader* would have done is sometimes a different story because *he* is different.

In the essays and the interview, the situations are contained in short anecdotes used to illustrate a principle. Beliefs are more openly stated in the essays, but their application is not always so clear as it would be in a story. When a man says he believes in "freedom" or "equality," he should allow the reader to see how that belief would change his actions in a specific situation. Otherwise the words have no more meaning than some memorized and oft-repeated pledge or creed. The *action* section following each selection provides further opportunity for you to check your understanding and the application of these beliefs.

180

FREEDOM AND RESTRAINT

The readings in this section present a variety of approaches to this generation's most-talked-about topic. The first is a small account of an incident in the life of a young man out of the mainstream of American life. There is no evidence that the check-out clerk in the A & P is a member of any minority group, nor is he oppressed in any visible way. When he sees restraint in action, he responds in one of the few ways available to him. It is an individual action, without large implications—just one young man who acts out of his own convictions, without being a member of any club or organization. He tells it as if he were speaking to a group of friends some time after it happened.

The second deals with a member of a larger group—the black graduate of a college, reporting on the kinds of discrimination he experienced as one of the few blacks in one of the country's top schools. It is a discrimination that would have been regarded as not worth mentioning a decade or so ago, when workers in the civil rights movement were trying to desegregate schools. But "racism" has taken on broader meanings in recent years, and this personal account does have larger implications for both blacks and whites.

The third reading selection pits cops against kids, but not in a sensational way. One police officer is sympathetic to some of the demands for experimentation from the kids in his precinct. He is anything but the stereotype of "pig." Yet the article is not necessarily a defense of either the police or the drug addicts and rioters in the troubled area of Haight-Ashbury. Instead, it is a clearly expressed, colorful invitation to do serious thinking about the value and limitations of the law, not only as enforced on the local level, but in the much broader context of man's freedom.

A & P

JOHN UPDIKE

In walks these three girls in nothing but bathing suits. I'm in the
third checkout slot, with my back to the door, so I don't see them
until they're over by the bread. The one that caught my eye
first was the one in the plaid green two-piece. She was a chunky
kid, with a good tan and a sweet broad soft-looking can with
those two crescents of white just under it, where the sun never
seems to hit, at the top of the backs of her legs. I stood there
with my hand on a box of HiHo crackers trying to remember if
I rang it up or not. I ring it up again and the customer starts
giving me hell. She's one of these cash-register-watchers, a witch
about fifty with rouge on her cheekbones and no eyebrows, and
I know it made her day to trip me up. She'd been watching cash
registers for fifty years and probably never seen a mistake before.

By the time I got her feathers smoothed and her goodies into
a bag—she gives me a little snort in passing, if she'd been born at
the right time they would have burned her over in Salem—by the
time I get her on her way the girls had circled around the bread
and were coming back, without a pushcart, back my way along
the counters, in the aisle between the checkouts and the Special
bins. They didn't even have shoes on. There was this chunky
one, with the two-piece—it was bright green and the seams on the
bra were still sharp and her belly was still pretty pale so I guessed
she just got it (the suit)—there was this one, with one of those
chubby berryfaces, the lips all bunched together under her nose,
this one, and a tall one, with black hair that hadn't quite frizzed

right, and one of these sunburns right across under the eyes, and a chin that was too long—you know, the kind of girl other girls think is very "striking" and "attractive" but never quite makes it, as they very well know, which is why they like her so much—and then the third one, that wasn't quite so tall. She was the queen. She kind of led them, the other two peeking around and making their shoulders round. She didn't look around, not this queen, she just walked straight on slowly, on these long white prima-donna legs. She came down a little hard on her heels, as if she didn't walk in her bare feet that much, putting down her heels and then letting the weight move along to her toes as if she was testing the floor with every step, putting a little deliberate extra action into it. You never know for sure how girls' minds work (do you really think it's a mind in there or just a little buzz like a bee in a glass jar?) but you got the idea she had talked the other two into coming in here with her, and now she was showing them how to do it, walk slow and hold yourself straight.

She had on a kind of dirty-pink—beige maybe, I don't know—bathing suit with a little nubble all over it, and what got me, the straps were down. They were off her shoulders looped loose around the cool tops of her arms, and I guess as a result the suit had slipped a little on her, so all around the top of the cloth there was this shining rim. If it hadn't been there you wouldn't have known there could have been anything whiter than those shoulders. With the straps pushed off, there was nothing between the top of the suit and the top of her head except just *her*, this clean bare plane of the top of her chest down from the shoulder bones like a dented sheet of metal tilted in the light. I mean, it was more than pretty.

She had sort of oaky hair that the sun and salt had bleached, done up in a bun that was unravelling, and a kind of prim face. Walking into the A & P with your straps down, I suppose it's the only kind of face you *can* have. She held her head so high her neck, coming up out of those white shoulders, looked kind of stretched, but I didn't mind. The longer her neck was, the more of her there was.

She must have felt in the corner of her eye me and over my shoulder Stokesie in the second slot watching, but she didn't tip. Not this queen. She kept her eyes moving across the racks, and stopped, and turned so slow it made my stomach rub the inside of my apron, and buzzed to the other two, who kind of huddled against her for relief, and then they all three of them went up the   cat-and-dog-food-breakfast-cereal-macaroni-rice-raisins-sea-

sonings-spreads-spaghetti-soft-drinks-crackers-and-cookies   aisle.
From the third slot I look straight up this aisle to the meat
counter, and I watched them all the way. The fat one with the
tan sort of fumbled with the cookies, but on second thought she
put the package back. The sheep pushing their carts down the
aisle—the girls were walking against the usual traffic (not that we
have one-way signs or anything)—were pretty hilarious. You
could see them, when Queenie's white shoulders dawned on them,
kind of jerk, or hop, or hiccup, but their eyes snapped back to
their own baskets and on they pushed. I bet you could set off
dynamite in an A & P and the people would by and large keep
reaching and checking oatmeal off their lists and muttering "Let
me see, there was a third thing, began with A, asparagus, no, ah,
yes, applesauce!" or whatever it is they do mutter. But there was
no doubt, this jiggled them. A few houseslaves in pin curlers
even looked around after pushing their carts past to make sure
what they had seen was correct.

You know, it's one thing to have a girl in a bathing suit down
on the beach, where what with the glare nobody can look at each
other much anyway, and another thing in the cool of the A & P,
under the fluorescent lights, against all those stacked packages,
with her feet paddling along naked over our checkerboard green-
and-cream rubber-tile floor.

"Oh Daddy," Stokesie said beside me. "I feel so faint."

"Darling," I said. "Hold me tight." Stokesie's married, with
two babies chalked up on his fuselage already, but as far as I can
tell that's the only difference. He's twenty-two, and I was nine-
teen this April.

"Is it done?" he asks, the responsible married man finding his
voice. I forgot to say he thinks he's going to be manager some
sunny day, maybe in 1990 when it's called the Great Alexandrov
and Petrooshki Tea Company or something.

What he meant was, our town is five miles from a beach, with
a big summer colony out on the Point, but we're right in the
middle of town, and the women generally put on a shirt or shorts
or something before they get out of the car into the street. And
anyway these are usually women with six children and varicose
veins mapping their legs and nobody, including them, could care
less. As I say, we're right in the middle of town, and if you stand
at our front doors you can see two banks and the Congregational
church and the newspaper store and three real-estate offices and
about twenty-seven old freeloaders tearing up Central Street because the sewer broke again. It's not as if we're on the Cape;

we're north of Boston and there's people in this town haven't seen the ocean for twenty years.

The girls had reached the meat counter and were asking McMahon something. He pointed, they pointed, and they shuffled out of sight behind a pyramid of Diet Delight peaches. All that was left for us to see was old McMahon patting his mouth and looking after them sizing up their joints. Poor kids, I began to feel sorry for them, they couldn't help it.

Now here comes the sad part of the story, at least my family says it's sad, but I don't think it's so sad myself. The store's pretty empty, it being Thursday afternoon, so there was nothing much to do except lean on the register and wait for the girls to show up again. The whole store was like a pinball machine and I didn't know which tunnel they'd come out of. After a while they come around out of the far aisle, around the light bulbs, records at discount of the Caribbean Six or Tony Martin Sings or some such gunk you wonder they waste wax on, sixpacks of candy bars, and plastic toys done up in cellophane that fall apart when a kid looks at them anyway. Around they come, Queenie still leading the way, and holding a little gray jar in her hand. Slots Three through Seven are unmanned and I could see her wondering between Stokes and me, but Stokesie with his usual luck draws an old party in baggy gray pants who stumbles up with four giant cans of pineapple juice (what do these bums *do* with all that pineapple juice? I've often asked myself) so the girls come to me. Queenie puts down the jar and I take it into my fingers icy cold. Kingfish Fancy Herring Snacks in Pure Sour Cream: 49¢. Now her hands are empty, not a ring or a bracelet, bare as God made them, and I wonder where the money's coming from. Still with that prim look she lifts a folded dollar bill out of the hollow at the center of her nubbled pink top. The jar went heavy in my hand. Really, I thought that was so cute.

Then everybody's luck begins to run out. Lengel comes in from haggling with a truck full of cabbages on the lot and is about to scuttle into that door marked MANAGER behind which he hides all day when the girls touch his eye. Lengel's pretty dreary, teaches Sunday school and the rest, but he doesn't miss that much. He comes over and says, "Girls, this isn't the beach."

Queenie blushes, though maybe it's just a brush of sunburn I was noticing for the first time, now that she was so close. "My mother asked me to pick up a jar of herring snacks." Her voice kind of startled me, the way voices do when you see the people first, coming out so flat and dumb yet kind of tony, too, the way it ticked over "pick up" and "snacks." All of a sudden I slid right down her voice into her living room. Her father and the other men were standing around in ice-cream coats and bow ties and the women were in sandals picking up herring snacks on toothpicks off a big glass plate and they were all holding drinks the color of water with olives and sprigs of mint in them. When my parents have somebody over they get lemonade and if it's a real racy affair Schlitz in tall glasses with "They'll Do It Every Time" cartoons stencilled on.

"That's all right," Lengel said. "But this isn't the beach." His repeating this struck me as funny, as if it had just occurred to him, and he had been thinking all these years the A & P was a great big sand dune and he was the head lifeguard. He didn't like my smiling—as I say he doesn't miss much—but he concentrates on giving the girls that sad Sunday-school-superintendent stare.

Queenie's blush is no sunburn now, and the plump one in plaid, that I like better from the back—a really sweet can—pipes up, "We weren't doing any shopping. We just came in for the one thing."

"That makes no difference," Lengel tells her, and I could see from the way his eyes went that he hadn't noticed she was wearing a two-piece before. "We want you decently dressed when you come in here."

"We *are* decent," Queenie says suddenly, her lower lip pushing, getting sore now that she remembers her place, a place from which the crowd that runs the A & P must look pretty crummy. Fancy Herring Snacks flashed in her very blue eyes.

"Girls, I don't want to argue with you. After this come in here with your shoulders covered. It's our policy." He turns his back. That's policy for you. Policy is what the kingpins want. What the others want is juvenile delinquency.

All this while, the customers had been showing up with their carts but, you know, sheep, seeing a scene, they had all bunched up on Stokesie, who shook open a paper bag as gently as peeling a peach, not wanting to miss a word. I could feel in the silence everybody getting nervous, most of all Lengel, who asks me, "Sammy, have you rung up their purchase?"

I thought and said "No" but it wasn't about that I was thinking. I go through the punches, 4, 9, GROC, TOT—it's more complicated than you think, and after you do it often enough, it begins to make a little song, that you hear words to, in my case "Hello (*bing*) there, you (*gung*) happy *pee-pul* (*splat*)!"—the *splat* being the drawer flying out. I uncrease the bill, tenderly as you may imagine, it just having come from between the two smoothest scoops of vanilla I had ever known were there, and pass a half and a penny into her narrow pink palm, and nestle the herrings in a bag and twist its neck and hand it over, all the time thinking.

The girls, and who'd blame them, are in a hurry to get out, so I say "I quit" to Lengel quick enough for them to hear, hoping they'll stop and watch me, their unsuspected hero. They keep right on going, into the electric eye; the door flies open and they flicker across the lot to their car, Queenie and Plaid and Big Tall Goony-Goony (not that as raw material she was so bad), leaving me with Lengel and a kink in his eyebrow.

"Did you say something, Sammy?"

"I said I quit."

"I thought you did."

"You didn't have to embarrass them."

"It was they who were embarrassing us."

I started to say something that came out "Fiddle-de-doo." It's a saying of my grandmother's, and I know she would have been pleased.

"I don't think you know what you're saying," Lengel said.

"I know you don't," said. "But I do." I pull the bow at the back of my apron and start shrugging it off my shoulders. A couple of customers that had been heading for my slot begin to knock against each other, like scared pigs in a chute.

Lengel sighs and begins to look very patient and old and gray. He's been a friend of my parents for years. "Sammy, you don't want to do this to your Mom and Dad," he tells me. It's true, I don't. But it seems to me that once you begin a gesture it's fatal not to go through with it. I fold the apron, "Sammy" stitched in red on the pocket, and put it on the counter, and drop the bow tie on top of it. The bow tie is theirs, if you've ever wondered. "You'll feel this for the rest of your life," Lengel says, and I know that's true, too, but remembering how he made that pretty girl blush makes me so scrunchy inside I punch the No Sale tab and the machine whirs "pee-pul" and the drawer splats out. One advantage to this scene taking place in summer, I can follow this up with a clean exit, there's no fumbling around getting your coat and galoshes, I just saunter into the electric eye in my white shirt that my mother ironed the night before, and the door heaves itself open, and outside the sunshine is skating around on the asphalt.

I look around for my girls, but they're gone, of course. There wasn't anybody but some young married screaming with her children about some candy they didn't get by the door of a powder-blue Falcon station wagon. Looking back in the big windows, over the bags of peat moss and aluminum lawn furniture stacked on the pavement, I could see Lengel in my place in the slot, checking the sheep through. His face was dark gray and his back stiff, as if he'd just had an injection of iron, and my stomach kind of fell as I felt how hard the world was going to be to me hereafter.

■ **Comment**

This story has a basic situation which could have been told in fifty words rather than five pages. The extra words provide the setting and describe the other store employees, the older customers, and the three girls who violated a store rule. From the first words, "In walks these three girls in nothing but bathing suits. I'm in the third checkout slot . . ." the reader has met almost all the important characters, and he knows that the storyteller is telling what happened "in his own words." Since the bathing suits are important, they are described with care; so are the aisles and the products for sale—including the Fancy Herring Snacks that flashed in Queenie's eyes as she discussed decent clothing with Lengel.

■ **Discussion**

In what way is "freedom" involved in this story?

What do you know about "Queenie"? about Lengel? about Sammy's parents? about the other customers?

Under what circumstances might Sammy have made a different choice?

■ **Action**

Write a restatement of this basic situation in fifty words or less. Then give at least three examples of how the writer improved on the basic situation with descriptive words that showed what the people or the place were really like.

Choose one of the situations in Freedom and Restraint. Retell it with the added descriptions that a more complete narrative would need.

Or

Write a description of the basic values of any two of the characters in this story.

LISTEN TO THE BLACK GRADUATE,
YOU MIGHT LEARN SOMETHING

BARRY BECKHAM

It was commencement day on College Hill and I was making my way leisurely across the green as if I had not a care in the world. Actually, I had many cares, and the graduation gown's length kept me from strutting. I was carrying a seven-inch baton, my class marshal badge was pinned to my chest. I spotted a black Brown graduate of two years earlier moving toward me.

We exchanged greetings. He looked at my badge and my baton.

"So you're the colored class marshal this year, huh? I was the one for 1964."

It was a joke of course, the sort of self-critical humor that blacks engage in with full knowledge of the truth that lies beneath the surface of the witticism. Every time a black man encounters discrimination, he must, if he is on his feet, have an appreciation for the intrinsic humor of the event, for prejudice itself is a product of the half-wit mind.

But he may have had something there, and every time I look back on my collegiate experience to try to gain a perspective on the zeal of black students on predominantly white campuses today, I begin with that put-down.

There were only twelve class marshals who would lead the line in its march down the hill, I was thinking. Weren't we all leaders or something on campus? Or had I been chosen only to add some color to the ceremony? Quickly, as if I were reviewing my notes before an exam, I recounted my four years: frosh basketball manager, Inter-House Council secretary, distinction in English lit, proctor of Hope College. . . .

So it must be that uncertain role I played; that confusion of what I was about, which gives shape to any comparison of my years in school with blacks in college this term. The overriding theme here must be this: role-playing.

Freshman week, 1962. I was bopping this time across the College Green. I saw another black face bouncing on tall shoulders, heading toward me, and I had to clear my throat to overcome the temptation to shout at him. Finally. It was another brother, and I felt safer, more comfortable. We shook hands and asked each other the same question at the same time, laughing at the verbal coincidence: "How many others have you seen?" Maybe two, maybe three, but not too many. Eventually, we counted about eight of us out of a class of 659.

It was only natural that we stuck together, and I can understand why this same kind of conscious separatism exists and baffles administrators on predominantly white college campuses today. The black students always sit together in the cafeteria, they insist. There we were, way up in New England, surrounded by white middle- and upper-classers who had prepared at Exeter, Lawrenceville, Groton; whose fathers were Wall Street brokers and resident surgeons and corporation lawyers; who had spent the summer in Switzerland; who would have a larger allowance for a month than I would see for a semester. In other words, the common ground between black student and white student is so uncommon, the possibility of a badly needed entente is so slight, that it shouldn't seem so unusual for black students to spend that perfect opportunity to mix and talk—at mealtime—with other blacks.

Even the New England accent wasn't our bag. I remember reporting to coach on the first day of basketball practice.

"Go put the balls on the cart over there," coach said.

I stood and looked around the gym.

"What cart?" I asked.

"What cart! What kind of manager will you make. Don't you even know what a basketball cart is?" I finally interpreted it: he meant *court*.

As the months passed on, however, and I became familiar with white students—a hockey game in the dormitory hallway, a casual discussion in the john, a borrowing of notes for a missed lecture—I found that these acquaintances would come over and join us at lunch. And we didn't mind; in fact, we welcomed it. But that entrance of the white student into the gastronomic coterie was always their decision—probably prompted by a degree of courage, a measure of curiosity and perhaps a belief on the part of some sensitive individuals that they knew why we sat alone.

When we were asked why we sat together, we would explain that it was elementary, my dear Watson. In human situations, contrary to the laws of physics, likes attract. And opposites, observing the attraction of likes, tend to be repelled.

Frequently, we black freshmen discussed our high-school experiences. Inevitably, after trading episodes, we came to the conclusion that we had had more fun and felt more comfortable in high school than we perhaps ever would at Brown. The milieu (of course we expected a change) was different, so strange. This was the question on our minds: why should black students attending one of the top schools in the country have to sacrifice so much to obtain a superior education?

Brown had been my first choice. When I told a guidance counselor I had been accepted by the seventh oldest university in the country, he said, "I didn't know you had applied to Brown," and I was instantly glad I hadn't told him.

All through my first semester of freshman year I kept my fingers crossed that the admissions office would not find out I had had my secondary-school class presidency usurped. It started with a speech I gave at a P.T.A. meeting in the evening. After I got home, I pulled out my chemistry book to prepare for the next morning's exam. I fell asleep, book in hand, awoke too late the next day, decided to stay home instead of arriving late and receiving a detention.

The day after my truancy, I explained to the assistant-principal-in-charge-of-discipline why I had been absent. Shouldn't the class president be truthful?

About a week later, I met the class adviser outside the nurse's office.

"I'd like to call a class meeting," I said.

"You ain't president no more," was his answer.

I got an audience with the principal: "This will make a better man of you, and don't worry, all information we send to Brown will say you're president."

There were several rumors advanced for my being taken out of office: the school was predominantly white and therefore most

Caucasian parents didn't want a black president anyway; a couple of Jewish parents had complained to the principal of my galloping with a group of nocturnal miscreants who were secretly dating their daughters (terrible kissers). So for half a semester during my freshman year in college, I lived with the fear that someone from my home-town would write the admissions office and inform them of my political impropriety.

It didn't take us long to agree collectively that we didn't especially want to come back to begin our sophomore years. We voiced our displeasure to the administration, and we received sympathetic ears. We complained, they listened, suggested. Number of problems solved: none. I conducted an informal, wide-ranging survey of students at other schools and found their situations were less encouraging. Black brothers at Harvard were complaining; brothers at Penn cried, actually wept on the weekends; Cornell and Dartmouth students were isolated, so were Princetonians. The remedy for me was simple: go to the Apple. My application for a transfer to Columbia College in the City of New York was rejected, and so I was back in Providence to begin my second year, resigned to make the best of it.

There just weren't enough of us, but no one ever suggested that we could amend this fantastic inequality of numbers. We took it for granted that the university had searched the country-side for qualified blacks. It wasn't difficult to reach the ego-building deduction that we were the only talented Negroes in the country who could pass the stringent admissions policy of Bruno-versity. Yet for this September, primarily through the recruiting efforts of its black students, Brown accepted 151 non-whites (of which 70 accepted Brown)—the greatest proportionate increase of any Ivy League school. Maybe there is more talent than we cared to imagine.

Whenever we congregated, the joke went, "Don't stand around together like this, man. If a bomb drops, they've got all of us." Another was: "If they ever have a race riot here, it will turn out to be a race massacre." So even if all of us in the class had come to one mind about a demand and had decided to march to the dean's office, the sheer insignificance of our numbers would have, as one Brown senior told me last year, "got each of you kicked in the butt and told to get back to the library."

Part of the survival kit which we drew from to maintain an equilibrium during our four-year stay included an imaginary little hole. There, periodically, we dropped little bits of our own culture—bits which were substituted for the magnitude of a larger, more dominant culture. A few used "look it" instead of "dig it." We substituted the terms "skin" for pornographic magazines, "tweed" for a cat who vined well, "jock" for an athlete, and "get laid" for sexual success.

Socially, we fell upon another phrase to explain our uncertain, confusing status: integrate or masturbate. With fewer than a half-dozen black Pembrokers available for the brothers to date, with little money to travel and barely any acquaintance of black Providence society, we resolved that we had to brave a slap in the face, a kick in the shin. We had to ask white girls for dates if we were to keep from becoming dust collectors on the weekends. Fortunately, we were luckier than a New Yorker I know who went to school in Colorado. He dated so many white girls during his first year ("I went crazy!"), the black sisters demanded that he either take his dates to bed or to the movies; but don't bring those white *skanks* to their parties!

Our reluctance to ask was well-founded, we thought to ourselves. Hadn't we been programmed throughout our segregated neighborhoods to stay away from white women? And why? Because we weren't equal, weren't human enough to touch them. So why were we reluctant to ask girls in liberal old New England? Because we were sure we'd meet noncompliance. Deep, deep down inside, we *thought* perhaps we weren't equal, or at least thought *they* thought it. What a role to play. On the one hand, realizing alumni all over the country were counting on us to go out into the world and hold our own against the demons from Harvard, Yale and Princeton; yet feeling inferior.

I don't think any of us were refused a date because of our skin color, but we certainly did take unusual precautions to ensure success. Occasionally, we acted with the kind of boldness that frightened us. I can remember meeting a girl from Risdy (Rhode Island School of Design) by whistling at her from behind. She stopped, turned, smiled, and we met. A date. Another time, I walked right up to a girl sketching on the sidewalk, sat down and started rapping. (If the girls had been black, the techniques used to meet them would have been less eligible for commendation. But to use these boldacious methods for white chicks—we were breaking new ground!)

Sometimes our audacity took the form of comedy. Once my room-mate and I had five girls posing in Wranglers on the grass. We were taking pictures of them. After the impromptu photo session, we took all the names and phone numbers down so "we can call when the pictures are developed." Since we had no film in the camera, the only thing that developed was a list of five possible chicks. Another score.

I don't think the brothers have so many hangups about their social roles now, and the reasons are two-fold. First, there is a substantial number of black foxes on campus, and secondly, the new sense of black pride on campus is nurturing a new attitude about what is called interracial dating. I asked a senior during my last trip on the hill about black-white romancing.

"It's done," he said, "but none of us take it seriously, nobody thinks he's in love." And we used to cry almost when a white Pembroker, after pushing your advancing chest away, would beg you not to take this thing seriously. Now the brothers are doing the admonishing.

I used to note with pride that Brown is the only college in the country offering a concentration program in Egyptology. The lamentable fact that not one course required the reading of W. E. B. DuBois or Frederick Douglass or Richard Wright wasn't so lamentable to me. (Last year they offered a course in black literature.) And none of us bothered to ask why, none of us demanded that all the chips—not red or white or blue, but black—be put on the historical table. As far as I was concerned, black history, in the words of that famous industrialist, might be the bunk. Having had no encouragement to think otherwise, through fourteen years of schooling, how was I to have the unusual acumen to perceive that our contributions to history had been neglected? How were we to know two Negroes were in that boat when George Washington crossed the Delaware, or that whites weren't the *only* abolitionists or that Thomas Jefferson had freed only a few of his slaves and had kept more than a hundred on his plantation? It didn't even seem strange to me to read this sentence in my History 52 senior-year text: "In the years between 1820 and 1869, Americans made it quite clear that theirs was to be an equalitarian and open society."

Recently, a Jewish student from City College in Manhattan said that he would lobby for a Jewish Studies Institute if that college pushed forward with its plans for an Institute of Afro-American Studies. The logical underpinning for his argument is that City is sixty-percent Jewish. I prayed I might find him in the street so I could shout: "What are you afraid of? Don't you realize that Jewish studies have not been neglected, buried or ignored? Did it ever occur to you that we all know more about Abraham's sacrifice than we know about Frederick Douglass' bondage? At least you have a great, living document (placed in every motel in the nation) of your people's history! Why, why are you so afraid of others getting a piece of the action?"

In contradistinction to today's blacks, a piece of the action is what we failed to claim. We weren't thinking of running a candidate for president of Hillel, but just a few aggressive gestures aimed at making our stay on campus more comfortable and less agonizing would have been in order.

But that City College student was appalled at the school's plans to make a separate effort to please its black students.

The most glaring legal example of this separatist posture which has kept minority groups an arm's length from the American dream is that doctrine enunciated in *Plessy v. Ferguson*. But every university in the country maintains separate admissions standards for different groups. Sons and daughters of alumni and alumnae are almost always given preference over other applicants to colleges. I have been told by a source whose ear is close to the administrative whisperings of my alma mater that one athletic coach reviews the admissions dossier of all jock applicants and *decides* which athletes are to be admitted so they can play for him. One of the few men in my class to be accepted to the Yale Law School insisted that his good fortune was in part related to his having changed his last name so it didn't sound Jewish. Really, universities—being no less American than other institutions—have always used discriminating admissions standards for different groups. Now that some of the more forward-thinking colleges are using guidelines for non-whites instead of against them, the administrations are being accused of unconscionably dispensing preferential treatment.

What would we have done with a substantial number of blacks on campus? Suppose we had been a hundred strong instead of fifteen weak?

I would have not only lobbied for courses in black history, but also for a course in racism which would illustrate how much of discrimination—that overt manifestation of prejudice, which exists in the mind—is gratuitous, unwitting. My comp teacher, for instance, gave me a "C" because I wrote "too much about Negroes." A fraternity member intercepted my progress across the Wriston Quad one Saturday to invite me to his fraternity's burlesque show. I wrote an "A" paper on Theodore Roethke and the bulk of the professor's comments centered around his opinion that I had outdone myself; or loosely translated, who would have expected a black student to do so well? These incidents, rooted unconsciously on preconceptions, on the peculiar brainwashing of the white set of the mind about the black man's role, had been sampled as far back as high school.

I remember sitting in elementary algebra (in the back, of course) during the first week and hearing the instructor say that the class was too big and one or two would have to be transferred to another section. I was the only black in the class. Naturally, a girl turned to me immediately and asked if I wanted to leave. The same year, I received a "B" in general science during the third or fourth marking period. Why was I exasperated? I had an "A" average that period. Herr Professor changed my grade when I pointed out the discrepancy. He had just assumed I could achieve no better than a "B" average no matter how well I had done. He hadn't even checked my average that term.

Because a course in racism has to put the sociological scalpel in the student's hand so that he may dissect the psychology of the white mind, I would make it mandatory that whites attend these courses. The arguments raised by black students for excluding whites from black-oriented instruction are specious and self-defeating. If it's the white man's sickness that spreads the germ of prejudice, why not *treat* the patient rather than abandon him. And why should black students, if they really feel black is beautiful and white is just all right, be afraid to discuss the reprehensible aspects of black life in front of white people? Confrontation, not separation, is the near-panacea. We should, in the words of the Reverend Hosea Williams, not be afraid of playing "political psychiatrists" for the sick, racist mind.

I'm not convinced that the instructors of these courses—on racism or black history—have to be black. In all fairness, the criterion should be whether he knows his stuff, whether he can get his stuff together. Even if this selection criterion were not used, it is doubtful that there are enough black scholars to fill the burgeoning demand for their services. Consider: there is a sociology professor at Brown who teaches a course in minority relations. Each year about page 128 in the text, on his lecture about the Negro in America, he becomes increasingly emotional, finally nearing tears, scratching his hair, stomping his feet, whining, "The black man in this country doesn't have a *chance!*" His performance is probably more effective in urging students to think about the American dilemma than any black professor's enumeration of civil-rights murders.

But maybe it's not a bad idea to have a black dormitory and recreation building and a dean of black students—a group of demands recently made by some black students.

My room-mate and I took pleasure in handing out honorary soul-brother cards to gentlemen of Hope College. We taught a couple of them how to slap five, we invited them into our room to dig Ornette and Miles, we even asked them what was happening, baby. One white student became so wound up in the beauty of black jargon (his room-mate was a black from Virginia), he would come into our room with, "Hey, man, man, what's happening, man. Oh, man, man, is it nice out today, man." He even *bopped*. Well, tried to.

Maybe the black students today can't take this kind of obsequious appreciation, maybe they feel it's not their business to teach a white how to be cool or tutor him in Chitlins 100, no more than it's the white's responsibility to instruct a black in the difference between a puncto reverso and passado. "Give us," say some blacks, "our own building where we can do the Four Corners, listen to Pharaoh Sanders, read brother LeRoi and—and just be black." Fine. But if the purpose of a college education is to afford you the opportunity to find out, why limit your vistas? Similarly, if black is beautiful, let's exhibit its beauty to the whole world rather than the same old people who see it everyday. It has long been my entrepreneurial proposition that if the Black Muslims would distribute their bean pie in the white market, they would get billions in revenue.

However, I don't think a black dean would have answered us in the same way a white dean did during one of our first-year meetings with the administration. Somebody complained that we were getting a superior education, but socially we were castrated.

The dean's answer: "Yes, but remember, there are a lot of white freshmen who are just as unhappy as you."

The black student didn't bother to press his argument, but all of us knew what he would have said: "The white student can date anytime he wants with anyone he pleases. The white student has money to go to the movies or a concert. He has friends who rent off-campus apartments. He has a car. He can afford to bring his girl friend up from Natchez. The white student is white. He belongs here. If he is unhappy, he must be dopey."

A black dean would have sympathized with us, would have

probably gone through the same kinds of traumas when he was an undergraduate, would have at least eased our apprehensions with: "I know how you feel, brother, it's hell up here in Providence Plantations." Does our experience corroborate what today's black students assert—that only a black dean can understand them, empathize, hear them? Does it take a black man to understand basic human emotions such as loneliness, frustration, bewilderment? Or does it just take a human being? Possibly the blacks are suggesting that they haven't encountered many of these human beings who are white college administrators, and they'd rather take their chances with a black dean than continue the quest for the great white hope.

At graduation, the rumblings among the gentlemen standing around the College Green after commencement were about future plans. What are you going to do in September? What are you going to do in September? What are you doing next year, next year, next year?

The silent understanding among the three of us graduating was that we had better get off campus fast. If anybody learned that all three of us had majored in English lit, they would surely accuse us of collusion for four years, investigate our records, check with our professors, reread our papers and *boom!* No degree. But we made it, two of us going to law school and the third to graduate school in English. We had no grand designs about changing the society, going back to our hometowns to work for a poverty program, or trekking down South to work for some voting-rights campaign. We still had the business of education to consider, of further development of our minds before we entered into our new roles of black Ivy graduate out to reap the full value of that hard-won (and long-endured) degree.

I was the first to tread the boards in this new role—black graduate on stage with a cast of thousands of whites in the spectacle of big business. I left law school to work as a public-relations writer. After three job changes, I am in a better position to comment on the thrust now among black students to major in Afro-American studies and go back and work among their own people.

One should major in anything he wishes, as long as he receives a broad exposure to the essential areas of knowledge. Law schools do not favor certain majors; nor do medical schools. Corporations looking for future vice-presidents are concerned with the man, not the concentration. So it should be remembered that to concentrate means to take a majority of courses in a particular area, not all. One could major in black studies and be exposed to the same number of courses in philosophy, sociology and history as an economics major.

No matter how exasperating the experience may be, I hope some black graduates will realize that getting a piece of the action requires getting to know the operating procedures of the white corporate structure. If he is to operate his own oil well, he would be better off working for Atlantic Richfield than for a poverty agency. But, as I said, the experience can be unnerving.

Scene: my first week as a public-relations writer for a corporation whose number of employees is about three times larger than the population of my hometown. I have left my jacket in my office, I enter the art department with my shirt and tie. I stand by the doorway until one of the artists ends his conversation. A secretary comes toward me.

"Are you a messenger?" she asks.

Surely, I must be dreaming, I think. I am so flabbergasted, so unprepared, I can only shake my head no. First the campus, then the job.

Through the whole six-month experience with that colossus of a company, it became clear to me that perhaps the black college graduate would do well to join a large corporation if only to perceive the thousands of average and below-average white performers. Perhaps nowhere in America is the myth of the inherent inequality of the black man more susceptible to annihilation than in business.

The depersonalization of the company would keep a sociologist busy for a lifetime. In the directories and on any written material, employees are referred to only by their first two initials and last names. Under no circumstances would John A. Doe be written other than J. A. Doe.

And the exasperation. After my first trip out of town, which resulted in my filing a discrimination suit against an auto-rental company—a suit looked upon by my manager as causing trouble to the company—I was called in by one of my two bosses. He told me to "fix up" the expense voucher because I hadn't used enough money. If the accounting department noticed that I could spend so little in one day, they might check previous vouchers of executives who had been more prodigal.

Writing was to be by company formula or it wasn't acceptable. I wrote a dedication speech for the president of the company that began: "I can't remember when I have been so excited about an opening." My immediate boss crossed it out, saying the use of the word "opening" was lewd. He was certain people would attach sexual connotations to it.

Sometimes you wondered if anyone was sane. In some introductory remarks for one executive, I used the term Black Tuesday. He removed the allusion because the audience was mixed, and he feared black anger. In a film about a black family that received entrepreneurial assistance from the company, the black girl's voice was dubbed with the white voice of a company executive's daughter. The black girl's voice sounded too "colored."

So the role continues to be the same, only the setting changes. High school, college, business. In each instance, it is the black man thrust upon the scene, bewildered, unfamiliar, abashed, like some character from Kafka floundering in his castle. If he comes out shouting, demanding a piece of the action, a part of the American dream which says, yes, you are a member of this society and we shall accord you your equal share—if he attempts to usurp that which patient bargaining has failed to obtain, he is called a radical.

Well, what other appellation would best suit those black students at Cornell with guns? That they were frightened, that they had been threatened were disregarded facts, discarded with the detritus of other relevancies. It was never supposed that they might have had the Birmingham Church bombings in mind; the slain civil-rights volunteers of the early Sixties; the dogs of Bull Connor. These are events that can convince any man he must arm to protect himself. Readers saw that front-page photograph of rifles, breeches open, cartridge chambers empty, and the registering in the minds was automatic: Militants. Radicals. Student Insurrectionists. So, few recognized the real symbol of the event: Fear. And if those students are fearful and mistrustful, is it their paranoia or a true index to the climate surrounding the black student who refuses to be an invisible man on the predominantly white campus that is the cause? Who can blame them for insisting on conditions that will preclude them from having to mouth the opening line of Ginsberg's *America?*

"America I've given you all and now I'm nothing."

Today's black student, for the most part, is something else.

Comment

This country seems to have developed a new professional in recent years. He is the expert on race relations, who lectures, writes, appears on panel shows, and constantly attempts to answer the question asked by the man in the cartoon on page 27: "Just what is it you people want anyway?"

The personal recollections of the young man who wrote "Listen to the Black Graduate . . ." are not necessarily representative of other black people or even other black graduates. Nevertheless, his experiences have the mark of truth. They communicate amusement, embarrassment, and anger as he encounters fellow blacks, school officials, white co-eds, and workers on the job. Each encounter is a situation; each offers many choices. He tells what his were, and he describes the beliefs behind them.

Discussion

Find an example of a general statement marked by the words: "It was only natural . . . ," "the common ground," "likes attract," or "the self-critical humor that blacks engage in." Do you understand what the author believes to be "common" or "natural"? Do you agree?

Does the author sound prejudiced toward any group of people? Does he seem to understand why the people who disagree with him behave as they do? Give an example.

Action
(Choose one.)

Write a response to this essay, in which you express your own agreement or disagreement. Refer to specific parts. You may agree with some and disagree with others. Did the author want too much? Did he sell out? Write any essay called "Listen to the _____," designating yourself as a member of some group such as Veteran, Older Student, Working Student, or Woman. Explain through incidents and statements what people should know about that group.

From **COP!**

L. H. WHITTEMORE

. . . Next evening, I met the cops at the Mexican cafe, where we ordered the same meal of chicken and rice. They commented that the mood of Haight-Ashbury seemed desperate, and they were right.

Later that night, at the station house, I learned how desperate the evening had been. We were told that an undercover narcotics agent had been out walking through the crowd unnoticed. As one of the police officers later explained, "This cop was well known in the Haight, but he could still make narcotics arrests. People just associated him with the uniform, you know? Once a cop is out of that uniform, his face doesn't mean anything. For some reason, when he's in uniform and makes an arrest, most of the time he doesn't get any trouble. The minute he gets out of the monkey suit, even showing 'em the badge, or the star, doesn't mean anything. The kids want to punch him right in the eye and knock him down. It just infuriates these kids, because they don't believe that narcotics should be against the law. And it infuriates them to be arrested for it or to see one of their friends being busted. They'll riot against the 'narkos' if they get the opportunity. They'll literally come down and drag that guy away from the cop, even if they have to kick him in the head to do it. They'll go right ahead and start slugging, with no compunction whatsoever. Among these kids, the laws against narcotics are a direct threat to a way of life, which is just what drug taking is for them."

On this evening, according to several cops I spoke to, the plainclothes "nark" moved among the young people who whispered, "Acid? Lids? Mescaline? Speed?" He paused casually next to a pair of black dealers from Oakland. After a minute he nodded to the two men and they motioned for him to follow them around the corner. The undercover man said, "Do you have any lids?" referring to marijuana.

"Acid," was the reply.

"Yes."

The transaction was made and then came the words, "You're under arrest." The agent moved quickly, handcuffing the men together and calling for a patrol car in the callbox nearby. As they waited for the car, the dealers began shouting to the crowd on Haight Street. Together they broke loose and ran around the corner, ducking into a saloon. They screamed at the Negro owner to protect them, that they were being arrested illegally, but the owner told them to leave. Just then, the radio car pulled up and two officers, plus the undercover man, attempted to drag the prisoners out of the bar.

"The kids on the street hate the 'narkos' so much," said one police officer who had been on the scene, "that right away they responded to the shouting. In thirty seconds everybody on that street knew there was something big on—the word spread like wildfire. Then the bottles and rocks started coming; glass was being smashed all over. It was as if they had been waiting all the time for something to happen, and as if they were ready for it when it came."

The patrol car was surrounded by a mass of angry, shouting people. Within minutes, the Haight-Ashbury district was shattered by surges of street violence and flaming Molotov cocktails. Colin and Gary and I were still in the restaurant when we heard the sirens and dashed toward the crowd, leaving their dinners of chicken and rice behind them on the table. I followed, but stayed a block away from the melee so as not to become involved.

Colin later described his initial feelings this way: "I don't mind an actual confrontation breaking out around me, but the thing that scares me is like knowing that the crowd was gathering for a real riot. I mean, at first you're on the outside and you have to go in there. You can think for a minute, and that gives you time to get scared. You know there are snipers, you know there are Molotov cocktails—you know all these things, but you're not yet in the middle of them. You become apprehensive, like,

'Hey, I can get hurt over there.' And then you start worrying yourself to death. It's that time for rationalizing that's bad."

When Colin pushed his way into the crowd he saw that the patrol car had no way of leaving the scene. "They were completely surrounded," he said. "They asked for a unit to respond and one did. No overresponse, just one unit. But they were trapped, so they called for more units."

One of the cops in a radio car responding to the scene recalled later, "The psychology behind it was 'Okay, you're there, the red lights are on, you got a lot of spectators coming around, so we'll leave! And if we do that, the crowd will go away.' Well, this didn't occur. Not in this particular instance. Good Lord knows why not. We left, the crowd stayed—even after the two dope sellers were taken out of there. Members of the crowd, the hard-core kids who come up to the street looking for narcotics and just to raise hell, they started picking up bottles and sticks and things like that, and they threw 'em at passing automobiles and buses.

"The crowd became unruly, and so that necessitated all the cops to return. This all took maybe five minutes. The first couple of units came back in and they took 'em on pretty heavy. So they brought in more units, and again they had to disperse the crowd. They dispersed it to a degree and left the area again. The crowd then moved to another location, half-way down the block. And the same thing began all over again. This occurred periodically. It was word of mouth, you know: 'Come down to Haight Street,' and so everybody was throwing bottles. Well, we put as many units as we had in the station up on Haight Street. And the crowds began to gather on this one corner, and they gathered and gathered and gathered. They just built up, so to speak, and it looked like a Mexican stand-off. You know—a policeman on each corner and the crowd milling about, back and forth. So once again we said, 'Let's leave the area. We'll try it again.' Of course, in the process of leaving the area, and of building up a substantial force, we were pretty disorganized. But we all left and the cops gathered in the station house to prepare themselves. One of the prime things, of course, is having enough power to put something down as soon as possible, and having wagons available, because if you have a prisoner, what are you gonna do with him once you got him? You gotta get rid of him somehow. So they called for wagons from outside districts. So while the crowd was gathering, we were preparing our next move."

Meanwhile, Colin had gone to a rooftop in order to prevent people from throwing things off it. I remained on the fringe of the disturbance. "I'm up there watching the action," he said, "and as soon as the cops left, the crowd started throwing more bottles, bricks, sticks—every kind of thing—at cars . . . and jeez, they hit a couple of buses real good. Busted the windows right out of them. And I could see it all going on down there. The most frustrating thing is to be in a position where you can see people doing things, things that are absolutely wrong, and being totally helpless to do anything about it.

"I spotted one particular individual," Colin went on, "who was actually acting like the commander of a rat pack. The kids were just following him around. You could see these little sporadic groups forming, away from the crowd itself, and then the bottles again. Many people in the crowd were spectators; not all, but a percentage of them were. Then, one group started smashing windows in the store directly underneath me! They were looting right below me, and I could hear the windows breaking and alarms going off. So I'm standing on the roof and what was I gonna do? Shoot ten people standing down below because they're burglarizing a store? I *could* have done it. I could have done it easily, no problem at all. It probably would have put a stop to it for quite a while—as a deterrent, you know . . ."

Gary, meanwhile, had been mingling with the crowd, trying to talk the participants out of being violent; but to little avail. At one point he saw me and threw up his hands despairingly.

The *Berkeley Barb,* a local underground newspaper, had a somewhat different version of the outbreak: "Ask any cop just what he was doing out there tonight, what it was all about, and the ones who answer you at all will probably say that they were defending the community against a riot by the hippies. It's no secret any more WHO starts riots, is it? When a cop speaks about defending society, what he means is defending one way of life by destroying those who would lead their lives another way."

The underground press has never been popular, to say the least, with policemen. However, Gary Cummings regularly combed the various papers for allegations of police brutality. After the "hippie riot," which ended with a "sweep" of thirty tactical cops through the street, Gary brought the following allegation in the underground press to Colin's attention: "The cops who had arrested us took us into the interrogation room, closed the door and proceeded to methodically, carefully and skillfully beat us up. They used a small sap or blackjack, their fists,

205

elbows and boots. They worked us over for about 15 minutes, it seemed. I could see very little, because I was protecting my face. . . . The cops concentrated on my kidneys, chest and groin. I found myself pleading with them to stop. They would not."

"The other side to that story," Colin said, "is that the kids wanted the police to beat them up. Not all of them, maybe, but a great many of them. This wasn't a riot in the same sense as Watts, for example. The kids—and many of them are much older than kids—tried their best to make the *police* break the law by beating them up. So maybe they succeeded, I don't know."

Gary, who had tried to calm the crowd through "establishing a dialogue," had not succeeded. "The sight of those cops in riot gear charging down the street," he said, "waving their clubs and using them on those fleeing kids, was enough to even frighten me." Gary told me he had witnessed one scene where an officer was rousting a young man off the street. "He told the kid to get going and started whacking him on the back with his stick. The kid started running and crying, 'I'm going, I'm going, I'm sorry, I'm sorry.' But the cop chased after him, clubbing him. He jabbed his stick into the kid's stomach, and when the guy fell, the cop kicked him in the ribs."

"That was a bad scene," said Gary, "and I'm inclined to think that it's society to blame, not so much the police or the kids. I mean, the whole thing boils down to a confrontation and anything can happen. It's really a minor battle in a big civil war, I think. But it's as if Haight-Ashbury was an arena, with the kids on one side and the cops on the other, each going wild, while the rest of society just sits back and chooses sides.

"These white kids, the hippies, have made police brutality a part of their lives by going against society. They're just beginning to catch up with the Negroes, and I think it helps them to identify with black people. Myself, I don't think I ever even thought about police brutality, because cops just weren't an important part of my life. For the average white person, the policeman never enters his life. They never even *talk* to a policeman. But you show me a black person and I can guarantee you—and I don't care who he is, a doctor or a lawyer or what—that he's had some kind of dealings with the police. And you show me the *average* black person and he's had *more* than one dealing with police. Now, I'm not saying that it's always been unfavorable. Sometimes it *is* favorable. But he's had dealings, while the average white person has never come into contact with a cop. The closest he's come to a policeman is the guy standing on the corner directing traffic. Or worse, the rich whites have had contact with cops because they get special favors.

"I know this one Negro civil rights leader named Lassiter, who went to jail for demonstrations. I heard on the car radio two days after he had gotten out of jail that the police had stopped him on the street. And they ran a check on him over the air. The guy in Communications said, 'Is that *the* Mr. Lassiter?' And the cop in the car chuckled and said, 'Yeah, it's him.' Well, the guy had just gotten out of jail two days before, and you *know* they didn't have any warrants for him. They just wanted to harass the guy.

"And here we get into the personality of the cop, which is something that's not supposed to matter insofar as keeping the peace and enforcing the law. But some guys, they don't care if it's a Negro or not. Some guys are just so prejudiced that they just like to whip a guy's head. They don't care—I mean, they use any excuse. The cat's a liberal, or his hair is that way, or he may wear a certain type of clothing. Wham!"

"It's hard to stay liberal on this job," said Colin. "It'll swing most anyone over."

"Like yourself?" I asked.

"Sure, like me. One of those kids yelled at me, 'You're causing the riot.' I told them to go home and some guy three rows back threw a bottle, and everybody was standing around, laughing, egging on the doers. It pisses me off. It's *impossible* to stay liberal as a cop, I think."

"But it shouldn't be that way," Gary joined in. "I mean, they have to put caliber people in these kinds of areas, who are willing to accept some sort of a challenge, who can go into an area and take a situation—even if the people he's dealing with are wrong—and take whatever crap is flying and try to apply some imagination to it—and just turn it around.

"This goes back to something I believe about the whole goddamn Police Department," Gary continued. "There's no psychological screening, as far as applicants go. And as far as assignments, it doesn't make sense to assign your most talented people to certain areas. I mean, it's true that in general, the worst policemen are assigned to ghetto areas or to big disorders.

"A cat you send to any area that is explodable should be your most talented person, not your most off-balanced. You should send a guy who has less hang-ups than anyone else and who's not gonna get excited about being called a pig and a honkie and so on. I mean, they pay a guy enough so that he should be able to take a little verbal abuse. And he should be able, if something does happen, to turn it around or at least turn it into something less explosive instead of more. And they don't do this. In fact, in San Francisco there isn't any real psychological testing, to see if a guy is prejudiced or not. They teach a guy the law, the regulations, and give him his orders, and he goes outside to judge things as right and wrong. But either the situation is too complex for that or the guy's prejudiced.

"And when I say prejudiced, I don't mean just Negroes. I mean prejudiced toward homosexuals, for one thing, and toward any racial group, or hippies . . .

"For example, there's a guy in the station who all the guys think is a homosexual. Now, I don't know if he is or not, and I don't care. All I know about the man is that he's a hell of a nice guy. He has a good mind and so on—but the guys take a real delight in needling him, not to his face but just throwing it out so he can hear it. Now, I just don't understand that—why a policeman gets so goddamn worried about homosexuals and things like that.

"But it's the same old stuff about crimes without victims. For example, prostitution. It's a crime, but there's no victim. No victim at all. Yet the department will tap the energy of any policeman to get whores and pimps and everybody else. Granted, if you have whores and pimps you always have offshoots—you're always gonna find things like stolen property and so on."

"Well, that's true," Colin said. "With prostitution you almost always have crime. They rob their victims, and—"

"Okay, okay. But once a broad robs a guy, arrest her for robbery! But until she does, leave her alone! It's a business, really. If she finds a customer, she's happy and he's happy. So forget about it! Now, if she robs him and he complains, then bust her for robbery!"

"Do you feel the same way about narcotics?" I asked him.

"Well. I've got nothing against pot at all. Grass, I mean. I don't think anybody needs speed, though. I've got nothing against most of the pills or grass. But anything like heroin, or speed . . . I've seen so many guys on speed, and I've seen what it does. Not only what it makes them capable of doing to other people, but what it does to them. But my feeling about grass is that it should be treated just like alcohol. I don't even think possession should be a misdemeanor. If you smoke so much grass that you get mussed up and can't handle yourself, then they ought to lock you up for the night for your own protection, just like they do with alcoholics. I smoke grass now and then."

"But you bust guys for grass, don't you?" Colin argued.

"It sounds hypocritical, but in unavoidable situations I have busted guys for grass. Yes, I have."

"Well," said Colin, "I'd say you were in conflict, all the way around. Especially with yourself."

"Is that so terrible? Look, I happen to be a cop just like you. I don't go around like our friend Fred did—busting guys for grass and keeping half of it to plant on somebody else he wanted to bust. Or like some guys who keep it to smoke themselves. And when a cop plants some narcotics on a guy, what can the guy do? What's the system gonna do? The system is going to say the cop is innocent. I mean, you think a judge is gonna take a citizen's word over a policeman's? Unless the citizen's got money or prestige? Otherwise the whole goddamn system would break down, if the judge couldn't believe that officer. The whole system would crumble.

"Of course, you're not gonna do that to a guy with money, because most truthfulness is equated with money. You might be the rottenest sonofabitch in the world; but if you've got money our society says, 'You must be righteous or some sort of truthful human being,' and in that case it's the reverse: then the *policeman* must be the bad guy. Then the cop is the bad one, the dishonest one, because he doesn't have that position or that money. That's just the way it is in our country. The guy with prestige can stand up in court and say, 'Well, I didn't do that,' and the court's gonna believe him; but if you're some poor slob, especially from a minority group, well, everybody knows they lie."

"My wife has read so much about police corruption," interrupted Colin, who had been married less than a year, "that she kids me, not too seriously, about not showing her all the money I get from people." Laughing, Colin added, "I really don't think she believes me that there's very little of that, at least in my experience."

"Well, corruption is hard to prove," Gary said. "But like, I go down to the colored bars after work, you know? And in one bar, all the chairs are hot. They were stolen from one of the big hotels in San Francisco. Now, it never went to court. The cops came in and busted the owner of the bar, but it never went to court. The owner told me, 'It cost me some money downtown.' So that's downtown that got paid off—the higher-ups. But the average cop in blue, like you and me, he's not going around making money."

Two nights later, Haight Street was returning to its normal state of suppressed chaos. Police had arrested more than ninety people in three days of periodic rioting. Forty-five had been injured, including eight cops. On one occasion, several hundred militant youngsters had pulled a large sidewalk trash bin into an intersection to form a barricade. They set it on fire while others dropped flaming Molotov cocktails into the street from rooftops.

Now, on the third night, two dozen helmeted policemen carrying long batons walked back and forth through the grimly quiet street, breaking up any gathering in their path. Squad cars cruised by, undercover men maintained serveillance, and a tactical patrol of fifty men was held in readiness.

The seemingly mindless outbursts of violence had presented an ugly enigma, even for long-time residents of Hashbury. One of them commented, "There are no real hippies here any more, only thugs and pseudo-hippies. I'm getting out."

The San Francisco *Express Times,* an underground paper, acknowledged the victory by the police: "Haight-Ashbury, deep in pain and boredom, suffering from lost dreams, unconsciously reached out for life-giving rebellion last week. It wasn't enough to do the trick. The Haight is still dying." According to this newspaper, the hippies' relationship with the police was humiliating. The cops had shown superior strength and organization while the residents of hippieville were fragmented and unsure of what they wanted. Many thought that this was only the beginning of what was to be a long, drawn-out battle for creation of a "free community" whose values were alien to that of the larger society. The outbreak was viewed as part of the student rebellion, the political rebellion, the social revolution. For the time being, the cops were in control.

To the youngsters who were involved, one of the most frustrating things about the hippie-police confrontation was the way in which they were trapped between two advancing walls of riot cops. As one participant put it to me, "Did you ever try explaining to a riot pig that you would love to get out of his way, but you see, there is this brother of his right behind you who wants you to go the *other* way, and if they would only get together and decide which way they both want you to go that you would be more than happy to go, but you can't go any-place right now—like you don't have the time to tell them that . . .?"

On the other hand, the feeling of solidarity among the police grew stronger during the confrontation and seemed to carry over into the following days. One of the tactical cops told me, "I've been on Haight Street for almost every uprising. I missed the one where they had to use gas. I can't say I was glad to miss it, because you work with these guys, and you know what they're going through, and you feel that just maybe if I'd been out there, somebody wouldn't have gotten hurt, or I would have been able to back up somebody. Like the young cop that got killed out here not long ago. I wish I had been there to help him. And of course I also know that it could have happened to me. It can very easily happen to any one of us at any given time. In jobs like a banker or a store clerk, you have a different thing entirely, because you don't really meet the hostility.

"I get angry. Now, this is the human angle, and you're not gonna be able to get away from this. I don't care what you do, we're not robots, we're people. We have emotions just like anybody else. Like I grabbed a guy one day and he broke my nose. I made the apprehension. I handcuffed him and I was ready to beat hell out of him. I didn't, however. But I think you get angry any time you come close to getting killed. It's just like driving an automobile and some drunk comes by doing eighty miles an hour, and he hits you broadside; and you get out and you'd really like to do that sonofabitch in, you know?

"But I got even more angry after this guy who broke my nose was booked on a felony charge, for forgery—and battery against me, of course—and they dropped the forgery charge because the checks were stolen and the person who owned the checks was subpoenaed and he didn't· show up in court. He had to testify, but he refused to show up. Now, this guy who broke my nose was out on bail for two other forgery charges prior to this. And he was allowed to plead guilty to one of the prior forgery charges, a misdemeanor forgery, for which he got six months in county jail. He also went up on the assault against me, which is a felony, and they let him plead guilty to a misdemeanor battery, which was six months. Now, that adds up to *twelve* months, but he served 'em concurrently! So, I was frustrated as hell . . .

"I've enjoyed being a tactical cop. It's a good job. Before joining this squad I was accused of police brutality. As a matter of fact, I received a captain's reprimand on one occasion. They held an investigation and to make everybody happy they reprimanded me. What was I supposed to tell my wife and family?

"It was right after Watts. Now, what sparked Watts? It was a drunk-driver arrest, something real simple like that. And they waited, and they waited, and the cops stayed at the scene; so a disturbance was created and the crowd went into a fit, but the cops didn't leave and it grew and grew and finally blew sky-high. So right after that, I was aware of this chain-reaction kind of thing.

"A kid escaped from a paddy wagon and I chased him. I was on a relief motorcycle with no radio on it, no red light; and so the wagon guys told me about it and I went off to find him. The patrolman who was chasing the kid caught him and I was right behind him. He caught the kid around the waist, but the kid twisted around and began throwing hands, you know? So I got off the bike and grappled with the kid. We wrestled on the ground and a big crowd gathered around us. Well, the kid ended up with a black eye. Later, he charged police brutality. See, the crowd had gathered. People were coming out of the houses—a Negro district, and the kid was Negro. I was thinking, 'Let's not make the same mistake as Watts.' So we handcuffed the kid but there was no way to transport him away from the crowd, and he was yelling and yelling for his people to help him. I sat him up on the deck of the motorcycle and rode him about a hundred feet, and then I saw the wagon coming and I waved it down. He claimed we had beat him up on the street. None of the people in the crowd substantiated that testimony, however. I was given a reprimand for transporting the kid on the motorcycle. But see, I was trying to avoid another Watts.

"I know one officer who got stabbed in the hand, and he physically took the guy apart. He shot him up."

It was inexplicable to Gary Cummings that Colin Barker would want to join the tactical patrol, but that is what he told us. Gary was a bit stunned, but Colin explained, "The foot-patrol beat is getting too dangerous. Not that I'm afraid, really, but the tactical force would be a good change of pace."

As for Gary, he eventually made friends with one of the few Negro radio-car men and began driving a steady beat with him.

One night, Gary expressed some of his most personal thoughts about his job to me.

"My main concern," he said, "is that, well, I have a feeling about what's going to happen. I have a feeling that this country is, within the next five years, going to become a police state. And I think the first person that's going to suffer is the black man. When I say suffer, I mean physically. I really believe this.

"I have an emotional hang-up here, because, like everybody else, I've been raised from birth to believe in the free-enterprise system. The capitalist system and so forth. Now, I'm not that hip on economics or politics. I'm not like a lot of guys who fling around words like 'fascist' and 'communist' and so on. I probably couldn't explain what fascism is, or bring in the economics of it or anything. I couldn't explain about communism either. But I see a lot of policemen who really *act* knowledgeable about it all. They say, 'Oh, there are communists down here starting riots in Haight-Ashbury.' And if you ask them to explain what communism is, or different types of communism, they can't.

"So we've been brought up believing in free enterprise and so on, and you hear the comparisons between our standard of living and Russia's, and you think, 'Hey, this country is great.' But on the other hand, half the evil in this country is because of the capitalist system. The slum landlords and so on. And the police really believe that they're hired to just go in and keep the peace, to keep order and so on. But they never ask themselves, 'Well, why aren't the middle-class kids out in a suburban area rioting?' I mean, why doesn't it ever *occur* to them to riot?

"It's the old thing about raising expectations and then not fulfilling them. I mean, you know you're gonna have trouble. If you do that to a child, you're in trouble. And obviously you're gonna have problems on the national level.

"Now, of course, any trouble we may have in San Francisco can be a result also of what may have happened in Cleveland or Detroit or Oakland. Because, say, if Watts breaks out, and a kid from there comes here, he's going to tell a kid up here, 'Man, you guys ain't shit. Because we've been *doing* it down there.' This is the attitude, you know. There's a pride about riots.

"And this is another thing I'm sort of afraid of. As far as riots, it's almost 'the thing to do.' I mean, they wait for summer. But why wait? Kids on the street will say, 'Man, just wait till the summer.' And you kind of wonder, well, why wait? Even if

213

he has no reason to riot, he's grown up with three or four years of rioting every summer. This has been a real part of the kid's life, see. A seasonal thing, like football season. He figures, you know, that this is *supposed* to happen.

"What I feel, and it might just be an emotional reaction or whatever, is two things: one, that not long ago, twenty-odd years ago, a modern, industrial, supposedly enlightened country put to death six million Jews and three million other Europeans. Just through their concentration camps. All fully justified, as far as *they* were concerned. Killing nine million people. Now, legally, the United States had no right to try those people in Germany for war crimes. It's against our constitution to do that. You can't try anyone for something that was not a crime when he did it. *We* made it a crime, after those acts were committed.

"It's not a crime, for example, for the state of California to put a man to death. The death penalty exists. But if in the future it's eliminated, do we then try the governor or the jury who sent a man to the gas chamber? Of course not, because it was legal to do it at the time. And in Germany, it was perfectly legal—those people were executed through sentencing by the courts. In one way or another, the Germans executed all six or nine million people through legal process. They were either judged undesirable, or whatever. And it was legal! So what are we gonna try them for, murder?

"I'm talking about the way a country can do terrible things under law. Which brings me to the other thing that worries me —that also, in the same period, California locked up an awful lot of Japanese. For—what did we say?—national security. We locked up Japanese. I knew some kids whose families had lost all their property, and really, it's a shame. Everybody else was protected by the Constitution, yet these people weren't. I don't know what we thought they were going to do . . .

"So, the Japanese were put in concentration camps in California. Now, as far as any rioting, it's possible—and the Negroes think this—that the same thing can happen to the twenty-million or so black people in this country. We've come a long way since the 1940's to now—but the United States has always been an expert at doing the impossible. We suddenly converted from making autos into making battleships and planes—that was a miracle. And I don't think this country would have any trouble getting rid of twenty million people. Especially when they're so identifiable. None, whatsoever. And all this country needs, I think, is the justification. The majority of the white population,

214

I think, already feels that it *does* have the justification, right now. It's frightening.

"So a lot of white liberals, like myself—and especially because I'm a cop—are going to have to choose. And I don't have a lot of encouragement, from reading history, that many white people will have any courage. Let's face it—everybody looks out for himself in the long run. And when it comes down to the point of death, well—you know the story of the guy who fell in love with the girl and they found out he had this fear of rats? So they put the cage up to his face with the rat coming toward him, and what was the guy's reaction? 'Not me, not me, not me! Do it to her!' And this was the one object, the girl, that he loved.

"I know, for myself, that I have a fear of pain and that I'm not ready to die or get killed. But, I don't know. When the thing comes down to a choice, the white liberal can go with his own people or, if the Negro will have him, he can go with the blacks. But how is he gonna move around? The Negro'll be too distrustful.

"One hope, and this is the crazy thing, is a place like Haight-Ashbury. Not so much the young plastic hippies, but the real rebels, the ones who want to defy authority. The hippies aren't the *only* hope or anything like that, but I think we're gonna need them as some kind of bridge, or alliance. I mean, they draw together all kinds of people, and there's some kind of communication between races and so on.

"But the people in control can always find a reason for something if they want to do it. I don't know if it makes much difference which political party is in power, either; but when Jack Kennedy was in, it seemed there was an attitude that this country had, that now it has lost. There was an enthusiasm. Like the Peace Corps. Here was a guy who got people to give up two and three years of their lives to do something. There was an attitude among the young that I think is missing now.

"I don't think very far ahead, for myself. Certainly not about being a policeman. For most cops, the uniform and the whole experience draws them closer to one side; they merge into a group. With me . . . with me, it has made me look at myself much more critically, as a human being . . ."

■ Comment

The thinking cop is a rare phenomenon in the writing of today. Television scripts, editorials, and essays tend to focus on issues, and either glorify the police officer as a much-abused hero or villify him as a pig, as the first representative of oppressive government policies. This excerpt from a longer book shows police at work, on the job, answering calls for help, being attacked by their opponents, and at the same time, expressing opinions that avoid extremes.

The excitement in the writing is achieved by the on-the-spot technique. The author rode around with these men, answered calls, and kept his tape recorder going. Then he compressed the material to give a vivid picture of two California policemen.

■ **Discussion**

In which of the episodes related here do you think the police should have reacted differently—either with more harshness or more tenderness? Discuss the problems of the "liberal" cop riding around with someone whose views are decidedly different. Can you imagine a situation in which the men would disagree about the appropriate action?

To what degree are the men on duty affected by what happened during the hours they were off duty?

■ **Action**

Summarize the activities in this article as they would be reported in one of the following ways: (a) an account on a police blotter; (b) at the awards ceremony of a policemen's organization; (c) in the editorial page of a revolutionary newspaper.

What happens—or what should happen—in a society in which the majority of the people disagree with the laws as written? How do factors outside the law—such as crowded living conditions—affect obedience to the law? Should those conditions be taken into account in law enforcement? Explain.

216

MONEY

The readings in this section move from the personal to the public and abstract; they include character, action, and idea. In the first selection, the conversations of people in a number of different areas are used by the author as the basis for her theory that people in New York City talk more about money than about anything else. In the second, a psychologist explains for businessmen how they can motivate employees to work more efficiently through goals in addition to money. He explores other sources of satisfaction in jobs. Finally, the short story deals with the appearance of money, prestige, and power as a means of keeping industry moving. The actual work done by the "man of power" is less important than his just being there, and that man exists anywhere, any time.

CITY VOICES

MARYA MANNES

Taxis:

Sixty-fifth, going east to Lexington: "Look at those cars double-parked. Ever see 'em get a ticket? Not them. Ain't a cop don't get his payoff for letting 'em park."

Broadway and Fiftieth, going south: "They're all crooks, from the Mayor down. You tell me, you tell me one thing this Mayor's done for this city! One thing! They're all lousy politicians."

Seventy-fifth Street, going west to Park Avenue: "Boy I could tell this Mayor how to clean up this mess. If he had any guts, he could do it. Now, if we had La Guardia. . . ."

To Idlewild: "So my son, he says, Pop you got to get rid of all that furniture, I'm gonna buy you modern, see he gets two thousand a month in that electronics business he works for, he likes to spend, but I say, look, your mother and I we bought that when we got married and it's good enough, and after she died, you know, it sort of keeps me company, I'm used to it. But these young people they always want new things, new things, even if they're made cheap, but what can I do, my kid's smart, he knows what he wants. . . ."

South on Seventh: "Oh boy, did I have a night—no, not drinking, just arguing with my wife. She always wants this, she wants that, she's got status on her mind, she says, Mannie, this coat ain't what they're wearing now, and I say what the hell's the matter with it, it looks okay, and she says I go out in this and I feel like a dog, this year it's wrap around or whatever. Same thing with furniture, now she wants a hot-tray, what do we need with a hot-tray, she don't cook, we always eat out. . . ."

Gramercy Park, going east: "So what, the Chinese are commies, they're there, ain't they, they run the place . . . so what are we doing with Chiang Kai-shek, he's just a small-time dictator? I don't get this Formosa bit. . . ."

Remodeled brownstone, two flights up, white room hung with abstractions:

". . . calligraphy."

"Yes, it's pushing outside its limits. . . ."

"What do you expect from the *Times?* They're just catching up with Wyeth. . . ."

"Mies once said. . . ."

"You feel the tension in this space. It pulls the vertical downward."

"Well, I thought $5,000 was big, but Kurt said it's a big picture, people are buying them big. . . ."

Hardware store, proprietor to customer; January: "Well, I sent the wife and kids down to the Fountainblue, I'm going next

week. Yeah, forty a day, but they're all like that, and anyhow you need a break in winter. . . ."

Delicatessen owner to friend: "Well I told Charlene—she's only sixteen, you know—I said, no, baby, I will not give you ten dollars to dye your hair, why do you want to dye your hair? and you shoulda heard the squawk that kid put up, crying and all, so her mother says oh let her do it, Irv, they're all doing it, so what's the harm, and I say at *her* age for Christ's sake, but you know women, they never let go. . . ."

Liquor store dealer to customer: "Sorry, I got no one to deliver, two of my boys didn't come in because of the rain. Honest, lady, it's terrible these days, nobody wants to work, they just stay away when they feel like it, so what, they get paid anyhow or they get another job. Nobody cares, I tell you, nobody cares."

Shoe store manager to customer: "Yes, you're right, they didn't match the sample. What can you do? They don't care, you see, they got no pride in their work, it's the same all over. The union protects 'em no matter what they do, why should they care?"

Passenger to bus driver: "But you always used to make this stop. . . ."

Bus driver to passenger: "Well we ain't now, so move on back, you're blocking the passage. . . ."

Apartment living room in the East Seventies, after dinner; the women, segregated: "Thank you, darling—it's only junk, but I loved the design."

"If they can clean they can't cook and vice versa. Marie is really a divine cook but quite crazy. She came in just before a large dinner the other night and said, Madame, he is there with a big knife again!"

"You have to use sour cream. It's no good without it. . . ."

"Do you really think I am? Well, I'm sticking to Metrecal for lunch, mostly."

The men, segregated: "I told Nelson I didn't think he could swing it, but. . . ."

"They're asking six thousand an acre now, so as an investment it can't. . . ."

"Hong Kong. They only cost ten bucks, made to order. . . ."

220

"I still maintain the economy can't take it. You pour nine billion into. . . ."

Women, anywhere in the city:

"Well, I'm not all that crazy about mink; there's too much of it around anyway. . . ."

"It was a doll of a dress, you know, kinda tight around here and loose here, with a darling collar. . . ."

"I always go to her, she knows my taste, the other day. . . ."

". . . so Mannie comes in and says what the hell you do to your hair, and I said for God's sake Mannie sometimes you get tired of your face. . . ."

"Well I told her, don't let him get away with it, he knows perfectly well what he's doing, why should she put up with it? she's got money of her own anyway. . . ."

Men, anywhere in the city:

"So I said, fifty thousand? What do you take me for?"

"As I get it, the deal is, a million down and. . . ."

"So if you sell for five, the least you ought to count on is. . . ."

"With that margin, I don't see how you can lose, especially if the amortization. . . ."

"So I said no dough, that job's worth two hundred a week or I. . . ."

"Sure you can take it off your tax, Ed told me. . . ."

I have eavesdropped in many cities: Rome, Paris, Berlin, Madrid; but nowhere have I heard more constant talk of money at all levels and in all places than in New York. And I do not mean talk in places and hours of business. I mean talk in good restaurants over lunch or dinner, talk in living rooms and theaters, talk in buses and on street corners, talk at cocktail parties, automats, and lunch counters. It is talk of money that animates the men, of deals, tips, investments, pay checks, overtime, and all the ways in which a dollar can be doubled. I eavesdrop in vain for the kind of talk I hear on the streets of Europe: French cabdrivers arguing about politics, men in British pubs fighting about the Labour Party, Italian masons fulminating about German tourists; talk of food and women, talk—on earth and street level—of ideas. All people talk of money sometimes, everywhere. But not for all people, everywhere, is money the addiction, the obsession, the stimulant, that it seems to be in New York. It is a large part of the clamor, and it is the voice—quite literally—of the man in the street.

Within the tall walls of New York are tens of thousands of voices talking of other things: of books and medicine, of plays and acting, of scholars and policy, of faith and death. Again, the glory of New York is this diversity, in which any man can match his own speech, whether in the vocabulary of psychiatry or art or religion or sport, or in the alien tongues and accents that make this city more than American. Walk on West Side streets or in the park and you will hear the heavy consonants and rounded vowels of the Austrian and German Jews who fled to the city in the thirties, or the high sibilant Spanish chatter of the Puerto Ricans—two sounds that have replaced the Irish brogue and the Italian recitative in much of New York. Babel it still is, though the idioms change.

But what, in his way of talking, marks the long-term or native New Yorker apart from most other Americans, who in turn recognize his difference? It is not merely a matter of Bronx or Brooklyn accents, unique to this city. It is a matter, very hard to define, of intonation and phrasing that produces a sophistication absent in the voices of the Midwest, the Far West, and the South. Unlike them, New York is a region only in attitude. The New York voice reflects its diversity, its foreignness, and, inevitably, the sense of superiority New Yorkers feel or come to feel. It says, without saying, We Know. And nowhere is this assumption of vantage more clearly evident than in the casual drawl of the upper-class, traveled man or woman, who throws words away as mink coats are tossed on chairs. To the Midwesterner, on the other hand, words are serious, and each syllable is given the same attention.

In the poorer purlieus, southern Negro and Puerto Rican influence has served to thicken and blur the New York speech so that much of what the young New Yorker of the streets has to say is impenetrable; only the spit of contempt comes through. I do not for a moment suppose this city is alone in the debasement of language by poor diction and almost total reliance on obscenity, but the street children of New York—of whatever origin and color —bring the Word to its knees. They do not speak; they rape.

Yet beautiful speech is here too, in abundance; where actors gather, where teachers explain, where singers practice their songs, and where young students from the far corners of the world translate their thoughts into English with awkward purity. The voice of New York is scored for a great orchestra, even if some of the instruments are stridently harsh. And if the chorus does not sing "Seid umschlungen, millionen!" the theme of the symphony is still freedom. Each voice, to those who listen, can be heard.

■ **Comment**

Like a radio reporter with a microphone catching the sounds of a city street, Marya Mannes tries to record the sounds of Manhattan in writing overheard dialogue. Before making any interpretation, she submits her collection to the reader. Then—pages later—she announces one dominant interest in all the conversations she has listened to. No matter what the occupation, income, or part of town, the people keep returning to the topic of money. Then she adds a comment on what cannot be heard by the reader, no matter how accurately the writer has reproduced the words spoken: the voice and accent of the speakers. "City Voices" refers first to what was said, then to the way it was said.

■ **Discussion**

Has the writer left out any important groups in her search to reproduce the sounds of New York? Has she overlooked places where the conversation would probably have been very different?

After reading the dialogue alone, did you have a different interpretation of what seemed to be preoccupying these people? In addition to money, what else came through?

For instance, which of the overheard conversations could have been used to show that these people are interested in their families? in politics? in art? in justice?

If a dialogue recording were made in your town, would it sound the same? Explain.

■   **Action**

Decide on one place for eavesdropping on different conversations—a shopping center, a bar, a bus stop, service station, or theater. Take down as much of the direct speech as seems typical. Use either pencil or a tape recorder.

Then, read it to the class and allow them to make their own interpretation of what seems to be the main interest of the people you overheard. Is it sex, war, religion, sports . . . ? Compare their interpretations with your own.

AS I SEE IT

An interview with DAVID C. MCCLELLAND

Every businessman faces the same problem: how to get the maximum efficiency from his employees. And every businessman runs head-long into the same frustration: No matter what incentive plan he introduces, some employees will do just enough to get by; others will work well below their potential—which is like running a plant at 60% of capacity.

Professor David C. McClelland of Harvard's Department of Social Relations is the leader of a group of psychologists from Harvard and the Massachusetts Institute of Technology who have been studying this problem for more than 20 years. Dr. McClelland's years of research have convinced him that many incentive plans fail because they are based on a false idea of why men work. The least important motive, he says, is money.

He also believes that it's possible to motivate people to put in a more productive day's work, to turn underachievers into achievers. He has demonstrated his theories, with considerable success, both abroad and in leading U.S. corporations. His ideas and methods parallel those of the noted Dr. B. F. Skinner, who formerly also taught psychology at Harvard.

I have a friend. He's about 65. His wife is dead. They never had children. He's worth, I'd guess, at least $30 million. Yet, every morning, he rushes down to Wall Street to make another million. The other day I asked him, Why? He looked puzzled; finally he replied: "I don't know."

From *Forbes* magazine, June 1, 1969. Reprinted by permission of David McClelland.

McClelland: For a psychologist that's an easy question. It's difficult only for those who think men work for money. Men really work to get various types of satisfaction from life—achievement, power. I'm not talking now about a man who doesn't have enough to eat. He works for money, certainly, but a man can eat only so much. Once you get above that bare-subsistence level, the other motives come into play.

In the case of your friend, I would guess that his two major sources of satisfaction are achievement and power; the notion that he's somebody. I am reminded of Andrew Carnegie. He said that when he made a million dollars he was going to quit. He made it at 30, then kept on going.

For people like that, money is a way of proving they're better than other people.

True, but executives love stock options. Doesn't that prove they are motivated by money?

McClelland: I think—well, that problem interests me because I'm involved right now in a lot of companies that are being started by people to whom I've given achievement-motivation training. Those people all want to start companies. They say they want "a piece of the action." An executive doesn't want to consider himself just a salaried employee. He wants to have a feeling that he owns a part of the company.

The way you describe it, beyond a certain point, money is merely a way of keeping score.

McClelland: Yes, and the reason it motivates people in a culture like ours is that we're achievement oriented. The money is a symbol that proves we're achieving.

I used to live in Latin America. A constant complaint among American businessmen there was that if you raised a man's wages, he simply worked four days instead of five.

McClelland: That's true all over the world. My favorite instance of this happened in India. A businessman from the U.S. complained to a former British colonial administrator that his people wouldn't show up for work. He said: "I've raised their wages to well above what Indian companies are paying, but they still won't show up." The Englishman replied: "I have a suggestion for you: Cut their wages." The Indian worker is not achievement-oriented; he'll work just hard enough to satisfy his needs for food and drink.

What makes achievement-minded people different from these people?

McClelland: In practically every country in the world, you'll find a minority group that is very good in business; in the U.S., the Jews and Quakers; in Africa, the Ibos—the Biafrans—are very good in business, and in Ethiopia, where I was recently, the Guragai; in Southeast Asia, the Chinese. What these minority groups have in common is a sense of being superior to other people. Once a group of people gets to believing they're better than anybody else, they'll go out and prove it.

Do these minorities you talk about have a high achievement rate because *they are minorities and, therefore, feel they must try harder?*

McClelland: That's what a great many people think. They'll say, "Jews are so good in business because they've been discriminated against." These same people, however, also will say, "Negroes *don't* do well in business because they're discriminated against." I say you can't have it both ways. My answer is that if you discriminate against somebody who's got achievement motivation, he'll counter-strive hard, but if he doesn't have achievement motivation he won't do anything. We've made studies that show that a man hears his parents keep talking about getting ahead, and picks up the idea from them.

Could you pinpoint for me why one businessman is born to succeed while another is born to lose?

McClelland: We've spent 20 years studying just this, 20 years in the laboratory doing very careful research, and we've isolated the specific thing. We know the exact type of motivation that makes a better entrepreneur. Not necessarily a better head of General Motors; I'm talking about the man who starts a business.

228

That man has a particular thought pattern; very simply, he's thinking all the time about doing something better, improving his performance. Now, he isn't necessarily thinking in competitive terms; sometimes he wants to beat the other guy, but that may not be essential. He's thinking in terms of constantly improving his own performance.

How can you spot such a man except by his actual performance, his track record?

McCLELLAND: We've developed tests. For example, we'll show a man a picture of another man sitting at a desk, and he'll say: "Well, he's a man working late at night and he's very tired. He wishes he could go home and have a beer and watch TV and talk to his wife." Show that same picture to a man who is achievement motivated and he'll say: "Well, it's a guy working very hard on a new contract for a bridge. He knows it's important for his promotion. And he does it, and the next day his boss is pleased, and he's pleased and his wife is pleased."

All I ever think about is girls. Could you teach me achievement motivation?

McCLELLAND: Of course. We've been teaching achievement motivation for the past seven or eight years. We've had a program in India; we've had an extensive program among black businessmen in Washington, D.C. These black businessmen turn on much faster than the Indians because, I think, the American system is a much more open system.

How do you turn them on? How would you turn me on?

McCLELLAND: Let's go back to those pictures I talked about. The top score a man can make for his story about each picture is 11. Suppose he gets a score of 3. We tell him, "Here's how you got your 3, for this phrase and this phrase and that one. And this is why. Now here is how you can make 11 on that picture. Now rewrite it." We'll have the man keep rewriting it until he can think in those terms easily and readily. This isn't the only thing we do.

What are some of the others?

McCLELLAND: There are some action strategies. We have found, for example, that people who think in terms of doing better generally like challenging tasks. And what's that? One that's moderately difficult, not too easy, not too hard. We have a very simple game. We put a peg on the floor in a room without furniture, give the man three rings and say, "Now throw the rings over the peg. You can stand wherever you wish." He obviously can stand right next to the peg and just drop the rings over, but he obviously isn't going to get much achievement satisfaction out of that. Or he can stand too far away to have any hope of ringing the peg. Or he can stand just far enough away to make ringing it a challenge but not far enough away to make it impossible—and this is what the person with high achievement motivation does. He'll move back if he succeeds in ringing the peg and forward if he doesn't. He'll zero in on the place where he gets the most satisfaction, the maximum distance where he can ring the peg. Many of the black businessmen in Washington I talked about stood very close to the peg initially; they had very low levels of aspiration because they anticipated failure. A lot of our training with them had to do with getting them to set higher goals and showing them that a little risk may pay off.

We translated this into their actual business problems. Here's a guy in Washington. He's running a hole-in-the-wall dry-cleaning establishment. The wholesaler is charging him much higher prices than he charges a white, because the man buys in small quantities and the wholesaler isn't sure he'll get paid. We say, "Why don't you get together with three or four of your friends so you can buy in large quantities?" His first reaction is, "How do I know I can trust them to give me my fair share?" We get him to accept the idea of risk.

We've been talking so far about entrepreneurs. Aren't there some people who work just because they take pride in what they do?

McCLELLAND: The kind of man you're talking about really has what I'd call a professional orientation rather than a business orientation. Now in many cases, the man who is concerned with doing a job right is a terrible entrepreneur. Don't get me wrong. I don't want to run him down, but he often is a poor entrepreneur.

We found this in farming. In a sense, the best farmer is the worst farmer—talking in terms of profits. He gets fixed on producing the maximum amount of milk out of his cows by breeding and feeding, the whole business. This guy gets so fixated on his cows that he doesn't even think about the fact that maybe he shouldn't be in milk that much.

That's true of some companies, too. They're more interested in making steel or planes than money.

McCLELLAND: It takes all kinds of people to make a good world. For example, I don't want my accountant to be a good entrepreneur; I wouldn't want him taking risks with my accounts. But I wouldn't put him in charge of a new business, either.

Describe the ideal entrepreneur.

McCLELLAND: He's interested in moderate risks. The entrepreneur type is not a gambler, because even if he wins he can't get any satisfaction from it because *he* didn't do it. The entrepreneur type is innovative because the old thing he did over and over again becomes too easy for him.

I tend to describe him as the ideal type, but I want to make it clear that he's different from a manager. When you have a giant like General Motors, other skills and other motives are necessary. Those guys have got to worry about managing people, power, getting decisions through, getting compromises.

If I understand what you're saying, a man who is a terrific entrepreneur may be a terrible manager.

McCLELLAND: Exactly. The example I often give is of the wonderful salesman who is promoted and he becomes the world's worst sales manager. He sits at his desk watching other people do what he did and he knows he can do it better and he keeps butting in. That kind of man is counterproductive because his job is to get other people to sell.

Doesn't the worker on the assembly line work for his pay check?

McCLELLAND: That's the most common error managements make. That's why they're always fussing around with incentive plans to get workers to work harder. These incentive plans often do more harm than good, because workers are not necessarily achievement oriented. On many assembly lines, the most important motivation is affiliation. Suppose people are doing a simple, repetitive task. It's absolutely boring. The only way they can stand it is by chatting with their fellow workers. Work to them is a kind of kaffee klatsch. Introducing incentive plans may disrupt the social, kaffee-klatsch atmosphere. In a situation like that, it might be far better to cut down the noise of the machines so that the workers can converse more easily.

Or take telephone operators in offices. They're not achievement oriented, either. What motivates them? Well, during the war, I knew one telephone operator who actually loved her job. The reason she enjoyed her work so much was that she knew everything that was going on. She was in the center of everything. She was the first to know when somebody was sick, when somebody was away, when somebody had a baby.

You get these telephone engineers and they begin to think about efficiency and the number of plugs an operator can plug in and they design a system without thinking of the operator. That's how it's done at Harvard. They have a completely impersonal system. They'd be a lot better off if they decentralized so that one girl could handle one building.

Is there some way you can determine whether a company *is achievement motivated?*

McClelland: There are a variety of ways. You can give the top executives of the company an achievement-motivation test. We did that with two companies in Mexico, both about the same size. The first was growing at a rapid rate; the second was a good, solid company, but it was growing slowly. When we gave the tests we discovered that the man who made the lowest achievement-motivation score in the first company did better than the man with the highest score in the second company.

You can make what we call "climate studies." By that I mean you can ask the workers whether they feel the company's standards are high, whether they feel they get recognition for good work, whether they feel the company is more apt to censure them if they are wrong than praise them if they are right.

There's another question you can ask: Do the workers feel the company is authoritarian or that it permits a great deal of self-direction?

You mean the company that gives its employees a great deal of freedom to decide what they should do will get better results than one that lays down strict guidelines?

MCCLELLAND: Where you find too great a demand for conformity, you'll find a low-performing company. We were called in some time ago by a soft-drink company. It was dissatisfied with the performance of its route salesmen. We talked with the salesmen; they all felt they were too severely regulated. We talked with management and management said this wasn't true. The managers said: "We keep telling these guys they should take more initiative."

It turned out that the men were right. There were regulations for everything, like, first thing in the morning, check your truck and make sure it's clean; then check your uniform, it must be laundered every three days. They had a list of rules about this long.

They also told the routemen: "This week your quota is so many cases." Now these quotas were set from the top. Management figured out what the company's growth rate should be for the year, then allocated the quotas region by region, and from the regions, the allocations went down to the guy on the route.

We said to the company: "Why don't you work it the other way, from bottom to top instead of from top to bottom? Let the men at the bottom set quotas for themselves and work up." They were a little nervous about doing this, but finally they agreed. And it worked. They did better than they'd ever done before.

It works out this way: If you ask a man, "How many cases do you think you can sell?" and he says 11,000, he's going to sell them because he's put himself on the line. He'll feel entirely differently about the goal he sets for himself than about the goal you set for him.

I never heard of a company that operated that way.

MCCLELLAND: That's what this soft-drink company said when we made our suggestion, but they tried it, and it worked.

■ Comment

The interview as a form for presenting ideas is popular in magazines and on television. In this one, a "social engineer" explains how people can be encouraged to work harder when they have jobs, to want to go into business, or to get a job when they have none. He mentions different attitudes in different nationalities, and speaks forthrightly on a number of the problems of management. Even the way people play games shows how they feel about work and challenge.

In a time when the whole idea of working for a living has been questioned, it is interesting to hear from a man primarily concerned with increasing production.

■ Discussion

What did you learn from this article that you had not previously known?

Have you ever found that you were able to accomplish more when you were approached in a way different from before? When did you work harder on high school homework? Did you do better work when you knew it would be collected day by day, than on long-range assignments?

What improvements would you like a social engineer to make in your school? What do you think he might do to increase "productivity" of written work or attendance at athletic events?

Comment on the Englishman's suggestion for increasing Indian productivity by cutting wages, after it had been found that Indians seemed happy making just enough money to get along on.

■ Action

This interview was originally published in a business magazine. Explain the way some of Dr. McClelland's ideas would sound to someone who is not primarily interested in increasing production. Are human rights less important than property rights, or do the two go together?

Imagine a society run by social engineers. In addition to increasing efficiency on the job, what other improvements might be made by these social engineers? Would you like to be "engineered" to have a certain number of children, to use certain products, to keep your weight at a healthful figure, to be rich rather than poor?

Apply Dr. McClelland's belief that man works for satisfaction other than money to your own observations of other people and of yourself.

234

A MAN OF POWER

Alberto Moravia

He was sitting opposite me, behind the big desk—as much as 12 feet long, perhaps—of antique carved walnut. The room was immense, with red damask on the walls and a frescoed, vaulted ceiling. There was no furniture in it except his desk, his armchair and my chair. I looked at him: He was wearing a dark suit, with a dark tie and a white shirt; he gave the impression of a soldier in civilian clothes. On the desk were writing materials of all kinds: a leather writing pad, a fountain pen, various pencils, a scribbling block, a roller blotter; but these were all new, as though they had never been used. There were also two telephones and an internal telephone. The room had only one door, the one by which I had come in. He had kept me waiting, therefore, for about half an hour for some special reason, difficult to divine, and not because he was writing or receiving a visitor.

From the desk, my eyes went on to the man himself. I realized for the first time that he had an aquiline nose and slightly swollen cheeks. Strange, for I had never noticed this before; I thought he had a straight nose and flat cheeks. The aquiline nose, with its narrow nostrils and a small, aristocratic prominence in the middle, denoted authority and the will to command; the swollen cheeks, vanity. Suddenly I became aware of something else: When I had entered, he had received me standing up behind the desk but without shaking my hand. "As I was passing through," I said, "I thought I would come and see you. I thought it might give you pleasure to see an old friend again."

He looked at me for a moment in silence with his curious pale, unmoving eyes and finally said: "A pleasure, yes, it is always a pleasure to me to see you. But as for coming to see me here"— and he emphasized the "here" by a pause—"that's another matter. You did right to come if you have something to communicate to me, something to ask me, something to propose; but you did wrong if you came simply to look me up."

The voice was slow, emphatic, weary, as though to bring home to me that he was speaking to me merely out of courtesy. "Why?" I asked.

"Because this is my place of work and I cannot afford the luxury of receiving friends like this, simply to have a little conversation."

"I see, you're very busy."

He started laughing, with a strange laugh, partly polite and partly ironical, which left his eyes completely motionless. "No, I'm not very busy. In fact, for the moment, anyhow, I have nothing to do. But it's also true, in a way, that I'm extremely busy."

"I don't understand; are you busy or are you not busy?"

He assumed a reasonable, didactic tone in which I suddenly recognized his best quality of former days—his lucid consciousness of his own manner of acting and his facility in translating it into clear argument. "I *am* busy doing what I was called to this position to do, and I am *not* busy, because, as I said, there is not much to do for the moment. But I am busy being what I am, yes, very busy."

"I'm sorry, but I still don't understand you."

He gazed at me for a moment, as though weighing the pros and cons of this conversation. Then he said: "And yet there's nothing obscure in what I'm saying. I have two things to do here: The first is what is called my work; the second, much more important, is the exercise of power."

"The exercise of power? I'm beginning to see. . . ."

"It's time you did. Well, then, why is the exercise of power so much more important than the work? Because, whereas the work is an ordinary job of a bureaucratic kind that, fundamentally, does not concern me in any way and that might be carried out by anybody, the exercise of power, on the other hand, is something that affects me closely, that concerns me personally and, I am convinced, requires a precise vocation and special gifts to tackle it."

"And you have this vocation and these gifts—isn't that so?"

He looked at me, hesitated and then, once again, led on by his own self-knowledge as if by a mirage, gave way to his own kind of almost ingenuous sincerity: "I did not think I had them. I was convinced, on the contrary, that I was in no way cut out for power. Naturally, I knew that power existed, but I wrote it off, judging it from a moralist's point of view, as a thing devoid of real importance. A thing not to be taken into consideration, especially on the part of an intellectual. Then, once I was in this room, seated in this armchair, I discovered in myself gifts and a vocation hitherto unsuspected. And, above all, I understood."

"What did you understand?"

"I discovered that, at a certain level and in certain situations, work no longer counts, is no longer anything more than one aspect—and not even the most important—of the exercise of power. And that this exercise is, on the other hand, in itself, even by itself, even without the accompaniment of a regular, proper job, an occupation, a profession."

He spoke with warmth and smiled at me with a victorious look, like a conjurer demonstrating and explaining the workings of his trick. I said, rather vaguely: "Oh, well, power is power, as we know."

"Tautological but exact," he commented with a smile. "Certainly, power is power. But let us be specific, please. In my case, what is power?"

I looked at him in surprise and repeated, like a parrot: "Yes, indeed, what is it?"

"Power," he began, in a soft, insinuating, didactic tone of voice, "is, in the first place, this dark suit, this dark tie, this white shirt. D'you remember my old trousers, my wind jackets? All that is finished."

"Power is in one's clothes? Quite right."

"Certainly: Quite right. And then power is this room in which I sit for six hours a day. Please observe the carpet, the hangings on the walls, the frescoes on the ceiling, this desk, my big chair, your small chair: All this is power."

"Clearly," I commented with conviction.

"My timetable is power. My arrival introduces—how shall I say?—a soul into a body that lies inert and apathetic. I am the soul of this part of the building. The soul of the anteroom where sits the usher who showed you in, of the adjoining room where sits my woman secretary. My soul, that is, my power, reaches on one side to the record office and on the other to the far end of the corridor. When I am not here, everything is suspended, is in expectation; when I am here, everything functions. That is power."

He was silent for a moment, and I had almost the impression that I could hear him panting with some kind of excitement. Then he resumed: "Inside this room, power lies in the two telephones that I can use both at the same time, holding one receiver in my hand and clasping the other between my cheek and my shoulder. It is also in this internal telephone by which I can communicate with the usher and with my secretary. It is in this writing pad, this inkstand, this scribbling block. It is true that I don't telephone, I don't communicate by the internal telephone, I don't write; but I could."

"Yes," I remarked, "these are, so to speak, the tokens of power, the significant signs. But power as an occupation—in what does that consist?"

He started laughing again, and replied: "Power as an occupation consists in transforming any sort of activity, including work, into manifestations of power."

"Explain."

"Well, for example: I leave this room to go to the bathroom, in order to fulfill a natural need. I go out with my head erect, my chest thrown out, my arms hanging at my sides, my eyes looking straight ahead. The usher, when he sees me, rises to his feet. There, then, is an act of the most ordinary, everyday kind transformed into a manifestation of power."

This time I, too, started to laugh. "It can't be denied," I said, "that, in spite of power, you've kept your sense of humor."

He laughed, too. "Very well," he said, "here's another example, in connection with work. You know what the firm is concerned with, that has its head office in this building. But the real work is entirely done by lower-grade functionaries. As one rises in the scale, the work becomes more and more a pretext, an opportunity for power; and finally, in the highest grades, it evaporates and disappears: Nothing is left but power, an end in itself."

"Give me an example."

"Well, I don't know. Let's suppose it has to be decided whether to open an office of ours in a certain foreign city. Is this office necessary, is it useful, is it functional, is it opportune? I don't know. I only know that the creation of this office allows power to manifest itself."

"And in what way?"

"That's simple: I draw up a report that is exhaustive without taking any definite line, then I have it typed and I ask for an appointment with the chairman. He receives me, I go in and explain the case and I ask him to read the report. He reads it, he comments upon it, I reply, we have a long discussion. Now, I ask you, which has been more important in this business, power or work? I say, power. In fact—does the chairman decide to create the office? He has exercised power. Does the chairman decide *not* to create the office? Equally, he has exercised power. Or again: Does the chairman demur, does he say neither yes nor no? For the third time, he has exercised power."

He looked at me, shook his head and smiled in a triumphant, ironical manner. "Yes," I said, "that's right. Nevertheless, this firm does not depend entirely on this sort of ritual. There are, there must be, practical results as well. . . ."

"Of course there are. There are, but in the lower grades, as I said before, just as in the higher grades there is what you call the ritual of power. Take, for example, the meeting that the board of directors holds annually in the board room on the ground floor. The board of directors is, in reality, composed of distinguished persons who do not direct anything. Yet at the same time, they do direct. Just as I myself do not do anything here but at the same time am extremely busy. They direct, because without their names and without their backing, the practical results would not be reached. Now, I, like you, once thought that a board of directors of this kind, purely honorary, served no purpose. But after having been present at the meeting and having listened to the speeches made by some of the members—speeches, let me emphasize, of an absolutely formal kind—I changed my mind; or, rather, I discovered an immense territory whose existence I had not previously suspected."

He had become serious now. And I, in turn, asked him seriously: "And what is this territory?"

Gravely, he replied: "It is, to be precise, the territory of that magical, enchanted, esoteric fact that is power. The boundless territory in which actions acquire a significance very different from the significance they have according to common sense, precisely because they are performed in the exercise of power. You spoke of ritual. Well, for once, without intending it, you used the right term. It is, indeed, a question of ritual."

At this point, I interposed. "There is, however, a difference between you and the chairman, for instance. You, so to speak, are acting a part; that is, you are conscious of the transformation

239

that power introduces into things. But the chairman is not. He believes in power, and that's that."

He started laughing, in a slightly unpleasant, even though friendly, way. "Another error, another piece of naïveté. The chairman is by no means unconscious of it, and not only the chairman but even my secretary, even the usher. This is the point: Man always knows what he is doing, even when it may seem that he doesn't know."

I made as though to rise. "I understand," I said. "Then the only thing for me is to go away. It seems to me that the little chat with a friend passing through is really impossible in this place of rites and ceremonies."

He rose, too, looked at me and then burst into a fit of amused, almost childish laughter. "All right, go away, then, I won't keep you. But in your case, too, the transmutation of values that goes with power has come about—and how! We've had a little chat, that's true; but this little chat, precisely because you have had it here, and with me, has been changed, as it progressed, into a manifestation of power."

"Of what power?"

"Why, of *mine*, of course!"

■ Comment

The two men in this story have no names other than "he" and "I." The names of the city and country where it takes place are not given. Only the appearance of the man behind the desk is described, as is the office itself. The man and his office are important. Other details are deliberately vague, for the story could take place anywhere. Power exists everywhere.

The "I" of the story is not really a character in the old-fashioned sense of being well rounded and defined. He is merely the old friend with the typical reactions that any reader could be expected to have, while the man behind the desk explains a job which seems peculiar but which exists in reality in a wide variety of ways. This is a story in which little happens beyond defining a worldwide "job."

■ Discussion

Explain the remark of the man behind the desk: ". . . at a certain level and in certain situations, work no longer counts, is no longer anything more

240

than one aspect—and not even the most important—of the exercise of power."

Think of some large institution or corporation. Who has the power? Who does the work seen by the public? What titles are given to the people in power? Does anyone control them?

What does power look like? (A motorcycle escort is one manifestation of it. What else?)

■ **Action**

Describe some encounter you have had in which you have felt very small in the presence of something large and overpowering—a building or an event.

Write a short story in which an outside visitor has something explained to him just as the narrator of this story does.

LOVE, HATE, AND OTHER STRONG FEELINGS

At first glance, these selections are about love. A closer look reveals other emotions, like resentment, resignation, and greed. But love is the topic— a man courting a girl, a girl being courted by a variety of men, and various marriages which took place or didn't last or were headed off by senior members of the family.

In the story about the man courting the girl, true love is more complicated than it appears on a valentine, and the reader may justifiably confuse the man with the "creatures of the sea" who are pursued by the female characters. "The Drearies," an essay which is really more of a list, explains the irritating things men do and say on a date—or in trying to get one. This is possibly a useful bit of reading for a man who has been wondering whether it will take more than hair oil to get the girls he sees on television commercials. For those who already have enough romance, it can be simply a recap of all the things they're glad they have sense enough not to do. The final selection is "The Dirty Part," which turns out not to be sex at all. Rather, it is social position and family approval and inheritance—the unromantic influences which blight or encourage romance.

Authors' treatments vary, from the personal to the humorous to the sociological. Strong emotions lurk behind them all.

CREATURES OF THE SEA

DAVID ELY

"Give me a little kiss."

With his eyes closed, Gregory turned his head lazily toward her, feeling the sand trickle from his neck. Their heads were so close he could feel her breath on his face.

"A little kiss," Louisa repeated.

He touched her lips with the tip of his tongue. Then, he pretended to bite her lips—watching her preparing dreamily to submit to that tiny outrage—but instead, kissed her quickly and rolled over again on his back in the hot sand.

She would not leave him alone. With one finger, she traced teasingly on his chest and then, propped on one elbow and studying his face with affectionate curiosity, traced over his arms and legs, too, with an electric swiftness. In retaliation, Gregory told her deliberately and precisely how he intended to possess her—there on the beach, at that moment, with a dozen bathers and plodding shell collectors as witnesses. Louisa pretended to be shocked, but he knew she secretly relished his voice, his words and the image of a forbidden ecstasy.

Thus, together, they teased and excited one another until Gregory could stand it no longer and broke away in a sand-scattering rush for the surf. The water restored his equilibrium, but as he plowed back out, smoothing his hair and kicking off the anklets of seaweed, he was still left with the aftertaste: Louisa again had been the one who had begun their little game of love, and once more, she had worsted him. She was always ready to arouse him in circumstances that led only to frustration. In fact, she seemed to delight in it, as though to prove to them both, over and over, that she was in control. Although they were as good as engaged, she refused what she delicately referred to as "completion." He padded across the sand. She sat on her folded legs, brushing her black hair, smiling mockingly at him, her breasts moving in concert with her busy, upraised arms; Gregory sat down several yards away, sardonic and chastened. For a moment, he watched her; then, as her movements became deliberately insolent, he glanced away, to forestall a further proof of her capabilities.

"Your mother's coming," he said.

All along the beach, middle-aged women wearing kerchiefs or straw hats browsed at the water's edge with baskets, looking for shells. Whenever they spied some likely treasure, they would bend over with little cries, presenting broad posteriors to each other. Overhead, the gulls soared, turned, wheeled, dived. The birds sought the meat, the women the hard bright husks. Between them, they scoured the beach.

Mrs. Wainwright scudded across the sand in blood-red slippers, holding up something, smiling with joy.

"Darlings—a lion's paw!" She swept up like an eager, knowing bird, fluttering and studiously gay. Gregory was aware of perfume, salt, suntan lotion and a suggestion of sweat.

"It's very good," he said politely.

Mrs. Wainwright flourished the shell in triumph, then delved into her basket. "Look at this!"

It was a giant conch, alive and dripping. She handed it to Gregory, then opened the basket. Inside were two more. She displayed them with smugness.

"How will you get the creatures out?"

"Get them out?" Mrs. Wainwright cocked her handsome head roguishly and placed a smooth hand on his arm. "If they're gentlemen, why, then," she said, "they'll just *walk* out."

Gregory felt her fingernails tapping gently on his skin. "And if they refuse?"

"Then I shall simply have to boil them out," Mrs. Wainwright said.

"Boil them?" Gregory examined the conch. The creature inside the shell had extruded an inch of its slimy self, cautiously. He touched it and it withdrew.

Louisa explained, in a matter-of-fact voice: "You put them in boiling water for a while and that kills them. Then you sort of dig them out."

"That sounds gruesome."

She shrugged. "No, the worst part is later. They always leave a piece of themselves inside, so you have to put them outside in the sun."

"Why?"

"To let the ants finish them off. But they stink to high heaven."

"A small price to pay," Mrs. Wainwright said, taking the conch from Gregory with an exaggerated tenderness. "If you had the true shelling spirit, my dears, you would be out with the rest of us—" She laughed and swung her hips, a merry widow. "But perhaps you find each other—more interesting!" Then she whirled, in a display of careless high spirits, and actually scampered off, calling out after she had reached the waterline: "Remember—we drink at five!"

Louisa and Gregory ran into the water for a final swim. He dived into one breaker; a second, close behind, knocked him over. Farther out, Louisa managed the onrushing waves with practiced timing, challenging the gathering crests, then eluding their power with swift plunges. She laughed and beckoned, but Gregory had turned toward the beach. Near his feet something yellow flashed and tumbled in the last reaches of the surf. He backed away with the Northerner's instinctive distrust of the treacherous life of Southern seas, until he saw that it was merely a shell and picked it up. It was cone-shaped and dappled with black. If Louisa had not come splashing in behind him with the next breaker, he would have tossed it back, for it was still a living thing.

"What's that?"

"Just a yellow shell."

Louisa snatched it from his hand. "My God," she said in honest awe. "A junonia!"

"Will it bite?"

Louisa did not smile. She cradled the shell in her palms and stared at it solemnly. "It's perfect—perfect! Oh"—she gave him a wide-eyed child's glance—"Mother will have a fit, a regular fit!"

"Why? Is it rare?"

She looked at him, again with the seriousness of a child. He almost expected her to say something, in the summing-up fashion of childhood, like: "You found a junonia!" but instead she remarked: "It *is* rare. Especially a perfect one. Mother's been shelling for fifteen years, and she's never found even a broken one." They toweled dry and prepared to leave. "She'll love you for this."

"In what way?" he asked in mock eagerness.

Louisa became a mischievous nineteen-year-old again and leaned against him as they passed beneath the first rank of palms. "I could devour you," she said in a husky Garbo voice, "utterly and forever." Her fingers scraped his arm, clawlike. Gregory laughed pleasantly, but felt the itch of desire, too, and at the same time was again uneasily impressed by the strength of her control. He was, at least now in the period of their informal engagement, her toy.

The late-afternoon sun cast palm shadows across the porch of the beach cottage which Mrs. Wainwright called her cabana. Gregory rocked in a wicker chair, a drink in his hand, gazing dreamily out across the Gulf, only half-listening.

"Sanibel," said Mrs. Wainwright, who had changed from her beach pants into a sleeveless cotton frock that displayed her unwrinkled tan arms and back. She smiled prettily at Gregory. "Shells!" In the kitchen, the conchs and the junonia were boiling in a pot on the stove, their fingerlike and defenseless bodies driven half out of their shells. In the bathroom beyond, Louisa was taking a hot shower. Wisps of steam floated through the screened porch door.

". . . one of the finest shelling beaches in the world!" Mrs. Wainwright was saying. "The Great Barrier Reef is best, of course. Poor Henry, he always promised to take me there—but then there was the war—and then, eight years ago . . ."

Her voice trailed off; Gregory cleared his throat in sympathy. She let him know by her lapse into unaccustomed silence that she still mourned; even so, she chose this moment to prop her sandled feet on the railing, which caused her frock to hike up above her knees. Gregory admired the legs briefly, then studiously followed a pelican's headlong dive for fish. When the pelican reappeared, ruffled, Gregory turned his head slightly. Mrs. Wainwright was watching him with a little smile, with moist eyes—but the frock was even higher. *God in heaven,* he thought, *am I being teased by the mother as well?*

"Sanibel is a lovely island," he said finally.

Mrs. Wainwright crossed her legs and sipped at her drink. "Henry and I spent our honeymoon here, you know. . . ." She rolled her eyes at Gregory, as if expecting him to have immediate and vivid images of Henry's joy. "Seeing you here with my darling girl—ah! Memories!" She laughed a twittering laugh. "And now, all I have are my shells. My lovely shells!"

Thus was Gregory reminded of the underlying reason for his visit, which was tacitly understood by them all. To "speak" to the mother, in the unavoidable absence of the father, to bow ever so slightly in the direction of the formalism of a vanished age.

"Henry was a lawyer, too, you know," she was saying. "That's why it seems so—so right, somehow. Yes. Right."

Gregory quickly took a swallow. This was cutting pretty close, he thought resentfully. Did this woman really believe that he was the kind of man who could be tugged and nudged and jostled into a declaration? After all, he was several years older than Louisa and was almost established professionally— was a man of the world, an experienced lover, even. He was tempted, for a moment, to speak to Mrs. Wainwright the way he had spoken to her daughter on the beach, to inform her precisely of the ways in which he could make her forget Henry completely. Afterward, he told himself, he would take the conchs and the junonia down to the beach and throw them far out into the water. The poor bastards.

"Tomorrow, they'll start to stink."

Louisa had come through the door in white slacks that looked thin, like pajamas. Her mother put her feet down and covered her legs with what seemed a regretful sigh.

"I've got some lovely ones inside, Gregory—you don't mind if I call you Gregory, do you? You seem almost like—like a son, already."

"Mother!" Louisa said sharply.

Gregory made a polite remark, speaking quickly to mask his annoyance. That "Mother!" had really been unnecessary. Then Louisa gently brushed the back of his neck with her fingertips and he noticed, as he followed her into the house, that the slacks were even thinner than he had at first believed.

"Chinese alphabets . . . lion's paws . . . pectens!" Inside, Mrs. Wainwright was displaying her treasures. They gleamed under their coats of varnish in cotton-lined boxes, the prizes of fifteen seasons. Gregory wondered how many pots of boiling water, how many legions of ants, had been required to dispose of the occupants. "Have you ever seen such a lovely olive shade?" On the couch Louisa lay with her shoulders back, gazing innocently through the window. "Look at the points on that one," cried Mrs. Wainwright, holding up a desiccated star-fish. Gregory nodded.

When Mrs. Wainwright had stepped into the kitchen to prepare the salad, Louisa came up to him softly. Gregory found himself tensing to deal with another assault, but she spoke instead: "Do you want to see Father?"

It was merely a photograph. It showed a bald man with large eyes, a handsome nose, a full-lipped, irresolute mouth. Gregory glanced automatically into the mirror above the table where the shells were displayed. No resemblance, of course; except, perhaps, a wry expression of male watchfulness.

That night, on the lonely beach, Louisa surprised him by not only permitting "completion" but actually demanding it. Gregory was by that time so uneasily attuned to the pattern of arousal and frustration that he was caught off guard—was even, it seemed, himself abruptly taken by her, suddenly possessed by thirsty, searching, impatient innocence. Rhythmically the sea broke on the sand, rushed silently up near their bare feet, with a sigh to sink away. . . . From the indeterminate rank growth behind the palms, a bird cried out wildly and on their blanket as they lay quietly watching the turning stars, they stirred and touched each other. Louisa waited serenely now, followed his lead with almost wifely obedience, until in her mounting fierceness she tore at his back with her strong fingers. Inexhaustibly the breakers charged at them, fell short, foamed in again, strewing bits of life along the sands for the birds to find at dawn. They watched the subtle play of phosphorescence among the waves that seemed to mirror the stars. She pressed his hand; time to go. They walked back, not touching; she kept a half-pace ahead. In the cottage, he caught a glimpse of Mrs. Wainwright in her robe, fondling her shells. The two women exchanged glances—that was enough. The story was told, understood, commented on. Louisa swept calmly out of sight to her room. Gregory skulked guiltily to his, the eyes of his hostess burning on his back. His afternoon jauntiness was gone—he had been raped by the daughter, was threatened by the mother. . . .

Tossing on his cot, he waited nervously for Mrs. Wainwright to plunge on him from the darkness. Or perhaps Louisa, return-

248

ing—or even, which seemed to him a quite reasonable prospect, the two of them, insatiable and terrifying. He cursed his weakness. After all, he was a man; he had just performed with credit in the possession of his fiancée. Did not the mother have a right to a vicarious sexual experience, after eight Henryless years? He twisted to one side. There, in the doorway, stood Mrs. Wainwright.

"I forgot to tell you. I'm going out shelling at dawn." She paused meaningfully. "I imagine you and Louisa will want to sleep late." She seemed to chuckle—and was gone. Gregory found himself sitting upright in bed, the sheet clutched at his chest, like a maiden aunt listening for burglars. Would Louisa come to him, then, with the sun? He promised himself that if she did, he would be the complete master this time. He flopped back, realizing, in chagrin, that he should have thought first of going to her; for if she came, it would still be on her initiative. His reaction had again been defensive.

This was his last night on Sanibel. Tomorrow, he would take a ferry to the mainland, then a taxi to Fort Myers, a helicopter to Tampa, a plane to New York. If he was to "speak" to Mrs. Wainwright, it would have to be during the day. Had Louisa sought to force the issue? That was ridiculous. In the first place, there was no need for him to speak to anyone except Louisa. They would not marry for a year or two anyway. In the second place . . .

He was awakened by Louisa, kissing him. He sought to draw her down to him, but she tickled him unbearably under the arms and slipped away, laughing; he accepted the fact that there would be no lovemaking that morning. The sun had risen hot and sharp. As they ate breakfast on the porch, they could see the women grazing along the beach. On a flat rock at the end of the porch, the remains of the conchs and the junonia were already putrefying.

"Why do you love me?"

Gregory considered the question seriously. They lay again on the beach, their toes touching, their hands locked and perspiring in the sun.

"You don't know!" Louisa bit his earlobe. "I'll tell you why I love you, then." She withdrew her hand and looked seriously up into the sky. "I love you because—you're so manly, so intelligent, so—all the things I'm not. I'm curious about you. . . ." She turned to him, her eyes unwavering and intense. "All these things—things I'll never know, except through you. Do you understand? Half of the world—in you! The male half. I'll find out . . . by living in you, by absorbing you! She bit him again.

"I'm not afraid," he said gallantly.

"Yes you are!"

She slapped his stomach sharply and ran off into the water, expecting his pursuit. But he lay there, wondering. Why *did* he love her? He did honestly and truly believe that they were bound to each other, yet, with him, it was chiefly a subconscious recognition—baffling, for he was unable to formulate it intelligibly in his mind. It was a yearning, not simply sexual, that tipped his every sense. She felt it, too, but in an easy, animal way. Before this visit, he had been relieved that there would be no father to face; but now, he wished he could have known old Henry, talked with him. There, he suspected, would have been an ally.

The moment arrived. His suitcase was packed, his bed was stripped. They sat on the edge of the porch eating grapefruit, watching some far-off children playing with a beach ball. Inside, Mrs. Wainwright was working on her shells. The odor of the decaying corpses on the rock was penetrating. Gregory wished she had placed her victims somewhere behind the cottage.

He could, of course, say nothing. He would write faithfully. So would she. In three months, the women would be in New York, shopping; then, at the end of the summer, Louisa would be back at Bryn Mawr and there would be weekends together. But his failure to speak would be contrary to all expectations; there was a heaviness in the air that seemed to cry out for the lightning stroke of clearly voiced intentions. "Madam, I have the honor to ask for the hand . . ." That would be foolish, naturally. Still, a touch of whimsicality would not be out of place: a slightly amused nod in the direction of the Victorian image, to set off the seriousness of his lawyerlike statements. "Mrs. Wainwright, I can hardly help feeling that you have observed something a bit beyond ordinary friendship developing. . . ." Something like that.

Or—the hell with it. Was he to be rushed into a declaration by Louisa's surrender last night? Surrender! He smiled at the idea. Even now—look at her eat that grapefruit! She dug into it expertly with a tiny spoon, ripping the pink flesh neatly from the rind, greedy and sure of herself, chewing rapidly, avidly, a drop of juice on her chin. Now she had finished. But no, she had simply laid the spoon aside. She was crushing the fruit between her strong young hands, squirting the last drops of liquid into her mouth. Gregory glanced down at his own grapefruit. He had botched half of the sections and would not bother squeezing out the rest. Louisa winked at him from behind the crumpled rind, as if guessing his thoughts.

"You're finished? Nonsense. You left the best part. Let me have it, then."

And she took his and began consuming it, scraping its sides raw, working it vigorously with her fingers into a funnel so that all the juice would trickle into her hungry mouth and not a drop be lost. Gregory felt a weakness in his stomach. Was it dismay at the prospect of speaking to Mrs. Wainwright? He did not know.

Leaning against the steps, turned sideways to watch Louisa's enjoyment of the grapefruit, he was aware of other natural processes as well: on the rock, the noisome remains of the conchs, of his junonia, over which the ants were busily clustered; inside the cottage, her lips set, her fingers competent and quick, Mrs. Wainwright herself, arranging her shells, straightening the giant conchs under the dead, wary eyes of poor Henry. . . .

Gregory rose suddenly to his feet. Louisa looked up at him with fond possessiveness, her mouth wet with juice, her hands still kneading the submissive rind. He took one last look at his junonia, the lovely yellow skeleton, the mottled shred of corpse.

"Gregory, dear boy."

Mrs. Wainwright smiled. In the shadow of the room, she looked younger. Looked like Louisa. Gregory thought: *They are both ravishing.* His voice strong, his manner alert and gay, he stepped forward confidently and began to speak, deliciously stung by the salt tide of his destiny, feeling a tremor of apprehension and desire, as a force much stronger than he reached down for him with tender certainty.

■ **Comment**

Both the title and the first line prepare the reader for the plight of the young man in this story. The "creatures of the sea" are as important "characters" as Gregory, Louisa, and her mother. There are the collectors and the collected. From the very first command—"Give me a little kiss" to the last inevitable obedience to a stronger force, this is a story of the imposing of will by some creatures on others.

■ **Discussion**

Assuming that in Gregory's "situation" he had the choices of getting married, running away, or continuing to court the girl, is his choice limited to the one he actually made? That is, do you see evidence in the way the story is told that prepares you for what he chose to do?

What kind of woman is Louisa's mother?

Give examples from the story of Louisa in action, either by what she does or fails to do. What impression do you get?

■ **Action**

Find all the references to the shellfish captured from the sea. How is Gregory made to appear like the fish? Do you like this use of fish as a symbol? Is it helpful in understanding the story?

Prepare an alternative for Gregory. At what point in the story might he have behaved differently? End your story in your own way.

Write a paper on "The American Girl as Predator." Use Louisa as one example. Add other man-stalking women you have known, and draw some general conclusions.

THE DREARIES

JEANNE SAKOL

DREARIES are the Inept Seducers who DO THE SILLY THINGS that both EXHAUST and EXASPERATE GIRLS.

DREARIES obviously regard the female intelligence as somewhat less than a hamster. Otherwise, why do they say and do such Dreary Things?

DREARY: "My regular girl friend is in Paris. Want to come out?"

DREARY: When you indicate your disinclination to sleep with him after a whirlwind courtship of nine minutes and punctuate this attitude with a harsh push, he says, "I'm glad you did that. I was just testing you."

DREARY: He tries to get you drunk and is quite amazed when you say, "Stop trying to get me drunk."

DREARY: He plays Peter Palm-reader, gazes intently into your hand for about six seconds, then says, "You are very sensual."

THE DREARY AT HOME

You're at his place three seconds. He sidles up. Says, "What do you want for breakfast?"

You're at his place because you couldn't very well say no because he said he forgot something so there you are waiting for him to get it, whatever it is, and suddenly PAM! He ricochets around like a runaway billiard ball, bolting the door, turning off the lights, turning on the music—and turning down the sheets. Couldn't *be* more neat.

Excerpt from "The Drearies" reprinted with the permission of Price/Stern/Sloan Publishers, Inc. from *The Inept Seducer* by Jeannie Sakol. © 1967 by Jeannie Sakol.

You're at his place. He says, "Come into my Trophy Room," which turns out to be his bedroom and has a girl's bra hanging on the wall. Winner of the Neat Award.

THE SPANISH ATHLETE OR BULL-SHIFTER

His illusions of grandeur thrill one person very much. Him.

" . . . this sex kitten was mad about me . . . her father wanted to buy us an £80,000 house . . . she was a sweet kid . . . but I'm too young to die!"

". . . this married woman kept giving me solid gold cigarette cases and cashmere dressing gowns . . . she was married to this rich, *older* man, if you know what I mean (smirk) . . . I had to get rid of her . . . very embarrassing, her crying on the phone . . ."

". . . no more English girls for me! Not after those Japanese girls. (Or those Swedes.) They *know* how to take care of a man . . . see what I mean? . . ."

". . . so this stripper I used to go with . . ." YAWN.

". . . really had the hots for me but I couldn't see hurting her . . ." YAWN.

". . . Bunnies are the sweetest girls—and smart? This one I know is a Greek scholar and . . ."

I KNOW, I KNOW.

At the precise moment you meet, the Spanish Athlete is expected at three different parties given by rich debs. He can't decide whether to spend Christmas on a private island in the Caribbean or a private mountain in Switzerland—not to mention a private penthouse housing three nymphomaniacs *who have the hots for him.*

I KNOW, I KNOW.

He opens his wallet and out fall 74 colour transparencies of girls in Bikinis having the hots for him. He opens his jacket to show the tie, shirt, belt, buckle, tie pin and broken rib given him by ardent *friends*.

He loves telling how women have submitted to him in

bathtubs
hammocks
broom cupboards

254

haystacks
ski lifts
fire exits
wading pools
and other unlikely exotica.

He is King of the Drear when he calls at midnight to say he's been having dinner with stars of stage, screen and telly commercials—and he could have brought you if he had thought of it in time—and now the thing he wants most to do is come over and *tell* you all about it. While you make him coffee. And give him an Alka-Seltzer.

THE NOODGE

He does Noodgy Things:

You're trying to make a phone call. He grabs the phone out of your hand and shouts into it. Or gets on the extension. Or jiggles the jiggler to disconnect you. FUN?

On the dance floor, he turns into a vibrating machine . . . jumping . . . leaping . . . shaking . . . gyrating around . . . shouting, "Come on! Don't you want to dance?"

He puts his arm around your shoulder and leans all his weight on you.

Walking along the street, he purposely bumps against you or trips you.

At a crowded party, he puts his arm around your waist, except that his hand comes out the other side under your armpit or drops casually below your waist.

He punctuates his conversation with little hits on your arm or jabs at your ribs.

He turns out lights in lifts.

HE SNAPS YOUR BRA STRAP THROUGH YOUR SWEATER.

HE DIGS HIS NAILS INTO YOUR ARM.

HE CRACKS YOUR FINGERS.

HOW THE DREARY WRECKS A RELATIONSHIP

in two minutes
    asks *your* advice about *his* sex problems with someone else.
in one minute
    describes in detail the ballroom dancing competition he saw on TV.
in four seconds
    calls it a relationship in the first place.

ALICE IN DREARYLAND

A Dreary asks you out. He comes to take you out. He says, "I hate going out."

A Dreary takes you to a Nakedy-Ann waitress place. He does not realize that girls do not wish to: (a) compete with naked waitresses; (b) have naked waitresses exert undue stimulation on their boyfriends.

GIRL REACTION: 'drather do it *myself*.

A Dreary takes you to a swinging discotheque. Then, confesses proudly, "I can't dance. I just love to *watch*."

GIRL REACTION: Nothing like sitting through a fabulous evening at a discotheque, I always say.

A Dreary gets you safely home and then hurls himself on your couch or bed and refuses to move. "I'm staying!" he says, firmly, until you call the fuzz or hit him with an ashtray.

A Chelsea model girl who seemed to attract this behavior tried a number of deterrents. The most effective: "Hit 'em full blast with hair spray. Works fast. Leaves no marks."

THE UNCOMMITTED OR INEPT OPERATOR

He should be named Ambassador to an unplanned nation. He is so incapable of MAKING ADVANCE PLANS, he cannot order the main course at the start of a meal . . . (. . . he may not *be* there, or something *better* may come along in the meantime . . .).

The Uncommitted can neither accept nor reject an invitation: "Can I let you know? . . . I may have to be in Rome." Or "A friend of mine is supposed to be driving down from Scotland."

He calls to make a date, but he can never quite do it.

UNCOMMITTED: "What are you doing Saturday?"

"Well, I'm not sure what I'm doing, because I may be in the country, but if I get back in time, do you want to do something?"

He is so afraid of MISSING SOMETHING that even when he is out with you, he gives the uneasy impression of *knowing* that something better is happening somewhere else.

TYPICAL FIRST MEETING WITH UNCOMMITTED

HE: This is a great party. I nearly didn't get here because I was supposed to be somewhere else.

GIRL: Oh?

HE: Have you made any plans for later?

GIRL: Not yet.

HE: Well, listen, I *have* to go to this other party and I'd love to take you but I'm supposed to be meeting these very important people but you know what I'm going to do?

GIRL: What?

HE: I'm going to call them and see if it's okay to *bring* somebody.

GIRL: Fine.

Then two things happen. EITHER, he disappears for an hour so you make other arrangements and then he's mad because you *couldn't wait five minutes* and he was *just about* to call these other people!

OR, he can't get these other people on the phone but decides to take you anyway, except that the people either don't show up or, if they do, are not especially important or glad to see him— or you.

At this point, he says, "There was another great party in town. We should have gone to that."

THE SINGLE DEADLY BLOW

One of these is enough to switch off most girls forever.
Why?

Because each is symptomatic of an almost pathologically inept attitude. To hang around this type of Dreary is to encourage further ineptness and ultimate disaster.

The man who says, "Be a good sport." or "Come on, be a good sport."

The man who says, "You can't win 'em all."

The man who says "Martooni" when he means martini.

The man who says "Ciao!" who is not Marcello Mastroianni.

The man who says, "All girls are alike."

AND MOST DREARILY:
The man who says, "What are you saving it for?"

OTHER PLACES, OTHER ROOMS

He loves to regale you with the great time he had last night, last weekend, week. And how he wishes he had taken you. Because you would *really* have loved it. Somehow, he feels this gives him retroactive points. He's so *sorry* he didn't think of it.

You feel sorry about that, too. In fact, your reaction to him in general may be summed up as follows, "Sorry about that!"

OTHER VOICES, OTHER WOUNDS

He loves to regale you with the harrowing time he had last night, last weekend, etc., when he ran into this old girlfriend of his and how much she looks like you and how rotten she was to him but how much he's still mad about her and isn't it all sad? Your reaction: "Sad!"

THE INEPT SNOB

He has a constricted Old School throat.

He tries to inflame you by dropping names, places, schools, recipes, continents and squash raquets.

He calls perfume scent.

He asks you where you went to school.

If he approves, he recites a long list of people who went there, too. You never heard of any of them.

If he disapproves of your school, he says condescendingly, "You do awfully well, considering your background."

He starts sentences WE ALWAYS:

had a Scottish nanny.

went to private schools in Switzerland.

got thrown out of private schools in Switzerland.

gave a dance at Christmas.

stayed with people in Palm Beach for Easter.

spent the summer with people in Greece.

had to fire the maids because they sneaked into his room.

The Inept Snob is always AHEAD OF HIS TIME.

He was in St. Tropez before Bardot.

He knew Mary Quant in the old days in Chelsea.

He saw Yoko Ono's bare-bottom film years ago, long before John Lennon discovered her.

He had the chance to invest in Radio Caroline but knew it couldn't last.

Len Deighton asks him for recipes.

He knew Richard Burton's first girl friend in Wales and the Rolling Stones when they were mere pebbles. He has some early shoe ads designed by Andy Warhol. He was taking people to Liverpool to hear the Beatles before Ringo joined them. He knew Joan Collins before Tony Newley got her when she was a skinny little kid running around the East End.

THE INEPT SNOB:

refuses to eat an ice lolly on the street.

makes you wear a black dress and pearls at night.

eats caviare even though it makes him sick.

When you invite the Inept Snob to a party, he says, "Who's going to be there?"

The most vile insult he can hurl is, "How terribly nouveau-riche."

He is one of 50 million British whose ancestors came over with William the Conqueror and whose grandfather "lost everything" in The Slump.

He reads "William Hickey," "The Queen," "Nova" and "Private Eye."

He once went on a double-date with Michael Caine's stand-in.

THE OUT-OF-DATE HIPSTER

He calls girls "chicks."

He uses "ball" as a verb.

He talks about "clap" and "syph" and "knocking shops" with enormous zest.

Using slang, he feels, is extremely *hep*.

■ **Comment**

A girl examines courtship in England by listing some of the things men do to repulse women completely. This chapter is taken from a book called *The Inept Seducer.* Not only is it advice for men who would be more successful with women; it is also a woman-to-woman way of sharing: "I've experienced this kind of thing. Haven't you?" The writer calls these men "drearies," a word apparently more popular in England than it is in the United States; but while this and a few of the other words (lolly, telly) are unfamiliar, the tactics are not.

■ **Discussion**

Which of the activities objected to by the writer are the result of the man's desire to impress a girl with his own irresistibility?

What would be some good responses to some of the ploys mentioned here?

Do you find (or have you found) that insults work better than soft answers?

Which of the remarks and actions sound completely unfamiliar to your own experience?

The author tells what she does *not* like. What do you think she *does* like?

■ **Action**

Classify some other human trait in the manner of "the drearies." Suggestions:

People who are never invited back
The talkers
The sad mopes
The angries
The ideal lovers

Write a paper explaining why some of the drearies probably behaved as they did—and what the girl might have done to improve the situation.

THE DIRTY PART

STEPHEN BIRMINGHAM

In a large stone house outside Philadelphia, surrounded by acres of venerable lawn, at the end of a long graveled driveway that is raked so often that each car approaching leaves fresh furrows in it, lives a certain little old lady with servants and roomfuls of family photographs. At tea time, on designated afternoons, she receives her brothers and cousins, her nieces and nephews and little grandnieces and grandnephews, most of whom live nearby, and, as she pours from a large, heavily embossed silver service, the conversation is witty and cultivated and intimate and gay. "Gentle talk," she calls it. Mostly it is family talk, but often it ranges to art, the opera, the symphony, the local dances. Politics is a rare topic; so is the theatre—unless, of course, someone "knows someone" who has made the unusual move of "going into politics," or is "taking a fling" at going on the stage. The talk, in other words, centers around "people we know." When tea is over, the children kiss their elderly relative good-by and leave with parents or governesses, and a few adults stay on for cocktails and a few of these old members of the family may remain for dinner. At eleven o'clock, the great doors of the house close for the night.

This lady is a member of one of Philadelphia's oldest and wealthiest and most distinguished families. At eighteen, she was the city's most beautiful and popular debutante. Strangers ask why she never married. This is a subject that is not discussed much in the family any more; the reasons why no longer matter much. But, if pressed for an answer, close friends will tell the story of how once, when she was a young girl, she fell in love. The man she loved was out of her class, and was Jewish—either one of which circumstances might have been remotely tolerable, alone. But together they made the situation impossible. She never fell out of love, never fell in love again. Once, it is said, she asked her father for permission to marry the man. Papa, very gently, explained that it was out of the question. She bowed to Papa's wisdom. This story, in its classic simplicity, presents a classic truth: love, among the rich, can be cruel.

Love among the rich is different simply because the rich are rich, and for no other reason. (F. Scott Fitzgerald's sensitive observation about the rich that they are "different" from you and me and Ernest Hemingway's flat-footed rebuttal of it, that they have more money, reveals only that one man understood the power of money and the other did not.) "Power," states an old Chinese proverb, "is ancient wealth." And it is to this thinking that most American rich, knowingly or not, subscribe. The adjective here is most important. In order for the power—the influence, the prestige, the ability to control other people and shore up reserves against the world's inequities—to be at its fullest, the money must age. This is why the newly rich are very different from the anciently rich. Money, like a good strand of pearls, improves and grows more lustrous with each generation that wears it.

This, of course, explains why so much of the talk among the *very old* rich is family talk. Money is part of the bloodline, inextricable from it, celebrated along with it so that the two are tacitly considered to be the same. Family money is a thing that, from generation to generation, must not only be preserved, but must also be enriched and fed and nourished from time to time, from whatever sources are at hand, resupplied from other wells of ancient wealth. Otherwise, any family fortune—unless the strictest rules of primogeniture are adhered to—dissipates quickly through division, taxation, and simple spending. Marriage, therefore—the right marriage—is of prime importance. "Love"—taken to mean romantic love, or even sex—must be subordinated to that, or at least made equivalent to that. Among the rich, money and love and marriage go together like a horse and a pair of carriages —the money being the horse that pulls the caravan. In upper-class love, money is always raising its ugly head. Before the demands of love can be met, the demands of money must be. In marriage, money is definitely the dirty part; sooner or later all the implications of that five-letter word must be faced.

The rich in America are often accused of living in the past, but this is not really the case. The past, the family, and where the money came from provide a textured background for what goes on today, but the true concern of the rich is for the future: where the money will go. A child is more than a child. He is also the carrier of the money into the next generation, and the one after that. This is the reason for the unquestioning obedience and observance of ritual and tradition that accompany upper-class child-raising—a process that Wilmarth Lewis compares to the Oriental practice of foot-binding. This constrictive atmosphere is designed not to stifle romantic love, but to put it in its proper perspective, to help the young see love for what it is. The attitude is that love is cheap. Money isn't.

"Bringing up a child is so difficult these days," a New York woman sighed recently. "At schools and colleges, there is getting to be such a *range* of people." Of course. At the so-called "rich-boys' schools," it is increasingly difficult to be sure that one's son will meet only other rich boys, who are likeliest to have rich sisters. There are apt to be a few poor boys in these schools nowadays, and there are even more apt to be rich boys who are "the wrong kind of rich." This means that, to compensate for schools that "open their doors to practically everybody," more attention must be paid to what goes on in—and who goes to—the private dancing classes, the parties, and the subscription dances where little boys meet little girls. "I have to screen my list of boys' names so carefully," says Mrs. William Tew, the social secretary, "to see that someone who doesn't belong, or of whom parents would disapprove, is not invited." Parents themselves begin screening the list of their children's friends even earlier—from the first days of nursery school.

Why is it considered so important for the rich to marry rich? There are many reasons. "It's better that way," says a New York mother. "Then the young people will have the same interests, the same backgrounds." Oil and water don't mix. Also—always —there is the question of the money. When rich weds rich, there is less chance that one of the partners is a fortune hunter (though there is nothing to prevent a person with a fortune from setting out to bag an even larger fortune; not all fortune hunters are poor). When money marries money, the union of wealth not only assures that the young couple will have few worries over household bills, and few arguments over who is spending too much of whose income, but it provides, for the generation following and the generation following that, an even greater financial cushion. There is less chance of the money's running out; instead, the wealth will grow more ancient, bringing even greater power and greater respectability, into perpetuity. This is why so many of the rich have a curious habit of growing richer. And, if there is one consolation for an old-rich-new-rich marriage, it is that, two generations from now the money will all be old-rich.

Still, the marriage of two rich young people is less like a giant corporate merger than it sometimes seems from reading the newspapers. Instead, the money is joined in a kind of polite legal handshake. It is set up in this manner by attorneys and the trust officers of banks. The money is only married up to a point. Beyond that, against the unfortunate but very practical possibility of divorce, it is kept separate. In this way, when Thomas M. Bancroft, Jr., (whose mother was of the banking Woodwards, and related to the Astors) married Margaret (Peggy) Bedford, of a considerable Standard Oil fortune, it was called "a perfect marriage," and the Bancroft and Bedford fortunes joined hands. When the couple divorced, to allow Mrs. Bancroft to become Princess Charles d'Arenberg, the two fortunes slid apart and returned smoothly to their respective sources. Alimony is considered untidy, and, when both parties to a divorce are wealthy, it is quite unnecessary. In contrast to the Bancroft-Bedford arrangement was the $5,500,000 share of another Standard Oil fortune demanded, and won, by Mrs. Winthrop ("Bobo") Rockefeller in the 1950's—a tabloid hullabaloo that causes all Rockefellers to this day to turn pale when it is mentioned in their presence.

Often things go wrong when two fortunes attempt to disengage themselves in a divorce action. One California bridegroom, in a happy nuptial daze, put his signature to a number of legal documents in the process of taking a wife, without reading any of them carefully. A year or so later, in the process of a particularly bitter divorce suit, he discovered that one item he had acquired—for reasons that are still unclear to him—was half-ownership of a piece of real estate upon which his wife's parents' swimming pool reposed. To the distress of his in-laws, and to the dismay of their lawyers who could devise no legal way of excluding him, he came regularly to swim throughout the divorce proceedings, sometimes bringing large parties of friends but always, he says, "Being careful to swim only at my end of the pool."

In the East not long ago, a pretty girl whose homes are in New York City and Sands Point, Long Island, was more foresighted about divorce. While she and her young husband were honeymooning in Mexico they decided, after a particularly altitudinous evening on the town, to get a Mexican divorce. As she explains, "We were having such a marvelous, glorious time—a perfect holiday. We got the divorce for a lark, mostly. We were there, it was easy to get, and we thought—after all—we might want to use it *some* day." With their speedily obtained decree, the couple flew merrily home to New York, framed the document and hung it on their bathroom wall where, from friends, it provoked appropriate laughter. But, says the wife, "Later on we got to feeling rather funny about it. We didn't really know whether we were married or not. Some of our friends said the Mexican thing wasn't really legal, but others said it was. If we weren't married, it didn't seem quite right for us to be living together. So we sort of drifted apart . . ."

They have continued to drift. The young woman remarried, but she and her first husband are still "the best of friends," and the first husband continues to sail his boat out to Sands Point on summer weekends to visit his former wife's parents and to call on his former wife who is sometimes there for the weekend too. Sometimes, if the second husband doesn't happen to be in the vicinity, the former couple appear at parties together, "acting just like newlyweds."

There is always a good deal of clucking and headshaking about the morals of the rich. And it is true that when there is plenty of money a divorce can be both cheap and easy. But among a larger and less publicized group of American rich, divorces are not supposed to happen. Divorce is not considered respectable or practical. It casts an unfavorable light upon the families, and on the way they live, and on the money. It blurs, rather than strengthens, the bloodline. And, because the press pays more attention to divorces among the rich (HEIRESS SEEKS DIVORCE, scream the headlines) than it does to divorces among the poor, a divorce can be embarrassing. In this group, a marriage is supposed to last and last and last. It need not be happy, but it should last. Husbands and wives may stop speaking to each other, but they should not separate. American Society has, in fact, erected for itself a few bulwarks—flimsy, perhaps, but bulwarks nonetheless—to try to see to it that its marriages do last. One of these is Philadelphia's antique rule against divorced people attending its Assembly Ball. And, in Philadelphia, when one of the well-placed Ingersolls told his mother that he was getting along poorly with his wife, his mother sympathized and said, "Then I think you should take a mistress, dear."

Caring for the wealth and caring for the bloodline, and seeing that each reaches a not only ripe but indestructible old age, go hand in hand, but—in assembling the perfect marriage—concessions can be made in one direction or the other. An ample helping of Old Family and less money, on one side, can usually be brilliantly matched with a smaller amount of family, and *more* money, on the other. And a great family name—of the magnitude of Adams, Talbott, or Howard—can make up for almost anything, even total poverty. An Englishman, who had been visiting in Philadelphia, said recently, "I think that if a rich, social Philadelphia girl married an aging alcoholic homosexual in a wheelchair without a penny to his name—if the name were Cadwalader or Ingersoll or Biddle or Drexel or Roberts or Wister or Chew—everyone would say, 'What a marvelous marriage!'"

For though a divorce may be awkward it is as nothing compared with the disaster—and the cost—that can result from a *mésalliance*. When the late William Woodward, Jr., married Ann Eden Crowell, a former actress and model, and the daughter of a Middle Western streetcar conductor, his parents were models of stiff-upper-lip behavior. And, when young Mrs. Woodward later accidentally shot and killed her husband, Mrs. Woodward, Sr.'s lip was the stiffest anyone had ever seen. "Bill Woodward would be alive today, if he hadn't married that actress," says one of the elder Mrs. Woodward's friends, and certainly no one can refute that statement. The Woodward shooting illustrated a couple of tangential points—that the young Woodwards were doing the customary upper-class thing in maintaining separate bedrooms, and that shooting one's husband does not get a woman, no matter how lowly born, removed from the *Social Register;* the younger Mrs. Woodward retains her place in its pages, along with her membership in the exclusive Piping Rock Club.

More recently, when the son of a wealthy Chicago manufacturer insisted upon marrying a pretty California girl of simple origins, the wedding was described by a guest as "all minks and Mr. John hats on the groom's side of the church, and all little cloth coats and bonnets on the bride's." It was hard to decide, this guest confessed, which side of the church looked more uncomfortable. The young husband, in an attempt to tone up his new in-laws in the only way he knew how, gave them a sizable gift of money. His in-laws then did something that, it seemed, they had always dreamed of doing should a windfall ever appear. They bought a pick-up truck and an enormous house trailer. When they drove this caravan to Chicago and parked it, complete with butane tanks and chemical toilets, on the sweeping drive of their son-in-law's parents' estate on the North Shore, the fiber that held the young marriage together began to weaken. Another cash gift was tried—it went for plastic awnings and window boxes for the trailer—before the young man headed for the divorce court, another unhappy reminder of the importance of "sticking to our kind."

"I've told my daughter," says one mother, "that if she wants to have a fling with a stranger she should for goodness' sake *have* it. But not for a minute is she to entertain the thought of *marrying* him." But runaway daughters are a recurring Society phenomenon, and look what finally happens to them. Popular candidates for these girls' partners seem to be chauffeurs, cowboys, ski instructors—with fewer chauffeurs than cowboys and ski instructors because so few people keep chauffeurs any more while, as Mrs. Tew says sadly, "Everybody skis, everybody goes West . . ." A Chicago debutante of a few seasons back ran off and married her cowboy. When last heard from she was in Wyoming, trying to raise money through her family and their business connections, to get her husband a ranch of his own. A San Francisco debutante, selecting a ski instructor, was last heard from in the mountains trying to raise money to buy *her* husband a ski lodge. Moving up fast to fill the spot being vacated by chauffeurs are service station attendants. Why? So many girls these days are being given little sports cars as graduation presents. Sooner or later, each little car needs gas. Will such marriages last? Hardly ever, in the opinion of Society. Furthermore, when the novelty of such a mixed marriage has worn off, when it is time for the knot to be untied, it cannot be untied without cost.

Several years ago, Patricia Procter, heiress to a Procter & Gamble soap fortune (and a distant relative, through a complicated series of marriages, to the runaway Gamble Benedict) decided to marry Thomas Greenwood, the good-looking son of a London greengrocer. There was the customary consternation in the New York social world in which Miss Procter moved. In fact, her peppery grandmother (a curious parallel, ten years earlier, to Gamble Benedict's grandmother, for Mrs. Procter was also her granddaughter's legal guardian and controlled her inheritance), expressed more than consternation. "Granny," as Mrs. Sanford Procter was called, was so put out with the whole situation that, when arguments and blandishments and entreaties failed, she refused to attend the wedding, a relatively flossy affair with a reception following it at the Colony Club in New York. Guests at the reception bravely tried to ignore Mrs. Procter's conspicuous absence, but as one guest put it, "Granny was everywhere in that room!" (Leaving the reception line, after politely chatting with the young bridegroom, another guest moaned, "Oh, God! He even has a Cockney accent!")

Things seemed to go well enough for the young couple after their marriage, but friends soon became concerned when the Greenwoods moved into an apartment at The Mayfair House on Park Avenue, a couple of floors away from Granny's apartment, and when the groom began to seem more interested in the prompt delights of room service than in going to his job as a car salesman in New Jersey, an employment he suddenly appeared to find decidedly dull. Trouble, of a predictable variety, was not far off. There were quarrels, a separation, a reconciliation, more quarrels, and all the while Granny was right where a good granny should be, just a short elevator hop away. Soon the affair erupted unpleasantly in the newspapers. Greenwood was suing Granny for alienation of affections. Mrs. Procter, Greenwood testified, "through her great wealth," had systematically gone about breaking up the marriage. But what Greenwood wanted, it seemed, was not his wife's love back. He wanted money. There was a public scene in which Granny, a small and erect figure in aristocratic black, made a dramatic appearance in court. Love letters, and the opposite of love letters, were hauled out of dresser drawers where they should have stayed, and were read, and terrible accusations—many too spicy even for the tabloids—flew shrilly about. In the end, Greenwood lost his case, and disappeared. The couple were divorced. Patricia Greenwood, a sadly disillusioned young grass widow, withdrew from New York social life. Mrs. Sanford Procter continues to winter in Manhattan and summer at her farm in Massachusetts, which is called "Fish House,"* where virtually every stick of furniture and item of decoration is in the shape of, or bears the stamp of, a finny creature—as though a reminder that a fish cannot survive outside its water.

Of young Mrs. Greenwood, her friends say, "She should have known. After all, the difference in their backgrounds. . . ."

* Not to be confused with the ancient Philadelphia men's club of the same name. . . .

■ **Comment**

In this article about love among the very rich, money, not sex, is "the dirty part." Situations about real people are used to show the attitude of "society" toward marriage to a partner from the right background. The author explains through examples: the marriage that never took place; the loveless marriage that did not break up; the marriage ruined by two different styles of living; and the marriage ended with death.

The author reports without approval or condemnation, leaving the reader free to match his own code against the one expressed here.

■ **Discussion**

How important is on Old Family name in choosing a marriage partner? for marrying someone approved by the older generation? for alimony in divorce arrangements? for the appearance of respectability?

In what ways is the attitude of your neighborhood toward marriage different from the attitudes expressed here?

Comment on the quoted remark of a New York woman: "At schools and colleges there is getting to be such a *range* of people." What do you think she means by *range*? Has it been true in your own schooling?

■ **Action**

Discuss the advantages of selecting a mate according to the rules adhered to by the society people discussed in this essay. Then discuss the disadvantages.

Describe the way "class" still plays a part by the way people you know depend on categories like name, address, school, and clothing. How would you know you had met someone unsuitable on the basis of a first talk with him? Would your own standards differ from those of your parents?

TRUTH AND LIES

This last section contains readings headed Truth and Lies, though in a sense the entire book has been an effort to disclose truth (or various truths) through definition, confrontation, and reconciliation. The readings are varied. There are Indian girls, a repairman, and three people alone in a people-less town. The settings are India, suburban America, and New York. The issues range from what to do on a free afternoon to survival in a literal sense.

It would be possible to find choices other than those made by the people in this essay and two stories. But the authors have made the choices as they see them. One argues for a change in the Western attitude toward leisure. Another is clearly on the side of his main character, a more sober and practical person than the others in the story. In the most complex situation, a man tells about his encounter with a young girl, which is misunderstood by the various other people involved. The bare events of the story are the sensational newspaper story that might have been written instead. But the story penetrates beneath the surface to reveal a variety of truths depending on each point of view.

AN IRREVOCABLE DIAMETER

GRACE PALEY

One day in August, in a quiet little suburb hot with cars and zoned for parks, I, Charles C. Charley, met a girl named Cindy. There were lots of Cindys strolling in the woods that afternoon, but mine was a real citizen with yellow hair that never curled (it hung). When I came across her, she had left the woods to lie around her father's attic. She rested on an army cot, her head on no pillow, smoking a cigarette that stood straight up, a dreamy funnel. Ashes fell gently to her chest, which was relatively new, covered by dacron and Egyptian cotton, and waiting to be popular.

I had just installed an air conditioner, 20 per cent off and late in the season. That's how I make a living. I bring ease to noxious kitchens and fuming bedrooms. People who have tried to live by cross ventilation alone have thanked me.

On the first floor the system was in working order, absolutely perfect and guaranteed. Upstairs, under a low unfinished ceiling, that Cindy lay in the deadest center of an August day. Her forehead was damp, mouth slightly open between drags, a furious and sweaty face, hardly made up except around the eyes, but certainly cared for, cheeks scrubbed and eyebrows brushed, a lifetime's deposit of vitamins, the shiny daughter of cash in the bank.

"Aren't you hot?" I inquired.

"Boiling," she said.

"Why stay up here?" I asked like a good joe.

"That's my business," she said.

"Ah, come on, little one," I said, "don't be grouchy."

"What's it to you?" she asked.

I took her cigarette and killed it between forefinger and thumb. Then she looked at me and saw me for what I was, not an ordinary union brother but a perfectly comfortable way to spend five minutes.

"What's your name?" she asked.

"Charles," I said.

"Is this your business? Are you the boss?"

"I am," I said.

"Listen, Charles, when you were in high school, did *you* know exactly what your interests were?"

"Yes," I said. "Girls."

She turned over on her side so we could really talk this out head on. I stooped to meet her. She smiled. "Charles, I'm almost finished with school and I can't even decide what to take in college. I don't really want to be anything. I don't know what to do," she said. "What do you think I should do?"

I gave her a serious answer, a handful of wisdom. "In the first place, don't let them shove. Who do they think they're kidding? Most people wouldn't know if they had a million years what they wanted to be. They just sort of become."

She raised a golden brow. "Do you think so, Charles? Are you sure? Listen, how old are *you?*"

"Thirty-two," I said as quick as nighttime in the tropics. "Thirty-two," I repeated to reassure myself, since I was subtracting three years wasted in the Army as well as the first two years of my life, which I can't remember a damn thing about anyway.

"You seem older."

"Isn't thirty-two old enough? Is it too old?"

"Oh no, Charles, I don't like kids. I mean they're mostly boring. They don't have a remark to make on anything worth listening to. They think they're the greatest. They don't even dance very well."

She fell back, her arms swinging on either side of the cot. She stared at the ceiling. "If you want to know something," she said, "they don't even know how to kiss."

Then lightly on the very tip of her nose, I, Charles C. Charley, kissed her once and, if it may be sworn, in jest.

To this she replied, "Are you married, by any chance?"

"No," I said, "are you?"

"Oh, Charles," she said, "how could I be married? I haven't even graduated yet."

"You must be a junior," I said, licking my lips.

"Oh, Charles," she said, "that's what I mean. If you were a kid like Mike or Sully or someone, you'd go crazy. Whenever they kiss me, you'd think their whole life was going to change. Honestly, Charles, they lose their breath, they sneeze—just when you're getting in the mood. They stop in the middle to tell you a dirty joke."

"Imagine that!" I said. "How about trying someone over sixteen?"

"Don't fish," she said in a peaceful, happy way. "Anyway, talk very low. In fact, whisper. If my father comes home and hears me even mention kissing, he'll kill us both."

I laughed. My little factories of admiration had started to hum and I missed her meaning.

What I observed was the way everything about this Cindy was new and unused. Her parts, visible or wrapped, were tooled for display. All the exaggerated bones of childhood and old age were bedded down in a cozy consistency of girl.

I offered her another cigarette. I stood up and, ducking the rafters, walked back and forth alongside the cot. She held her fresh cigarette aloft and crossed her eyes at it. Ashes fell, little fine feathers. I leaned forward until I was close enough for comfort. I blew them all away.

I thought of praying for divine guidance in line with the great spiritual renaissance of our time. But I am all thumbs in that kind of deciduous conversation. I asked myself, did I, as God's creature under the stars, have the right to evade an event, a factual occurrence, to parry an experience or even a small peradventure?

I relit her cigarette. Then I said, with no pacing at all, like a person who lacks aptitude, "What do you think, Cindy, listen, will you have trouble with your family about dating me? I'd like to spend a nice long evening with you. I haven't talked to someone your age in a long time. Or we could go swimming, dancing, I don't know. I don't want you to have any trouble, though. Would it help if *I* asked your mother? Do you think she'd let you?"

"That'll be the day," she said. "No one tells *me* who to go out with. No one. I've got a new bathing suit, Charles. I'd love to go."

"I bet you look like a potato sack in it."

"Oh, Charley, quit kidding."

"O.K.," I said. "But don't call me Charley. Charley is my last name. Charles is my first. There's a 'C' in the middle. Charles C. Charley is who I am."

"O.K.," she said. "My name is Cindy."

"I know that," I said.

Then I said goodbye and left her nearly drowned in perspiration, still prone, smoking another cigarette, and staring dreamily at a beam from which hung an old doll's house with four upstairs bedrooms.

Outside I made lighthearted obeisance to the entire household, from rumpus room to expanding attic. I hopped onto my three-wheeled scooter and went forward on spectacular errands of mercy across the sycamore-studded seat of this fat county.

At 4 A.M. of the following Saturday morning I delivered Cindy to her eight-room house with two and a half bathrooms. Mrs. Graham was waiting. She didn't look at me at all. She began to cry. She sniffed and stopped crying. "Cindy, it's so late. Daddy went to the police. We were frightened about you. He went to see the lieutenant." Then she waited, forlorn. Before her very eyes the friend she had been raising for years, the rejuvenating confidante, had deserted her. I was sorry. I thought Cindy ought to get her a cold drink. I wanted to say, "Don't worry, Mrs. Graham. I didn't knock the kid up."

But Cindy burned. "I am just sick of this crap!" she yelled. "I am heartily and utterly sick of being pushed around. Every time I come home a little late, you call the police. This is the third time, the third time. I am sick of you and Daddy. I hate this place. I hate living here. I told you last year. I hate it here. I'm sick of this place and the phony trains and no buses and I can't drive. I hate the kids around here. They're all dopes. You follow me around. I hate the two of you. I wish I was in China." She stamped her feet three times, then ran up to her room.

In this way she avoided her father, who came growling past me where I still stood in the doorway. I was comforting Mrs. Graham. "You know adolescence is a very difficult period . . ." But he interrupted. He looked over his shoulder, saw it was really me, and turned like a man to say it to my face. "You sonofabitch, where the hell were you?"

"Nothing to worry about, Mr. Graham. We just took a boat ride."

"You'd better call the police and tell them Cindy's home, Alvin," said Mrs. Graham.

"Where to?" he said. "Greenwich Village?"

"No, no," I said reasonably. "I took Cindy out to Pottsburg—it's one of those amusement parks there on the other side of the harbor. It's a two-hour ride. There's dancing on the boat. We missed a boat and had to wait two more hours, and then we missed the train."

"This boat goes straight to Pottsburg?"

"Oh yes," I said.

"Alvin," said Mrs. Graham, "please call the police. They'll be all over town."

"O.K., O.K.," he said. "Where's Cynthy Anne?"

"Asleep probably," Mrs. Graham said. "Please, Alvin."

"O.K., O.K.," he said. "You go up too, Ellie. Go on, don't argue. Go on up and go to sleep. I want to talk to Mr. What's-His-Name for a couple of minutes. Go on now, Ellie, before I get sore.

"Now, you!" he said, turning to me. "Let's go into my den." He pointed to it with a meaty shoulder. I went before him.

I could not really see him through the 4 A.M. haze, but I got the outlines. He was a big guy with a few years on me, a little more money, status, and enough community standing to freeze him where he stood. All he could do was bellow like a bull in his own parlor, crinolines cracking all around him.

"You know, sonny," he said, leaning forward in a friendly way, "if you don't keep away from my kid—in fact, if I ever see you with her again—I'm gonna bring this knee right up"—pointing to it—"and let you have it."

"What did I do?"

"You didn't do anything and you're not going to. Stay away. . . . Listen," he said intimately, man to man. "What good is she? She's only a kid. She isn't even sure which end is up."

I looked to see if he really believed that. From the relaxed condition of his face and the sincere look in his eyes, I had to say to myself, yes, that's what he believes.

"Mr. Graham," I said, "I called for Cindy at her own door. Your wife met me. I did not come sneaking around."

"Don't give me any crap," he said.

"Well, all right, Mr. Graham," I said. "I'm the last guy to create a situation. What do you want me to do?"

"I don't want you near this place."

I pretended to give it some thought. But my course was clear. I had to sleep two hours before morning at least. "I'll tell you what, Mr. Graham. I'm the last guy to create a situation. I just won't see Cindy any more. But there's something we ought to do—from her point of view. The hell with me . . ."

"The hell with you is right," he said. "What?"

"I think a little note's in order, a little letter explaining about all this. I don't want her to think I hate her. You got to watch out with kids that age. They're sensitive. I'd like to write to her."

"O.K.," he said. "That's a good idea, Charley. You do that little thing, and as far as I'm concerned we can call it square. I know how it is in the outfield, boy. Cold. I don't blame you for trying. But this kid's got a family to watch out for her. And I'll tell you another thing. I'm the kind of father, I'm not ashamed to beat the shit out of her if I have to, and the *Ladies' Home Journal* can cry in their soda pop, for all I care. O.K.?" he asked, standing up to conclude. "Everything O.K.?

"I'm dying on my dogs," he said in a kindlier tone. Then in a last snarl at the passing stranger he said, "But you better not try this neighborhood again."

"Well, so long," I said, hopefully passing out of his life. "Don't take any woolen condoms." But when he cantered out to look for me, I was gone.

Two days later I was sitting peacefully in my little office, which is shaded by a dying sycamore. I had three signed-for, cash-on-delivery jobs ahead of me, and if I weren't a relaxed guy I would have been out cramming my just rewards. I was reading a little book called *Medieval People,* which I enjoyed because I am interested in man as a person. It's a hobby. (I should have been a psychologist. I have an ear.) I was eating a hero sandwich. Above my head was a sign in gold which declared AERI AIR CONDITIONERS. Up the Aeri Mountain, Down the Rushing Glen, Aeri Goes Wherever, Man Builds Homes for Men.

The telephone gave its half-turned-off buzz. It was Cindy, to whom I offered a joyous hello, but she was crying. She said three times, "Oh, I'm sorry. Oh, I'm sorry. Oh, I'm sorry."

"I am too, honey." I thought of how to console her. "But you know there's some justice to it. Your daddy's really planning a lovely future for you."

"No, Charles, that's not it. You don't know what happened. Charles, it's terrible. It's all my fault; he's going to put you in jail. But he got me so mad . . . It's my fault, Charles. He's crazy, he really means it."

On the pale reflection in the colorless window glass, I blanched. "O.K.," I said. "Don't cry any more. Tell me the truth."

"Oh, Charles . . ." she said. Then she described the events of the previous evening. Here they are. I have taken them right out of Cindy's mouth.

"Cindy," Mr. Graham said, "I don't want you to go around with a man like that—old enough to be your father almost."

"Oh, for godsakes, Daddy, he's very nice. He's a wonderful dancer."

"I don't like it, Cindy. Not at all. I don't even like your dancing with him. There are a lot of things you don't know about people and things, Cindy. I don't like you dancing with him. I don't approve of a man of that age even putting his arm around a teen-ager like you. You know I want the best for you, Cindy Anne. I want you to have a full and successful life. Keeping up your friendship with him, even if it's as innocent and pleasant as you claim, would be a real hindrance. I want you to go away to school and have a wonderful time with fellows your own age, dancing with them, and, you know, you might fall in love or something. . . . I'm not so stupid and blind. You know, I was young once too."

"Oh, Daddy, there's still plenty of life in you, for goodness' sakes."

"I hope so, Cindy. But what I want to tell you, honey, is that I've asked this man Charles to please stay away from you and write you a nice letter and he agreed, because, after all, you are a very pretty girl and people can often be tempted to do things they don't want to do, no matter how nice they are."

"You asked him to stay away?"

"Yes."

"And he agreed?"

"Yes, he did."

"Did he say he might be tempted?"

"Well . . ."

"Did he say he *might* be tempted?"

"Well, actually, he said he . . ."

"He just agreed? He didn't even get *angry*? He didn't even *want* to see me again?"

"He'll write you, honey."

"He'll write me? Did you say he'll write me? That's all? Who does he think I am? An idiot? A dope? A little nitwit from West Main Street? Where does he get off? That fat slob . . . What does he think I am? Didn't he even *want* to see me again? He's gonna write me?"

"Cindy!"

"That's all? That's what he wanted me for? He's gonna write me a letter? Daddy . . . Daddy . . ."

"Cindy! What happened last night?"

"Why do you go stick your nose in my business? Doesn't anything ever happen to you? I was just getting along fine for five minutes. Why do you always sit around the house with your nose in my business?"

"Cindy, were you fooling around with that man?"

"Why can't you leave me alone for five minutes? Doesn't anyone else want you around any more someplace? What do you want from me?"

"Cindy." He gripped her wrist. "Cindy! Answer me this minute. Were you?"

"Stop yelling. I'm not deaf."

"Cindy, were you fooling around with that man? Answer!"

"Leave me alone," she cried. "Just leave me alone."

"You answer me this minute," he shouted.

"I'll answer you, all right," she said. "I was not fooling around. I was not fooling. You asked me. I was not fooling. I went upstairs where the lifeboat is and I lay down right underneath it and I did it with Charles."

"What did you do?" gasped her father.

"And I ruined my blue dress," she screamed. "And you're so dumb you didn't even know it."

"Your blue dress?" he asked, scarcely breathing to hear the answer. "Cindy Anne, why?"

"Because I wanted to. I wanted to."

"What?" he asked dimly.

"I wanted to, Daddy," she said.

"Oh, my God!" he said. "My God, my God, what did I do?"

Half an hour later Mrs. Graham returned loaded with goodies from the KrissKross Shopping Center. Cindy was crying in the kitchen, and in the TV room Mr. Graham sat in his red leather-ette, eyes closed, his pale lips whispered, "It's statutory rape. . . . It's transporting a minor . . ."

Cindy, my little pal, came lolling down the courtroom aisle with a big red smile, friend to the entire court. She wiggled a little in order to convey the notion that she was really a juvenile whore and I was not accountable. Nobody believed her. She was obviously only the singed daughter of a Campfire Girl.

Besides—philosophically and with a heavy hand—I had decided my fate was written. O.K., O.K., O.K., I said to the world and, staring inward, I overcame my incarceration anxiety. If a period of self-revelation under spartan circumstances was indicated, I was willing to accept the fact that this mysterious move of His might be meant to perform wonders. (Nehru, I understand, composed most of his books in jail.) Do not assume any particular religiosity in me. I have no indoctrinated notion about what He is like: size, shape, or high I.Q.

Adjustments aside, I was embarrassed by the sudden appearance of my mother, who had been hounded from home by the local papers. She sat as close to me as the courtroom design would allow and muttered when apropos, "She's a tramp," or "You're an idiot." Once we were allowed to speak to each other: she said, "What a wild Indian you turned into, Charles."

Was she kidding? Was she proud? Why did she even care? Me, Charles C. Charley, puffed and scared, I am not the baby who lay suffocating under her left tit. I am not the boy who waited for her every night at the factory gate. I am not even any more the draftee who sent her portable pieces of an Italian church.

"What kind of a boy was your son?" my stupid lawyer asked. She peered at him, her fat face the soundboard of silence. "I said, Mrs. Charley, what kind of a boy was your son?"

After a few disengaged moments she replied, "I don't know much about any of my boys; they're a surprise to me." Then her lips met and her hands clasped each other and she hadn't another comment on that subject.

My legal adviser, a real nobody from nothing, was trying to invent an environment of familial madness from which I could not have hoped to recover. "That is certainly an odd name, in combination with his last name, Charles C. Charley, Mrs. Charley. How did this naming come about?"

"What is your name, sir?" asked my mother politely.

With a boyish grin he replied, "Edward Johnson, ma'am."

"Ha! Ha! Ha!" said my mother.

When it was my turn, he asked, "And weren't you in love with young Miss Graham, that flirtatious young woman, when you lost your head? Weren't you?"

"Generally speaking," I replied, "there's love in physical union. It's referred to in Western literature as an act of love."

"That's true," he said, not cerebrating noticeably. "And you loved Miss Graham, didn't you?" Here he pointed to her where she sat. Her hair had been washed that early morning. She wore a golden Chinese slip of a dress with little slits, probably to flash her tan calves through. Her sweet round rump nestled in the hard pew of the law.

"I suppose I did," I said.

At last the attorney for the prosecuting victim had a chance at me. He had known Cindy since she was an even younger child than she was a child at present, he said, using just those words. He was close to tears. Not a hair was rooted in his head. This is description, not adventitious comment, which I can't afford, since I am unpleasantly hirsute.

Even now, time having awarded some dimension, I don't understand his line of questioning nor the line of questioning of my own brainless lawyer. I had pleaded guilty. I was not opposed to punishment, since our happy performance, it turned out, had a criminal aspect. Still they talked. I realize they had their training to consider—all those years at school. Men like these must milk the moment or sleep forever.

"Well," he began, blinking a tear, "Charles C. Charley, you have told us that you loved that little girl at that moment but did not love her before or after and have not since?"

"I have no reason to lie," I said. "I am in the hand of God."

"Who?" the judge shouted.

Then they all mumbled together in an effort to figure out what could be done with the contemptible use of pious nomenclature. They could not say, of course, that we are not in the hand of God when, for all they knew, we were.

Mr. Graham's gleaming attorney returned to me. "Mr. Charley, did you love Cindy Graham at that moment?"

"I did," I said.

"But you do not love her now?" he asked.

"I haven't thought about it," I said.

280

"Would you marry her?" he demanded, twisting his head toward the jury. He felt sly.

"She's just a child," I said. "How could I marry her? Marriage requires all sorts of responsibility. She isn't ready for anything like that. And besides, the age difference . . . it's too great. Be realistic," I adjured his muddled head.

"You would *not* marry her?" he asked, his voice rising to a clinch.

"No, sir."

"Good enough to force sex on but not good enough to cherish for life?"

"Well," I said calmly, refusing to respond to his hysteria, and without mentioning names, "actually it's six of one and half a dozen of the other."

"And so you, a mature man, an adult, you took it upon yourself, knowing something about the pitfalls before a young girl, this child, still growing, Cynthia Anne Graham, you took it upon yourself to decide she was ready to have her virginity ravaged to satisfy your own selfish rotten lust."

After that little bit of banter I clammed up. Because Cindy was going to live among them forever, I was so silent that even now I am breathless with self-respect.

These castaways on life's sodden beach were under the impression that I was the first. I was not. I am not an inventive or creative person, I take a cue from the universe, I have never been the first anywhere. Actually, in this case, I was no more than fifth or sixth. I don't say this to be disparaging of Cindy. A person has to start somewhere. Why was Mr. Graham so baffled by truth? Gourmets everywhere begin with voracious appetites before they can come to the finesse of taste. I had seen it happen before; in five or six years, a beautiful and particular woman, she might marry some contributing citizen and resign her light habits to him. None of my adversaries was more than ten years my senior, but their memories were short (as mine would be if I weren't sure at all times to keep in touch with youth).

In the middle of my thinking, while the court waited patiently for a true answer, Cindy burst into wild tears, screaming, "Leave him alone, you leave him alone. It's not his fault if I'm wild. I'll tell the whole world how wild I am if you don't shut up. I made him do it, I made him do it. . . ."

From my narrow-eyed view the court seemed to constrict into a shuddering sailor's knot. Cindy's mother and father unraveled her, and two civil-service employees hustled her out. The opposing lawyers buzzed together and then with the judge. A pair of newspapermen staggered from one convulsive group to another. My mother took advantage of the disorganization to say, "Charles, they're bugheaded."

The paid principals nodded their heads. The judge asked for order, then a recess. My attorney and two cops led me into a brown-paneled room where a board-meeting mahogany table was surrounded by board-meeting chairs. "You didn't give one sensible answer," my attorney complained. "Now listen to me. Just sit down here and keep your mouth shut, for godsakes. I'm going to talk to the Grahams."

Except for some bored surveillance, I was alone for one hour and a half. In that time I reviewed Cindy and all her accessories, also the meaning of truth. I was just tangent to the Great Circle of Life, of which I am one irrevocable diameter, when my mother appeared. She had had time to go shopping for some wheat germ and carrots and apples full of unsprayed bacteria. The state of her health requires these innocent staples. Mr. and Mrs. Graham followed, and my little grimy Cindy. Mrs. Graham kept tissuing some of the black eye stuff off her smeared cheeks. Mr. Graham, sensible when answering or questioning and never devious, said, "All right, Charles, all right. We've decided to withdraw charges. You and Cindy will get married."

"What?" I said.

"You heard me the first time . . . I'm against it. I think a punk like you is better off in jail. For my money, you could rot in jail. I've seen worse guys but not much worse. You took advantage of a damn silly kid. You and Cindy get married next week. Meanwhile you'll be at our house, Charley. Cindy's missed enough school. This is a very important year for her. I'll tell you one thing. You better play it straight, Charley, or I'll split your skull with a kitchen knife."

"Say . . ." I said.

My mother piped up. "Charles," she said, "son, think about it a minute. What'll happen to me if you go to jail? She's very pretty. You're not getting younger. What'll happen to me? Son . . ." she said.

She turned to Mrs. Graham. "It's hard to be old and dependent this way. I hope you have plenty of insurance."

Mrs. Graham patted her shoulder.

My mother regarded this as invitation to enlarge. "When you really think about it, it's all a fuss about nothing. I always say, let them enjoy themselves when they're young. You know," she said, her eyes hazy in the crowded past, "at least it gives you something to look back on."

Mrs. Graham removed her hand and blushed in fear.

"Don't you want to marry me?" asked Cindy, tears starting again.

"Honey . . ." I said.

"Then it's settled," Mr. Graham said. "I'll find a good house in the neighborhood. No children for a while, Charley, she's got to finish school. As for you," he said, getting down to brass tacks, "the truth is, you have a fair business. I want my accountant to go over the books. If they're what I expect, you'll be cooking with gas in six months. You'll be the biggest conditioning outlet in the county. You're a goddamn slob, you haven't begun to realize your potential in a community like ours."

"I wish I could smoke," I said.

"No smoking here," my lawyer said, having brought my entire life to a successful conclusion.

In this way I assuaged the people in charge, and I live with Cindy in events which are current.

Through the agency of my father-in-law I have acquired a first-class food-freezer and refrigerator franchise. If you can imagine anything so reprehensible, it was obtained right out from under the nose of a man who has been in the business for thirty years, a man who dreamt of that franchise as his reward for unceasing labor in the kitchens of America. If someone would hand me the first stone, I would not be ashamed to throw it. But at whom?

Living with Cindy has many pleasures. One acquires important knowledge in the dwelling place of another generation. First things first, she always has a kind word for the future. It is my opinion that she will be a marvelous woman in six or seven years. I wish her luck; by then we will be strangers.

■ **Comment**

The story of a man in his thirties forced to marry a teen-ager could have been told in a lot of ways, each with its own special kind of truth. Each of the main characters in addition to Charley could have recited the events— the outraged father, the bewildered mother, the businesslike lawyer, the eager girl, each telling a familiar story according to his own slant. But the strength of this story comes not just from the suggestion of what all those different truths might have been, as represented by special interests. The story goes so far beyond stereotypes that although the reader realizes how others might see it, he also sees a complete human being, complete with a rueful look at himself and his world. In a sense, Charley enters a whole new world when he marries Cindy and goes into business with his father-in-law. Time will never catch up for his wife. In the one life he has to live he has "done the right thing," but from the standpoint he makes the reader see he is living the wrong thing as payment for one impulsive evening.

■ Discussion

How clear are the events in the story? Are you sure in every case exactly what is happening? Are you ever surprised by what the narrator Charley chooses to tell or leave out?

Can you understand the motivations (reasons for doing things) of all the characters? Do you understand one more than any of the others? How happy is the ending? How happy would it be for another man, without Charley's philosophical ideas?

■ Action

Get rid of everything except the dialogue in this story, and see what you would have to add to make it into a short play.

Write a paper describing Charley's ideas on love, family, fate, and business.

Write a paper explaining the general proposition "The truth is never the same to the individual and to the public hearing about him." Refer to events in the story to prove your point, as you compare the way this story would sound to the people in Cindy's neighborhood or those attending the court hearing or readers of the newspaper with what you know of the story as a result of having "met" Charley.

AN INVITATION TO SERENITY

SANTHA RAMA RAU

Years ago, when I was a child of ten, I learned a casual lesson that has stayed in some remote part of my mind ever since. It was one of those small moments of awakening that often seem quite trivial but grow imperceptibly in importance as the years go by.

My sister and I had returned from four years of schooling in England, and along with our mother were spending a year in my grandmother's large, sprawling household in a provincial town in the north of India. Among the many members of that household, my particular companion was a girl cousin two years older than I.

It was a passing question of hers that I still remember as something far more profound than it seemed at the time. Sometimes in the long, hot afternoons, when the adults took a siesta before teatime, she and I would creep down to the guava orchard, where we were forbidden to pick fruit until it was ripe. We used to pick it anyway because we loved the crisp, mouth-puckering taste of the green guavas dipped in the salt we carried in the cup of a hand. Our morning lessons were over and our household chores—sewing on buttons, picking flowers for the prayer room— all were done. We had the whole lovely afternoon ahead of us before the grownups awoke, my cousin's music teacher arrived and I had to do extra work on my Hindi, much of which I had forgotten in England.

On one such afternoon I asked my cousin, "What are we going to do today?"

She thought a moment and said, "Nothing."

"But you must do *some*thing." My English education had taken firm hold. I could easily picture a distant study hall in which a girl sat staring dreamily out the window. I could hear the brisk voice of the teacher interrupting her.

"Mary, what are you doing?"

A guilty jump from Mary. "Nothing, ma'am."

"Nothing? You shouldn't be doing *nothing*. You should be doing *some*thing."

"Yes, ma'am" (meekly accepting the idea that it was wrong to be merely idle, dreaming or thinking).

But when I said the same thing to my cousin, she looked puzzled and demanded, "Why?"

I couldn't then and haven't since been able to formulate an answer to that "Why?" Seeing the expression on my face, she added, as though it explained everything, "I like just sitting here and watching the kites wheeling about in the sky." She calmly and quite naturally had assumed that left to my own devices, I too would find something equally fascinating to do. In fact, I wandered about, rather cross and bored, read a little and finally fell asleep.

My malaise of that afternoon was, after all, only a tiny example of what has become a growing and formidable concern of modern Western society—the satisfactory use of leisure time. The superficial reasons for the existence of the problem are easy to state and obvious to the most casual observer. In recent years in America the short work week, the early age for retirement, the good health that results in longevity, the countless uses of machines and short cuts around the house to lessen the housewife's efforts in her home, have given American men and women alike an unimaginable (to Asians) amount of leisure time. The trouble is that according to professional studies, far too many Americans are finding themselves frighteningly ill-equipped to confront what Freda H. Goldman, of the Center for the Study of Liberation for Adults, terms that "strange and disquieting new freedom we call leisure."

All work and no play may make Jack a dull boy, but even worse is the sad fact that when age or circumstances place Jack in a position where there is no further work required of him, he is bewildered and lost and frustrated. He doesn't by then know *how* to play, or how to justify to himself what he can think of only as "idleness." Can he, with complete confidence and enjoyment, say something equivalent to: "I like just sitting here and watching the kites wheeling about in the sky"? In one way or another, however he cares to phrase it, Jack's training (like mine in those far-off days) surely makes him say to himself, "The devil finds work for idle hands."

In India the problem—in this form—doesn't arise because quite simply, with the exception of the paper-thin class of the privileged that lies over the vast mass of nearly 500 million Indians, most of the people are overworked and underpaid or unemployed and threatened with starvation. In neither case could one say that the overwhelming majority had much "leisure" with the pleasurable connotations that the word carries in the West.

But there are other and more searching reasons too, reasons that concern the structure of Indian society and the attitude toward living that it engenders. For leisure in the end is a concept in your mind. You can be a carpenter and be deeply satisfied with your work. Equally, you can build, say, bookshelves in your basement and be deeply satisfied with this as a leisure-time activity, expecting no financial gain from your efforts. The difference in the satisfactions is deep within you, is complicated and important and, in my opinion, reflects your entire view of living.

Perhaps I can best explain what I mean by describing the kind of life that I found so strange at the age of ten, and later so rewarding. It is common to most of Asia, where society is still dominated by the large and inclusive family unit. In India we call it a "joint family," meaning merely that if not under the same roof, at least within the same compound or group of buildings live several generations of people related by blood or marriage. Each family is, then, a small community of its own.

The household in which I found myself that summer when I returned to India was quite unremarkable to Indian eyes, but seemed bewilderingly exotic to me. I had already become accustomed to boarding-school life, interspersed with vacations spent with my parents in city apartments or rented houses of manageable size. Visits with my English friends convinced me that an ordinary family unit meant simply parents and their children living in one home. But here in India, family living was quite another matter. The vast, endearing, confusing bustle of dozens of relatives of all ages, with their endlessly diverse temperaments and activities, flowed through our house and compound like a tide that appeared at first to have no discernible pattern. My great-grandmother, incredibly old and frail, attended by her woman servant, threaded her way through our days, remote and smiling peaceably. There was my grandfather with his infectious laughter, lavishly indulgent of the small children. My grandmother managed the entire household with easy competence, allotting chores to the various women in the family, supervising the cooking and keeping a sharp eye on the work of the servants. Most important, she controlled the finances. Under her unobtrusive government my aunts, uncles and cousins conducted their separate yet intertwined lives—jobs, school, college—all realistically aware that her unclouded eye noticed who was slacking on homework, who deserved a treat, who was in emotional or professional difficulties.

Besides the members of the "immediate family" there were nearly always second cousins, great-aunts, great-uncles and yet more distant relatives, who had come to visit for a few days or a few months. (It was considered impolite to say exactly how long you were going to stay. It would seem as if you felt there was a limit to the generosity the household could offer you.) Eventually this large and continually varying complex of people became individuals in my eyes, and I acquired my special favorites among them—a handsome and glamorous uncle who was a crack shot and could actually *drive a car;* a widowed aunt who was endlessly patient and affectionate with us children, since she had none of her own, and who would listen to the most trivial trouble with clucking concern; a delightful, tennis-playing cousin who brought his college friends to play on our court and who teased me unmercifully about my English ways (I adored him); and finally the cousin already mentioned, who was my special friend.

To American youngsters, I dare say our life in such a family might seem most sadly lacking in entertainment and excitement. It did not seem so to us. Admittedly we had no television set or radio, seldom went to the movies and never to the theater. The only formal amusements I can remember were occasional music festivals, when whoever in the family was interested went in a party of assorted adults and children to listen to the singers and instrumentalists. Rarely there was that peculiarly North Indian entertainment, a poetry contest, which we all loved. We sat on the ground with the rest of the audience, choosing our favorites among the poets and shouting, "*Va, va!*" when a competitor produced a particularly elegant turn of phrase or a specially subtle and witty play on words. But what were our other leisure-time activities; children or grownups, what did we actually *do*? Well . . . when I look back on it . . . well, nothing much. What happened, happened for the most part inside us—and I can't remember ever being bored or at loose ends once my English uneasiness had begun to wear off a bit.

To me the pleasantest time of day was the early evening after tea, when my older cousins came back from college on their bicycles, or more sedately by *tonga* (a one-horse carriage gaily decorated with bells and ribbons and paper flowers), and were greeted with shouted questions about how the history test had gone or who had won the ping-pong championship. The men of the family had returned from their various occupations and my grandfather had taken up his place, sitting cross-legged on a wooden platform in the courtyard, leaning against white, cotton-covered bolsters and puffing on his hookah. He would call all the children to him, settle us down in a chattering, nudging group around him, and after detailed inquiries about the alarms and excursions of the day, launch into his inexhaustible fund of funny or strange stories out of the long annals of our family history.

Almost always we were joined by my widowed aunt, who sat knitting or sewing something for one of the children, and by other grownups, who added explanations and comments to the narrative. Frequently we were interrupted by, say, an uncle's asking if anyone wanted to go with him to see the gardener's new goat, or somebody's announcing that the sweets vendor was sitting on the veranda and didn't we want something to snack on, or my grandmother's reminding one of us about unfinished homework and then returning across the courtyard to the kitchen, where the cook sat cleaning vegetables in the open door. Sometimes callers would arrive, be offered tea or lime water, and sit with us to listen to my grandfather and intersperse his stories with comparable ones from their own family adventures. Sometimes the man with the dancing bear would come along and ask if we wanted a performance, or the man who sold glass bangles from Benares. (He always commanded our full attention because it was very important to have the most supple hands in the house, the ones that the smallest-sized bangle would slip over.)

At the time, these evenings just seemed an amusing and absorbing way to spend the time. Nothing was, so to speak, "accomplished." But now I realize that they carried an extra dimension and gave us all a genuine involvement with our heritage, both personal and cultural. They even gave us a most immediate sense of our country's continuing history. After all, it is very different to read, for example, the history of the Indian Mutiny of 1857 in a book and to be told about it firsthand from a great-grandmother who was about ten years old at the time it occurred.

Apart from these uneventful daily hours of leisure we had, as well, our Special Occasions. Among them were the various religious festivals that punctuate the Indian year with days of sparkling excitement. The ones I liked the best were *Holi* and *Divali. Holi,* which can be considered either a spring festival or a thanksgiving for the winter harvest, was a marvelous time for practical jokes; for knocking on somebody's door, and when he appeared, dousing him with colored water from a bicycle pump; for careening around the streets in clothes brilliantly stained with indigo or scarlet, all for the joy of springtime. *Divali* involved us all in decorating the house and outlining windows and roof with tiny oil lamps, and later carrying the lamps down to the river with the girls of marriageable age in the house. There they set the little earthenware bowls adrift on the great Ganges where it meets the Jumna. The girls whose lamps, still lighted, reached the other side of the river would get married within the year. The suspense was terrific.

Festivals were always accompanied by visits to the temple. It was a painful and exasperating business to begin with. My hair had to be oiled and scraped back neatly; a *tika,* the mark Hindu women often wear, had to be put on my forehead; and I had to be dressed in my best clothes, which I hated. But it all was compensated for in the temple, where I could watch the women in their bright saris exchanging news and gossip; the children running about in the courtyard, absorbed in their own games; the holy men deep in meditation or reciting the Scriptures, quite impervious to the bustle around them.

We would return to the house, tired and a bit peevish, to be given an early supper; and then sometimes my grandmother would pull out her huge, worn copy of the *Ramayana,* one of the great epics of Hindu mythology, and read to us about the exploits of the good King Rama and his devoted wife Sita, about her kidnaping by the Demon King of Lanka (Ceylon), and all the thrilling battles, escapes and victories that went into Sita's recapture. My grandmother would send us to bed with our heads full of gods and demons, too bemused even to whisper to one another from under our little tents of mosquito netting.

There were other special occasions too, of a more personal nature. One was provided by my eldest cousin's graduation from college and the elaborate ritual of choosing a husband for her. Horoscopes arrived from various suitors as soon as word got around that my family was ready to arrange a marriage for her. We all read them eagerly. We looked at the accompanying photographs and discussed the desirability of each young man. Most of us (the children, that is) argued fervently in favor of the best-looking of the suitors, whose horoscope promised that he would be a "leader of men" and win "great fortune." We interpreted this to mean that he would somehow become a maharaja and were delighted at the idea of having a maharani as a cousin. Our elders, more prosaically, inquired into family backgrounds and the prospects of the young men in their different jobs. When at last one of them was chosen (he appealed to our cousin and found favor with our elders, though he disappointed me), there came the delicate business of refusing the others. Each of the horoscopes was returned, with the formal and appropriate explanation that on consultation with the family priest it was found not to "match" that of the prospective bride, that the two horoscopes taken together did not augur a happy married future for the young people.

After that came the excitement of meeting the chosen young man when he and his parents were invited to tea. My cousin, pink with embarrassment, sat in a corner, the end of her sari pulled over her head, and demurely said not a word. Her fiancé was almost equally silent. The elders set about arranging the practical details while we scuffled just outside the door, giggling and evesdropping and speculating.

All these events—marriages, graduations, engagements, as well as births, illnesses, deaths—were woven into the fabric of our family life. But between, of course, there were the long stretches when "nothing happened," when we simply continued our day-to-day lives. So when I wonder what we did with our leisure time, I realize that for the most part what we did was no more than to share in the lives of the people around us, giving and receiving the most ordinary kind of human contact. Of course, we also had our own special interests and activities that we pursued on our own—I wrote poetry in fat, messy notebooks and read voluminously; my cousin had her passionate interest in music; my mother was an ardent social worker; one aunt was a devoted gardener; another, deeply religious, spent hours in meditation and in the study of philosophic treatises; my favorite uncle had his shooting trips and his beloved dogs. But even those family members who had no particular hobby or private occupation never seemed to be restive or worried about how to occupy their time. There was too much living going on all around them, living in which they were a cherished and necessary part, for them to see leisure as a "problem."

Perhaps the most obvious difference between the kind of family life I have described and the modern American counterpart is that we were always involved with people representing several generations. None of us thought that leisure time was to be spent primarily with our own age group. I remember one time, years later, when I had just returned from college in America, that my grandmother asked me with patent skepticism, "Is it really true that old ladies sometimes live alone? Alone even in a *hotel?*"

"Yes," I admitted. "Sometimes."

"Even if their children are living in the same town?"

"Well, yes," I said rather defensively. "Some of them prefer to have a place of their own."

"How sad!" she said in wonderment.

"But," I insisted, "lots of them *like* to be independent."

"I meant, how sad for the younger generation," she answered sharply. "How will they ever learn to grow old?"

It is surely a question many Americans must be asking themselves—not necessarily how to grow old gracefully but rather how to grow old with a sense of fulfillment.

In her own way my grandmother was stating one aspect of the complexities of what we usually call leisure, meaning a time of freedom and delight, or of irresponsibility and the feeling that at last we can do whatever we want to do whenever we feel like it. An Indian joint family may never give its members that particular kind of leisure, but it will compensate them with the thought that they are never unneeded.

I believe that a sense of being needed, either in work or in family relations, is a fundamental necessity of any human being. It is easy to understand, then, why there are no colonies of "senior citizens" in India, no special resorts where the elderly gather, unwanted by the younger generations and helpless to know what to do with themselves during their declining years of leisure time. Old people in India always know that they have a position of honor in the family, that they will be needed in matters as diverse as initiating a young bride into the ways and running habits of her new home or offering experienced business advice or gauging the proper size of a daughter's dowry. Throughout their lives they will have the confident security of fulfilling their roles as wife and mother, or husband and father and breadwinner, eventually to become respected elders who can arbitrate family disputes and act as the moral conscience of the household. (Among my earliest memories are waking to the smell of incense from my grandmother's prayer room, her wavering voice singing a devotional song to the image placed there, her demand that we younger ones take off our sandals, make our proper obeisance to the deity and realize that a spiritual presence always accompanies our everyday acts.) The old people always know that they will be taken care of if they are sick, that they will be wanted to provide help and comfort if others have troubles, that they will always be surrounded by people of different generations and that they will die, as they have lived, among people who made up their intimate world.

In contrast, in America (although it may be different in deeply rural areas, about which I know virtually nothing) the first thing a young married couple looks for is a "place of their own" away from the family. When they have children, yes, it is an occasional Sunday lunch with Granny or a family get-together for Thanksgiving or Christmas; but it isn't a day-to-day sharing of the sorrows and joys, the calamities and excitements—the *life* of a family.

One can't, of course, put the clock back. America has already evolved a civilization that is gradually spreading its influence across the world. In India, as in most parts of Asia, the measured life of the large joint family is slowly breaking up, and in the cities it has almost entirely disappeared. As industrialization intensifies, as modern concepts of the roles of men and women become more modern (or perhaps I mean "more Westernized"), we too will have to face the complexities of the use of leisure time. Clothes for the entire family will not be sewed by the women in the house; cooking a meal will no longer require hours of preparation—of grinding spices by hand, of sifting rice from the chaff, of drawing water from the well for everything and heating it over charcoal burners. In short, there will be time on our hands. And what will we do with it?

In the end we all must come to terms with the way of living that surrounds us, must not be taken by surprise by "leisure" at an age when we are not equipped to handle it, must not regret past conditions that left no room for such a problem. In America, as anywhere else in the world, we must find a focus in our lives at an early age, a focus that is beyond the mechanics of earning a living or coping with a household, something that can be a continuing involvement—a hobby, an occupation, call it what you will—something that *lasts,* something that is beyond even human relationships. I am reminded of a Chinese saying: "If you wish to be happy for a day, kill a pig. If you wish to be happy for a week, take a wife. If you wish to be happy all your life, cultivate a garden." The value of the garden is that you are always looking ahead. What is planted this spring must be nourished throughout the year. Plans must always require a stretching of activity and of the mind into the future—next year, the year after —and whatever its form, surely the purpose of leisure time is to offer not only enjoyment (watching kites, if you will) but also interior satisfaction of accomplishment and self-expression.

■ **Comment**

"An Invitation to Serenity" could be an enlarged version of a situation in the first part of this book. In its basic form, two girls are faced with an afternoon free of tasks, with "nothing to do." The choices facing them are to enjoy contemplation, to hang around being bored, to insist on meaningful work, or to sleep. Each makes a different choice, and the author insists that the girl brought up in India knows more about how to enjoy life than does her cousin who was educated in England.

She uses the incident to introduce an entire comparison of the Indian and Western styles of life.

■ **Discussion**

Explain the author's belief that leisure is a concept in the mind.
Can people "work" harder in their spare time than they do in a paid job?
What are the advantages of the kind of family community in the author's household? What are the disadvantages?

What were the things people did in the times when "nothing" happened? Which of them would you classify as "something"?

■ **Action**

Compare the Eastern and Western attitudes toward leisure time, as explained by the author. (Include house chores, marriage customs, usefulness of old people.)

Gather evidence from commercials and magazine advertisements to show what Americans regard as the appropriate use of leisure time.

Imagine an American city with an Indian attitude. What changes would come about in architecture, economics, purchasing?

Describe an American household as Miss Rau describes an Indian one, beginning "The household in which I found myself that summer . . ."

From EARTH ABIDES

GEORGE STEWART

He came to the Pulaski Skyway about noon. Once before, as a boy of fifteen, he had driven there with his father and mother. Then the streaming traffic had half terrified him; trucks and cars had come roaring in, seeming to converge from all directions, and then suddenly to drop out of sight again as they went off onto the down-ramps. He remembered his father gazing anxiously, this way and that, to watch the traffic-signs, and his mother nervously giving advice. But now, Princess slept on the front seat beside him, as he speeded along the Skyway by himself.

Far ahead now he saw the high towers of the sky-scrapers, pearl-gray against a cloudy sky; there had been a shower, and the day was cool for mid-summer.

When he saw those towers, his feelings were strangely stirred. Now he knew, what he would not have been quite able to explain before, why he had headed for New York, even unconsciously. This, to every American, was the center of the world. According to what happened in New York, so in the long run, he could only think, it must happen elsewhere—"Falls Rome, falls the world."

When he came to the clover-leaf above Jersey City, he stopped in the middle of the Skyway to read the signs. No brakes squealed suddenly behind him; no horns blared; no truck-drivers bawled obscenities at him for blocking the road; no police-men shouted through loud-speakers.

"At least," he thought, "life is quieter."

From far off, he just caught the sound, some bird squawked twice—a seagull probably. The only other sound was the nearly imperceptible murmur of his own idling engine, as drowsy as the hum of bees.

There at the last moment he flinched from trying either of the tunnels. Untended, they might have gradually filled with water, and he had a vague fear of being trapped. He swung north, and at last crossed by the empty George Washington Bridge, and came to Manhattan.

Stretched out between its rivers, the city will remain for a long time. Stone and brick, concrete and asphalt, glass—time deals gently with them. Water leaves black stains, moss shows green, a little grass springs up in the cracks. (That is only the surface.) A window-pane grows loose, vibrates, breaks in a gusty wind. Lightning strikes, loosening the tiles of a cornice. A wall leans, as footings yield in the long rains; after years have passed, it falls, scattering bricks across the street. Frost works, and in the March thaw some flakes of stone scale off. (It is all very slow.) The rain washes quietly through the gutters into the storm-drains, and if the storm-drains clog, the rain runs still through the gutters into the rivers. The snow piles deep in the long canyons, drifting at the street corners; no one disturbs it. In the spring, it too runs off through the gutters. As in the desert, a year is like an hour in the night; a century, like a day.

Indeed the city is much like the desert. From the asphalt and concrete-coated soil the rain runs off both ways into the rivers. Here and there in a crack the subtle grass and the hardy weeds grow up a little, but no tree or vine or tall grass takes root. The very shade trees by the avenues, lacking man's care, die in their shallow pockets. The deer and the rabbits shun the empty streets; after a while even the rats go away. Only the flying creatures find there a refuge—the birds nest on the high ledges, and at morning and evening the bats fly out and in through the few broken windows. It will remain a long time, a very long time.

He turned south on Broadway, thinking to follow it clear to the Battery. At 170th Street, however, he came to a very official-looking STREET CLOSED sign with an arrow directing him to detour eastward. He could have driven past the sign and ahead, but he felt a caprice to yield docilely to instructions. He drove over to Amsterdam Avenue, and then went south again. His nostrils let him know that the Medical Center must have been one of the last points of concentration, and that the detour sign had been put up to give directions around it.

Amsterdam Avenue was vacant too. Somewhere in these vast accumulations of concrete and brick and mortar and plaster, somewhere in all these cave-like holes that men called rooms, somewhere certainty, some people must be living. The catastrophe had been nearly universal, and in overcrowded Manhattan the disease had probably raged even more severely than elsewhere. Also, he thought, what he had come to call the Secondary Kill might have been more severe in a wholly urbanized population. Nevertheless, he had already learned that a few people had survived elsewhere, and surely among the millions of Manhattan there would be some. But he did not bother to blow his horn; a mere straggler here and there he had found to be of little interest to him now.

He drove on, block after block. Everything was quiet and motionless. The clouds had broken, and the sun stood high overhead, but the sidewalks were as empty as if the sun had been the moon and the hour had been three in the morning. Even then he would have seen a beat-walking policeman or have met a night-hawk cab. He passed an empty playground.

A few cars were parked along the curbs. He remembered that his father had driven him through downtown Manhattan on a Sunday when even Wall Street lay deserted. This was much the same, but worse.

At last, near Lewisohn Stadium, nuzzling around an entry-way, two thin-looking dogs supplied the first sign of life. In the next block he saw a few pigeons fluttering about, not many.

He drove on, passed the red-brick buildings of Columbia University, and stopped in front of the high, still unfinished cathedral. It was unfinished now, and so it would remain.

He pushed at the door; it swung open; he entered. Momentarily he had a horrible thought that he might find the nave piled with the bodies of those who at the last hour had gathered there to pray. But there was no one. He walked down a side aisle, and went into the little chapels of the apse, one after another— those where the English and the French and the Italians and all the others of that teeming polyglot city had been invited to kneel and worship. The sunlight streamed in at the stained-glass windows; it was all as beautiful as he remembered from before. He had a wild desire to throw himself on his knees before one of the altars. "There are no atheists in fox holes," he remembered, and the whole world now was nothing but a huge fox hole! But certainly what had happened did not inspire one to think that God was particularly interested in the human race, or in its individuals.

He walked back along the main aisle. Turning, he looked up the nave, and let its grandeur beat in upon him. He felt a little choking in the throat. This, then, was the end of all man's highest striving and aspiration. . . . He went out to the empty street, and got into the car again.

At Cathedral Parkway he swung east, and defying traffic signs entered Central Park and went south along the East Drive, thinking that on a summer day people might go to the Park as they would have done ordinarily. But he saw no one. From his previous visit as a boy he remembered squirrels, but he saw no squirrels either; starving dogs and cats had apparently accounted for them already. On a meadow he saw a bison bull grazing; not far off, a horse. He passed the back of the Metropolitan Museum, and saw Cleopatra's Needle, now doubly orphaned. At Sherman's statue he swung into Fifth Avenue, and a tag-end of verse popped into his mind: "Now all your victories are in vain."

An island within an island, the green oblong of the Park will remain. It has open soil where the rain penetrates. The sun shines upon it. In the first season the grass grows tall; the seeds fall from the trees and bushes, the birds bring in more seeds. Give it two seasons, three seasons, and the eager saplings are sprouting. Give it twenty years, and it is a jungle of second growth with each tree straining upward to gain light above its fellows, and the hardy natives, fast-growing ash and maple, crowding out the soft exotics which man once planted there. You hardly see the bridle path any more; leaf-litter lies thick on the narrow roads. Give it a hundred years, and you walk in full-grown forest, scarcely knowing that man was ever there except where the stone arch still spans the under-pass, making a strange cave. The doe walks in the woods, and the wild-cat leaps upon the rabbit, and the bass jumps in the lake.

In the tall windows of the fashion shops, the mannequins still postured strangely in gay costumes, their jewelry flashing. But Fifth Avenue lay before him empty, as quiet as Main Street of Podunk on a Sunday morning. The windows of one great jewelry store had been smashed. "I hope," thought Ish, "he found the diamonds good eating, poor guy. No, I hope he was somebody who liked pretty stones because they were pretty, like a child picking them up on the beach. Perhaps, with his diamonds and rubies, he really died happier." On the whole, however, there was little disturbance along Fifth Avenue. "The corpse is laid out in good condition," he thought. "Yes, Fifth Avenue makes a beautiful corpse."

A few pigeons fluttered up at Rockefeller Center, disturbed now by the sound of a single motor. At Forty-second Street, yielding to a whim, he stopped the car in the middle of Fifth Avenue and got out, leaving Princess shut up.

He walked east on Forty-second Street, the empty sidewalk ridiculously wide. He entered Grand Central Terminal, and looked in at the vast expanse of waiting-room.

"Waugh!" he called loudly, and felt a childlike pleasure as an echo came reverberating back from the high vault, through the emptiness.

He wandered back to the street, and a revolving door caught his eye. He pushed against it idly, and found himself in the lobby of a large hotel. Flanked by huge chairs and davenports, the lobby led on to the desk.

Standing just inside the door, he had a moment's idea of approaching the desk and entering into an imaginary conversation with the reservation-clerk. He had telegraphed from—well, Kansas City would be a good place. Yes, and his reservation had been confirmed! What were all these excuses now? But the insane notion faded. With a thousand rooms empty and the poor clerk gone—who knew where?—the joke was not very funny.

At the same time also he noticed something different. Over all the chairs and davenports and cigarette-stands and marble floors lay a distinct layer of gray dust.

Perhaps, not being a housekeeper, he had not previously noticed dust, or perhaps this place was particularly dusty. No matter which! From now on, dust would be a part of his life.

Back at the car, he slipped it into gear, crossed Forty-second Street, and continued south. On the steps of the Library he saw a gray cat crouched, paws stretched out in front, as if in caricature of the stone lions above.

At the Flatiron Building he turned into Broadway, and followed it clear to Wall Street. There they both got out, and Princess showed interest in some kind of trail which ran along the sidewalk. Wall Street! He enjoyed walking along its empty length. With a little observation he discovered that there was some grass, weeds rather, showing green here and there in the cracks of the gutter. He remembered the family story that an early Dutch settler, one of their ancestors, had owned a good farm in this vicinity. His father, when the bills were high, used to say, "Well, I wish we had held on to that farm on Manhattan Island." Now Ish could take the land back for all that anybody cared. Yet this wilderness of concrete and steel and asphalt was the last place where anybody would really care to live now. He would trade that Wall Street farm for any ten acres in Napa Valley, or even for a small corner of Central Park.

He walked back to his car, and drove south on Broadway still, the little distance to the Battery. There he gazed across the expanse of the lower Bay toward the ocean. This was the end of the road.

There might be communities left in Europe or South America or on some of the islands, but he could not go to find out. Right here, doubtless, his Dutch ancestor had come ashore some three hundred years ago. Now he, Ish, had rounded the full circle.

He noticed the Statue of Liberty. "Liberty!" he thought ironically. "At least, I have that! More than anyone ever thought of, when they put the lady up there with her torch!"

Close to the shore of Governor's Island a large liner was beached. She must have been run aground at high tide, and now at low tide she loomed up far above the water, canted at a crazy angle. Secretly infected before leaving Europe, before long with passengers and crew alike dead and dying, that ship must have made desperately for port—for a port which itself had strangely ceased to send out signals. No tugs came out to meet her. Perhaps a dying boatswain on the bridge lacked even the crew to drop an anchor, and with dimming eyes merely steered her toward the mudbank. There she would rest, and doubtless the waves would wash up mud against her obstructing bulk, and in a century she would be almost indistinguishable—the rust-covered center of a little island with trees growing up around her.

Going on, Ish swung off through the East Side, struck a noisome area again at the great center of Bellevue Hospital, turned west and found the same difficulty around Pennsylvania Station and the adjoining hotels, and finally went north on

Eleventh Avenue. He turned into Riverside Drive, and noticed that the sun was getting low over the smokeless smokestacks of the Jersey shore. He was just wondering where he should spend the night when he heard a voice calling out, "Hi, there!"

Princess burst into a frenzy of barking. Stopping the car, he looked back, and saw a man emerging from the entryway of an apartment house. Ish got out to meet him, leaving the barking Princess in the car.

The man advanced with outstretched hand. He was completely conventional-looking, well shaved, wearing a tropical-worsted suit, with even the coat on. He was middle-aged and overweight, with a smiling face. Ish half expected him to break into the conventional shopkeeper's greeting "Well, sir, what can I do for you today?"

"Abrams is the name," he said, "Milt Abrams."

Ish fumbled for his own name—it was so long since he had thought of it. Introductions over, Milt Abrams took him inside. They went into a pleasant apartment on the second floor. A blonde-haired woman, about forty, well dressed, almost smart-looking, was sitting at a cocktail table, and there was a cocktail shaker before her. "Meet—the Mrs." said Milt Abrams, and from the way he hesitated, Ish knew that the Mrs. merely covered up his embarrassment. The catastrophe would scarcely have spared a husband and wife, and there had been no opportunity for any ceremony since. Milt Abrams was obviously conventional enough to let this worry him even under the circumstances.

The Mrs. looked at Ish with a smile, possibly at Milt's discomfort, "Call me Ann," she said. "And have a drink!—Warm martinis, that's all I can offer you! Not a scrap of *ice* in New York City!" In her own way she was as typical a New Yorker as Milt.

"I tell her," said Milt. "I keep on telling her, not to drink that stuff—warm martinis are poison."

"Think of it," said Ann, "spending a whole summer in New York City—and without a *scrap* of ice!" Nevertheless, she seemed to have overcome her dislike of warm martinis sufficiently to have got on the outside of several of them.

"Here, I'll offer you something better," said Milt. Opening a cupboard, he displayed a fine shelf of Amontillado, Napoleon brandy, and selected liqueurs. "And," he added, "they don't call for ice."

302

Obviously, Milt was a natural connoisseur in liquor. The bottle of Chateau Margaux that he produced for dinner was further proof.

Chateau Margaux over a meal of cold canned corned beef was not perhaps all that could be wished, but the wine was plentiful enough to produce in Ish a slight and happy befuddlement. Ann was definitely befuddled by this time.

The evening passed pleasantly enough. They played cards by candlelight—three-handed bridge. They drank liqueurs. They listened to records on a tinny-toned portable phonograph which had the great advantage of not needing electric power, but of being wound up by hand. They talked—as you might talk on any evening. "That record scratches . . . I haven't won a finesse yet. . . . Let me have another glassful."

It was a kind of make-believe. You pretended there was a world outside the windows; you were playing cards by candlelight because that was a pleasant thing to do; you did not trade reminiscences or talk of what you might think anyone would talk about under such circumstances. And Ish realized that this was proper and right. Normal people, and Milt and Ann seemed to be certainly normal, did not concern themselves much with either the distant past or the distant future. Fortunately, they lived in the present.

Yet, as the cards were dealt and played, by incidental remarks here and there, Ish put together a great deal of the situation. Milt had been part-owner of a small jewelry-store. Ann had been the wife of someone named Harry, and they had been prosperous enough to spend summers on the coast of Maine. The only work for pay that Ann had ever done had been to sell perfume in one of the more exclusive shops, as a kind of lark during the Christmas rush. Now the two of them occupied a fine apartment, vastly better than even Harry had been able to provide. The electricity had failed immediately, because the dynamos which supplied New York had been steam-driven; the water supply remained apparently at normal, and this prevented any sanitary problem.

Actually they were marooned on Riverside Drive. Being ordinary New Yorkers they had never owned a car, and so neither of them could drive. Automobiles were mysteries to them. Since all public transportation had now disappeared, they were left wholly afoot, and neither was of an age or temperament or physique to enjoy walking. Broadway, with its still well-stocked food- and liquor-stores, formed their practical eastern limit, the River lay to the west; they wandered up and down the Drive, perhaps half a mile north and south. That was their world.

Within these narrow limits they did not think that anyone else was living. As to what might be happening in the rest of the city, they had not as much idea as Ish. To them the East Side was as far off as Philadelphia; Brooklyn might as well be Saudi Arabia.

Once in a while, indeed, they had heard cars go by on River-side Drive, and on rare occasions they had seen one. They had been wary, however, about approaching any of the cars, because from loneliness and a sense of helplessness, a fear had come upon them, and they had a kind of bug-a-boo terror about roving gangsters.

"But everything was getting so quiet that I really wanted to see someone. You weren't driving fast," said Milt almost diffidently, "and I saw you were alone, and didn't look bad, and had an out-of-town license."

Ish started to say that he would give them his pistol, but checked himself. Firearms were as likely to create as to solve difficulties. In all probability Milt had never fired a gun in his life, and he did not look like an apt learner. As for Ann, she gave the impression of being one of those excitable women who would be as dangerous to friend as to foe if she ever started cutting loose with a pistol.

In spite of having no motion pictures and no radio and in spite of lacking even that great and continual show of the passing populace of the city, still Milt and Ann did not seem to be particularly bored. They played cribbage, alternating with two-handed rummy—for high, but of course mythical, stakes. As the result, Ann now owed Milt several millions of dollars. They played endless records—jazz, folk-songs, dance-tunes—on the tinny phonograph. They read uncounted volumes of mystery stories which they got from the circulating libraries on Broadway and left strewn around the apartment. Physically, he guessed, they found each other attractive.

But if they were not bored, neither did they seem to have much pleasure in life. There was a great vacantness somewhere. From shock they were walking in a kind of haze. They were people without hope. New York, their world, had vanished; it would never live again in their time. They had no interest when Ish tried to tell them what had happened in the rest of the United States. "Falls Rome, falls the world."

Next morning Ann was having another warm martini at

breakfast, and still complaining that there was not a scrap of ice in New York City. They urged him to stay longer; they urged him even to stay permanently. He could certainly find himself a girl somewhere in New York, they said; she would make a fourth for bridge. They were the pleasantest people he had found since the catastrophe. Yet he had no desire to stay there with them, even if he could locate a girl for a fourth at bridge—and other things. No, he decided, he would strike back for the West again.

But as he drove off and they stood at the entryway of the apartment-house and waved to him, he almost turned back to stay a while longer. He liked them, and he pitied them. He hated to think what would happen when winter struck, and the deep canyons between the buildings were clogged with snow and the north wind whistled down the groove of Broadway. There would be no central heating in New York City that winter, though indeed there would be plenty of ice, and no need to drink warm martinis.

He doubted whether they could survive the winter, even though they piled broken furniture into the fireplace. Some accident would quite likely overtake them, or pneumonia might strike them down. They were like the highly bred spaniels and pekinese who at the end of their leashes had once walked along the city streets. Milt and Ann, too, were city-dwellers, and when the city died, they would hardly survive without it. They would pay the penalty which in the history of the world, he knew, had always been inflicted upon organisms which specialized too highly. Milt and Ann—the owner of a jewelry store, a salesgirl for perfumes—they had specialized until they could no longer adapt themselves to new conditions. They were almost at the other end of the scale from those Negroes in Arkansas who had so easily gone back to the primitive way of living on the land.

The Drive curved, and he knew that they would now be out of his sight, even if he turned around. He felt the warmth and fullness of tears in his eyes—Good-bye, Milt and Ann!

■ Comment

The title for this selection might have been "Last of the Species," or "Alone in the City." But "Earth Abides" suggests the *Bible,* a fitting source for a story about the end of mankind: "One generation passeth away, and another generation cometh; but the earth abideth forever." Earth in this case includes everything made by man or Nature—all the plants, stores, automobiles, and highways. Only human beings have been threatened with extinction as the result of a swift plague. The author speculates "What if . . ." there were only a few people left on earth. How would they live? Alone or with each other? Would they plan for a future? Have a religion? Make laws? How much of the past would they be able to keep? Would they have to go back to the beginning and retrace the same steps, make the same mistakes?

The situation illustrating some of these problems is found in this chapter, in which the main character, Ish, who has traveled cross-country (on free gas) encounters a couple in a New York apartment. These few people exemplify different ways of dealing with the problem of survival.

■ Discussion

Science fiction is a way of commenting on the present by writing about the future. What comments about the present does the author seem to be making? Do you think the story was written after Hiroshima? Comment on the different street signs which now exist and which would have no meaning in the situation presented here.

These three people spend time together drinking and playing cards. Is there other possible action you would have had them do if this had been a story you wrote? Defend another choice, or explain why what the author had them do was as plausible as anything else.

If *you* were driving around an almost deserted New York, what would you do? *Is* suicide a strong probability? Is there a reason for continuing the human race?

■ Action

Discuss suicide as a possible alternative for the people in this situation. What moral or other reasons would you have for insisting that man begin again?

Describe a world of the future in one of the following ways: a world in which people are not allowed to make mistakes; people are rewarded for spending and punished for saving; population is controlled by law; complete freedom exists in every way. (Or any other speculation you care to make.)

What education are people now getting for survival in a world without daily mail delivery, air-conditioning, canned food, and other conveniences? Would such education be a good idea, or would it encourage acceptance of large-scale destruction? Pull all your ideas together in an essay or speech about Education for the Future, if you could design any curriculum you wanted.